BUILDING WITH LIME

Revised Edition

A practical introduction

STAFFORD HOLMES and MICHAEL WINGATE

PRACTICAL ACTION
Publishing

Intermediate Technology Publications Ltd
trading as Practical Action Publishing
Schumacher Centre for Technology and Development
Bourton on Dunsmore, Rugby,
Warwickshire CV23 9QZ, UK
www.practicalactionpublishing.org

© Stafford Holmes and Michael Wingate 1997, 2002

First published in 1997

Revised edition 2002

Reprinted with updates and corrections 2003

Reprinted 2006, 2008, 2013

ISBN 978 1 85339 547 5

Photographs by Stafford Holmes
unless otherwise stated
Illustrations by Terry McKenna

Since 1974, Practical Action Publishing has published and disseminated books and
information in support of international development work throughout the world. Practical
Action Publishing (formerly ITDG Publishing) is a trading name of Intermediate Technology
Publications Ltd (Company Reg. No. 1159018), the wholly owned publishing company of
Intermediate Technology Development Group Ltd (working name Practical Action).
Practical Action Publishing trades only in support of its parent charity objectives and any
profits are covenanted back to Practical Action (Charity Reg. No. 247257, Group VAT
Registration No. 880 9924 76).

Typeset by Dorwyn Ltd, Rowlands Castle, Hants
Printed in India by Replika Press Pvt. Ltd.

About the cover
The Ithnasheri Dispensary was designed as a hospital for the Khoja community in Zanzibar.
The foundation stone was laid in 1887.

This remarkable building successfully blends Indian, Arabic and Zanzibari styles. The open
central courtyard and external balconies facing the harbour provide ample shade and
encourage air circulation. The Bombay architect has incorporated a wide range of decorative
features and finishes in the design. These have been beautifully executed and demonstrate the
high level of craftsmanship that can be achieved by developing skills in the use of local
materials.

The coral ragstone was burnt to produce an excellent lime which was used as the binder
for much of the building's fabric, including floors, walls, finishes and decorative enrichments.
Lime-based mixes were used for running moulds, cast moulds and hand modelling to
represent carved timber, ashlar masonry and pilasters with ornately decorated capitals, all of
which form an integral part of the building.

Contents

Acknowledgements   vii
Dedication   viii
Foreword   ix

1   **An approach to using lime**   1
   1.1   Lime: a versatile binder   1
   1.2   Characteristics of limes   2
   1.3   Air limes, hydraulic limes, and those in between   4
   1.4   What limes do in buildings   4
   1.5   Specifying building limes   6

2   **What lime is and how it is prepared**   8
   2.1   Introduction   8
   2.2   Preparation   9
   2.3   Hydraulic limes   12
   2.4   Pozzolanic additives   14
   2.5   Magnesian limes   14

3   **Tools and equipment**   16
   3.1   Tools for lime   16
   3.2   Plant and equipment   17
   3.3   Setting-out tools   23
   3.4   Plasterers' tools   28
   3.5   Masons' tools and additional equipment   42

4   **Limewashes**   49
   4.1   Uses and qualities   49
   4.2   Preparation of a basic limewash   50
   4.3   Additives to the basic limewash   53
   4.4   Applying limewash   56
   4.5   Performance standards and trial mixes   58

5   **Lime mortars**   60
   5.1   Definition of mortar   60
   5.2   Performance   60
   5.3   Basic materials for mortar   63
   5.4   Additives   65
   5.5   Mortar preparation   67
   5.6   Mortar from non-hydraulic (Class A) quicklime   70
   5.7   Mortar from hydraulic (Class C) quicklime   71

	5.8	Mix proportions	72
	5.9	Application of mortar	72
	5.10	Trial mixes	75

6 Plain lime plastering for interiors — 77

	6.1	Introduction	77
	6.2	Tools	77
	6.3	Backgrounds	77
	6.4	Materials for lime plastering	83
	6.5	Plain lime plaster application	88
	6.6	Texture and finishes	98
	6.7	Ceilings	99
	6.8	Gauging with gypsum or plaster of Paris	101

7 External renders and thrown finishes — 103

	7.1	Introduction	103
	7.2	Tools	105
	7.3	Backgrounds	106
	7.4	Materials	106
	7.5	External lime render, mixes and applications	110
	7.6	Thrown finishes	112
	7.7	Traditional Indian renders	117
	7.8	Lime gauging, daub and earth finishes	120
	7.9	Gauging with Portland cement	121
	7.10	Identification of faults	122

8 Decorative plasterwork — 127

	8.1	Introduction	127
	8.2	Run mouldings	127
	8.3	Cast moulds	134
	8.4	Pargeting	138
	8.5	Modelling stucco *in situ*	140
	8.6	Depeter	143
	8.7	Carved and diapered plaster	144
	8.8	Sgraffito	146
	8.9	Italian stuccos	148

9 Stabilization and other mixes incorporating lime — 152

	9.1	Earth stabilization	152
	9.2	Daub construction	154
	9.3	*Pisé de terre* or rammed earth	156
	9.4	Lime-stabilized earth bricks and blocks	157
	9.5	Lime and cow dung rendering and pargeting	163
	9.6	Renders and slurries for soil structures	164
	9.7	Roof finishes	166

CONTENTS

9.8 Tar and lime coating 167
9.9 Calcium silicate bricks and components 168

10 Substructure: floors, roads and lime concrete 171
10.1 Floors and paving 171
10.2 Roads 178
10.3 Lime concrete 182
10.4 Hydraulic mortar and concrete specifications 186
10.5 Lime concrete canal lining in India 189
10.6 Water mortars for making lime concretes 190

11 Limestone recognition, testing and standards 193
11.1 Field investigation 193
11.2 Geological origin of rocks 194
11.3 Limestone recognition 195
11.4 Field tests for lime 203
11.5 Field tests for sand, pozzolans and mortars 216
11.6 Field tests for soil stabilization 223
11.7 Standard test methods 227
11.8 National standards 237

12 Maintenance guidelines 240
12.1 Introduction 240
12.2 Structural movement 240
12.3 Roof coverings 241
12.4 Rainwater goods above ground 241
12.5 Drainage below ground 242
12.6 Sanitary fittings 242
12.7 Maintaining wall finishes 243
12.8 Maintaining ceilings and decorative plasterwork 246
12.9 Metalwork 249
12.10 Floors 249
12.11 Roads and paths 250
12.12 Vegetation 250
12.13 Summary 251

References and bibliography 252

Glossary 259

Appendices 280
1 Proposed classification of building limes by hydraulicity 280
2 Pozzolans: natural and artificial 282
3 Sieve gauge and mesh size conversion table 285
4 Select list of national standards 286
5 Minerals associated with common limestone chemicals 290

6 Chemical analysis of hydraulic limes and natural cements   292
7 Effects of the addition of pure limes to natural hydraulic   293
   limes
8 Suitability of soils for the addition of lime   294
9 Recommended quantities of gypsum for gauging internal   295
   lime plaster
10 Comparative crushing strengths of mortars and associated   296
   building materials
11 Properties of bricks and blocks   297
12 Comparative compressive strengths of traditional British   299
   lime mortars with those given in some European standards
13 Conversion tables   300

Index   301

Acknowledgements

Some books flow sweetly from the author's experience and imagination with little apparent help from outside sources, but this is not that sort of book. The experience of the present authors when working with lime has served to confirm what others have already noted, often long ago, but many of those notes are inaccessible today. We hope that readers will be encouraged to root out some of the source material which has inspired us.

From earlier centuries we have been greatly inspired by the enthusiasm and clarity of three engineers: John Smeaton, L.J. Vicat and Capt J.T. Smith. From the early twentieth century we would particularly want to draw attention to the report by A.D. Cowper for the Building Research Station in England.

Our enthusiasm was first fired by John Ashurst, John Schofield and Robin Spence. The latter two can be taken as representatives of two large networks – first the 'Wells School' spreading out from the work of the late Professor Robert Baker on the West Front of Wells Cathedral, and very much responsible for the revival of the use of non-hydraulic limes, and secondly the expertise which came together in the buildings advisory work of Intermediate Technology Development Group. Members of this group have championed the use of indigenous hydraulic limes and pozzolans.

In recent years both Eurolime and the Building Limes Forum have opened up a great exchange of information and we have drawn on the work of many of their members. Some members have offered considerable help towards parts of this book, in particular Neville Hill, Rory Young, Pat Gibbons, Tim Meek and Douglas Johnston.

Much within the chapters on plastering has evolved from work with Jeff Orton who has given generously of his time to the development of those sections of the book. We have also benefited from the substantial book written by another plasterer, William Millar, a hundred years ago. John Norton and Hugo Houben have both kindly given permission to draw on their work with earth building techniques.

We are grateful for the administrative support given throughout the preparation of this book by Rodney Melville & Partners. For work behind the scenes our special thanks go to Beverley Bradford who typed the manuscript, then retyped it over and over again as the authors endlessly revised their text.

At different stages in the preparation of the first edition of this book the publishers received help from DFID and from the Tony Bullard Trust, to whom we are grateful for making the book possible.

Dedication

Tony Bullard worked for Intermediate Technology Development Group (ITDG) for about four years, starting early in 1985. He is most remembered in the organization for his work on building materials. During a two-year stay in Kenya he was instrumental in establishing a thriving programme of work, which has contributed to the creation of many jobs and has since expanded into housing. Tony always had a great interest in binders, and particularly the alternatives to Portland cement, such as lime. He contributed to the improvement of lime production and use in Malawi and Zanzibar. Even after leaving ITDG, Tony stayed in close touch, and helped to produce information leaflets on binders as late as 1992.

From ITDG Tony moved to Oxfam to work with refugees, and from there to the United Nations Centre for Human Settlements, as a building materials adviser to Afghanistan, in late 1991. He was asked to establish a field programme for resettlement in eastern Afghanistan in late 1992. It was on his way from Peshawar to project sites he had identified that he was tragically killed by gunmen, on 1st February 1993, at the age of 35.

In remembrance of Tony, a Trust was established in his name, by friends, family and former colleagues. It aims to further some of the ideas for which he worked, by supporting education and information activities aimed at improving livelihoods and living conditions in Africa and Asia. The Tony Bullard Trust has made a substantial contribution to the realization of this book, for which we are very grateful.

Within ITDG, Tony is remembered by his former colleagues as a hard worker with a great commitment to development work. Though cut short tragically, his life touched many of us. Tony would have greatly appreciated this book, and it is fitting that it is dedicated to his memory.

Foreword

The most common raw material for making lime is limestone, which is one of the world's most abundant minerals, widely available in many countries. Lime has many other uses, but this book is specifically about its use in building and construction, for which it has a proven track record through several millennia. Despite this long and successful history, in recent times it has been largely neglected whilst ordinary Portland cement has dominated the market. *Building with Lime* seeks to rectify this situation. The book is a revised, updated and improved edition of the very successful one of the same title, by the same authors, published by the same organization in 1997. The Intermediate Technology Development Group, of which ITDG Publishing is the arm concerned with publications, concentrates on promoting the use of suitable and affordable technologies, particularly in developing countries.

The size of building bricks or blocks is never accurate enough for them merely to be stacked up one upon another to build a sound wall. They require a bedding mortar to take up irregularities and so provide a stable structure. It is necessary that the mortar is spreadable in use, but also that it then sets hard enough to have sufficient strength to take the weight imposed on it as the building process continues above. A degree of adhesion of mortar to bricks or blocks is also desirable to enhance the properties to the wall. Strength and adhesion need not be greater than to be compatible with the bricks or blocks. Often lime-based mortar will be ideal and indeed this is true not only in developing countries but also in industrialized countries.

Lime is produced by heating limestone in a kiln and then the resulting quicklime, which is an unpleasant material to handle, is usually made ready for use by first slaking it with water. A basic mortar of sand mixed with slaked lime hardens by taking carbon dioxide from the air, but this process, although reliable, is slow. Since ancient times other materials, such as volcanic ash, have been mixed in and if they have suitable properties, they react with the slaked lime, accelerating the rate of set. Such reactive additives are known as pozzolans, and a variety of natural and artificial ones have been used. Some limestones themselves contain impurities which, after heating in the kiln, provide reactive material to give so called hydraulic lime.

In addition to use for bedding bricks and blocks, lime-based mortars can be used successfully for indoor plastering and outdoor rendering of walls;

additives can enhance performance. Lime wash can be applied thinly to wall surfaces to give an attractive finish.

Some of the advantages of using lime-based material are that, in walling, the slower setting rate gives time to accommodate some of the movements which otherwise would give rise to stress and, especially in the case of render finishes and lime wash on walls, there is sufficient permeability for the wall to breathe, allowing water vapour to escape.

Lime can be used for floors, ceilings and for making stabilized blocks from clayey soils. Fine decorative work can be achieved with lime, particularly if it is mixed with a little gypsum plaster. Where a sufficiently developed infrastructure exists, calcium silicate bricks can be made from lime and a suitable silica sand.

Ordinary Portland cement is available worldwide, engineers have been educated in its use not only for civil engineering but also for building and construction, and guidance for its use is widely available. However, use of lime should be investigated, particularly where the availability or price of ordinary Portland cement might mitigate against its use. The possibilities of using local materials and labour for production and the advantages in using lime might prove attractive and should be borne in mind in decision making.

Details of simple tests for materials are included in *Building with Lime* which concludes with a bibliography, a glossary of terms, appendices and a useful subject index. The book provides information on all aspects of lime use to inform decision makers, educate those wishing to revive or improve existing use, facilitate development of the necessary skills or help encourage best practice in the use of the product.

The authors, Michael Wingate and Stafford Holmes, are United Kingdom based professional architects not only with great enthusiasm for lime but also with much knowledge and experience. They have made inputs into projects in many different countries and have been involved with various groups promoting the use of lime. *Building with Lime* is an important and comprehensive book which can be expected to be in demand worldwide.

Ray Smith
Building Materials Consultant
Member and one-time ITDG Panel Chair

1

An approach to using lime

1.1 Lime: a versatile binder

When it is used well, lime is quite simply the best and most versatile binder in the world. There is a wide variety of limes which might be produced from differing materials and with various production methods. The approach taken in this book is to show how to make the best use in building works of each type of lime, whether extracted locally or from further afield. Every sort of lime has its own particular virtues and limitations.

Building lime has been used as a binder for building work for thousands of years, due to its unique setting properties and the exceptional smoothness which it offers when it is worked. Its versatility is shown by the wide variety of uses to which it is put. Structural elements for which lime mixes may be used, in appropriate designs, include foundations, walls, floors, vaults and roofs. Lime is also used for many finishes including paints, plasters, renders, and decorative work such as cornices and hand-modelled stucco.

Although lime has in the past been used in many of the greatest buildings throughout the world, it is also particularly suitable for one- and two-storey buildings and as a low-cost versatile binder for today.

The successful use of lime in construction depends on the craftsman's knowledge and skill; indeed, the same might be said of many other materials. Once understood, lime is a soft and forgiving material which amply rewards care and patience in its use and produces work with great aesthetic quality. The craftsman will learn to recognize and select sound and appropriate materials to ensure the best results. There is no substitute for skill and experience, but these can be developed in a short space of time provided that the appropriate knowledge is available.

This book is intended as a starting point for those considering lime as a building material, and as a general reference to the broad range of uses for lime in construction. The abundance of limestone worldwide means there is a high probability that this valuable low-cost resource will be available in geological formations not too distant from wherever it is required.

The use of lime has a well-documented and fascinating history. It is hoped that the technical information on how lime has been used successfully in the past, and is being used today, will assist a general understanding, and enable initial experience and skills to be developed.

The many environmental benefits to be gained by a return to appropriate uses of building limes are significant. These include the ability to manufacture locally on a small scale and to produce a binder at lower temperatures, using less energy than most currently available binders. In addition, by increasing local production and availability, associated transport, pollution and cost may be correspondingly reduced.

1.2 Characteristics of limes

Although each lime is different, and some may perform in very special ways, there are certain characteristics which are typical of most limes and set them apart from other binders such as cement, gypsum and clay.

Stickiness The root meaning of the word lime is 'sticky material'. It binds gently, and the stickiness gives good adhesion to other surfaces.

'Workability' (dependent on plasticity and water retention) This is easier to feel than to describe. It is the ability of a mortar or plaster to remain smooth and mouldable even against the suction it may experience from porous building materials. The mix can penetrate and fill voids in a background to give a good key. Less workable mixes would become stiff and awkward as the water is sucked away from them. Good workability greatly assists good workmanship, helping to achieve full joints with good bonding to the other materials involved. This is what makes lime-based mixes such a pleasure to use.

Durability When used carefully, lime is exceptionally durable. An outstanding example is the Pantheon temple in Rome which has a lime concrete dome spanning over 43 metres (142 feet). This has survived for nearly nineteen hundred years.

Soft texture This contributes to the comfortable feel and charming appearance of lime surfaces. It also helps lime to cushion the joints between stones or bricks and prolong their life.

'Breathability' (high porosity, high permeability) This group of characteristics also allows lime mortars to protect the other materials in a building by handling moisture movements through the building, protecting masonry materials from harmful salts. 'Breathability' greatly assists the drying out of buildings and the avoidance of condensation problems, which contributes to the comfort of people using the buildings.

Low thermal conductivity This property affects the surface temperatures within buildings, making lime plasters in cool climates feel warmer to the touch than cement plasters. The higher surface temperatures (in cool climates) contribute to a feeling of comfort. In warm climates lime plasters also improve comfort conditions due to this property.

Interior of the Pantheon in Rome; the dome rises to a height of 43m above the floor

Autogenous healing   When buildings made with lime are subjected to small movements they are more likely to develop many fine cracks than the individual large cracks which occur in stiffer cement-bound buildings. Water penetration into these fine cracks can dissolve 'free' lime and bring it to the surface. As the water evaporates, this lime is deposited and begins to heal the cracks. That is how some old buildings on poor foundations distort rather than fail.

Protection   In many ways soft lime mortars and paints can be used to give protection to buildings, particularly from severe rain. They can act sacrificially to protect the structure.

What most (but not all) limes do not provide is great strength, but for one- and two-storey buildings great strength is not needed, and even much larger buildings can be designed for low-stress materials if the geometry is correct. Great strength is the special characteristic of Portland cements, but for general building purposes this brings some disadvantages. Cement mortars are typically stiffer and less permeable. When used in conjunction with softer materials or on weaker backgrounds this can sometimes cause serious problems by trapping moisture and creating high local stresses.

1.3   Air limes, hydraulic limes, and those in between

There are two ways in which limes may set, either by a slow combination with carbon dioxide gas (a component of the air) in a process called *carbonation*, or by combination with silicates and aluminates in the presence of water in what is called *hydraulic set*. Nearly all limes set to some extent by carbonation, which is the only way that the purest limes gain strength. The hydraulic set is a property exhibited by limes which contain active clay impurities. In many cases the proportion of these impurities is low and the carbonation remains important, but for some limes the hydraulic set is predominant.

In later chapters of the book, these two methods of setting will be described in greater detail, but at the outset it is worth noting that where strength is particularly important or where lime must set in permanently damp conditions then hydraulic limes are the most appropriate. Where they are not available, similar results can often be achieved using a pozzolanic additive with an air lime. These additives would be some form of active clay or silica from natural or artificial sources and are described in Chapter 7 and Appendix 2.

The air limes tend to be 'fatter' than the hydraulic limes; that is to say, they hold more water in their pastes (which are known as 'lime putties') and retain this water tenaciously against the suction of porous backings. This, and the slow setting, are exactly the properties which are needed for plastering work. The fatness gives the workability which is also important for mortars.

Often what is needed are the good working properties of a fat lime with the advantages of some hydraulic action to give an early set in difficult conditions. Many of the under-exploited middle ranges of lime can provide just that.

1.4   What limes do in buildings

Lime is suitable for use in all building elements and finishes from foundations to roofs, provided that an appropriate lime is selected. Both the diversity of limes and the use of simple additives give the versatility.

The slaking of quicklime with excess water is a simple and inexpensive process. The production of limewash by this method can enable a local low-cost paint to be readily available. Improving weathering qualities by additives or producing a limewash of any desired colour by the addition of pigments is also a simple process.

Lime can bind sand or other aggregates to form a mortar for masonry walling. A lime mortar will typically be easy to use and has been shown to play a major part in the durability of historic structures.

Similar mixes, but perhaps with different aggregates, are used for internal and external coatings to improve wall surfaces. The external coatings, called renders, help with weathering protection and may improve appearance. The internal coatings, called plasters, make rooms easier to clean, reduce the risks of vermin and insects, and generally make a significant improvement to hygiene. The plaster gives a surface which can be bright and attractive in itself or can form a base for decoration. It is also incombustible and can be used to improve fire resistance, an attribute particularly useful for timber-frame buildings.

Lime as a decorative medium, either in two-dimensional patterns or for relief modelling, has been employed extensively. Hand-modelled shapes, and cast and *in-situ* mouldings using lime as a base, can be seen on every continent. Individual expression by the decoration of buildings with enrichments of this nature has been common to all societies throughout history.

Soil in various forms has been used widely throughout the world for building. Lime is one of the most compatible materials with soil structures. Soils with varying degrees of clay content may be stabilized by lime. This improves the soil's resistance to erosion by water. In addition, the permeable and relatively soft render and plaster coatings are well suited to earth walling. Lime's ability to stabilize soil can be used to make solid floors and stabilize soil structures.

Before Portland cement became available, lime concretes were used for many applications in building works and in civil engineering. Survivals from ancient Rome include the structural core for walling, floors, cisterns, baths, aqueducts, vaults and domes. In more recent times, lime–ash mixes have been used to make upper floors in mills, factories and homes. Harbours, canals, bridges and the foundations for large structures in the eighteenth and nineteenth centuries made extensive use of lime concrete.

Lime is an excellent material for repairing and protecting old buildings, particularly where existing materials must be conserved. The strength and porosity of the lime mix can be judged precisely in order to match or be less than those of adjacent material. The binder used in the original construction of most historic buildings is frequently lime, making this the natural choice for a compatible repair material.

1.5 Specifying building limes

Probably the most readily obtainable internationally recognized standards in connection with lime are those from America, India, Britain, Germany and France. These have been developed over many years and are extensive. Most standards specify test procedures and performance levels for lime generally, not only building limes. Most standards refer to pure, fat, or air limes, and cross-reference to qualities required for mortars and renders which may be of different materials. The standards, however, are useful guidelines to quality and there is common ground on test procedures and apparatus. Physical requirements for lime putty, dry hydrate, consistency and quality are stipulated throughout. This information is drawn together and described in Chapter 11.

Calcium carbonate occurs in many forms, of which one of the most common is limestone. The formation of limestone often involves a sedimentary process. Sediment may contain widely varying quantities of silica, alumina and other minerals and compounds. A wide variety of setting properties is possible between pure lime and eminently hydraulic lime. It is important, therefore, to consider which limes are available and the most suitable, in order that the appropriate classification is selected and specified for the task in hand.

The raw materials available, production methods used, and the standard of workmanship will all have a major effect on final quality. It is important, therefore, not only to understand the various requirements dictated by a building, but also local conditions, before finalizing a specification. It is quite possible that local materials, although not 'standard', will be suitable provided appropriate methods of preparation and application are employed.

The use of untried local materials can be both exciting and rewarding provided serious failures are avoided! If well tried and tested principles are followed through, it is possible that untried local materials may be used with success. If this is the intention, then small-scale trials will be essential. An example might be to make sample wall panels for artifically accelerated weathering tests, or to watch the natural weathering over several years.

Initially, when unfamiliar materials are to be used, a specification may be given in terms of the performance required which may offer only general guidance on selection and proportioning. After experience of these local materials has been gained, further field trials and perhaps even laboratory tests can be carried out to help firm up future specifications. These may then be given in terms of materials and workmanship rather than 'performance'. It is important to remember that, however thorough a specification may be, there is no substitute for good workmanship.

This book describes a great variety of ways in which limes can be used, but the selection of method must pay due regard to local regulations. It is unfortunate that over the last century there has been a rapid decline in the use of lime for building. This decline has been so extensive in some countries that there are standards and regulations that are no longer appropriate or adequate. Where building regulations regarding limes are unsatisfactory they should be changed.

2

What lime is and how it is prepared

2.1 Introduction

Safety

Quicklime is very dangerous. It can combine vigorously with water to generate a great amount of heat which can cause sudden and unpredictable spitting. Quicklime in your eyes can blind you and badly stored quicklime has been known to start fires when it became wet.

Other forms of lime are far less dangerous, but like Portland cement, are caustic and will dry out your skin.

Before using or specifying limes, check on safety procedures which are described in the section on slaking later in this chapter.

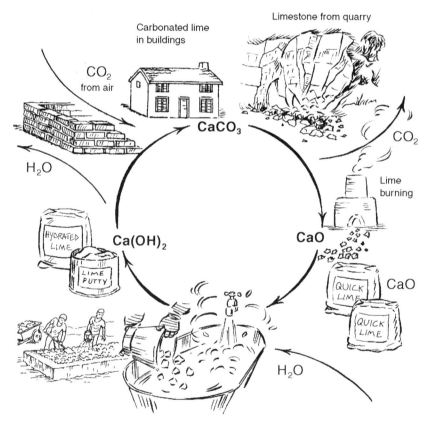

The lime cycle

The lime cycle

Lime does not occur naturally but must always be manufactured. In the manufacturing processes the material passes through several stages, as follows.

The raw material is *calcium carbonate* which is usually quarried as limestone, but may also be found as chalk, coral rocks or shells.

When this is heated in a kiln it undergoes a chemical change, giving off carbon dioxide gas and forming *calcium oxide*. This is commonly known as quicklime or lump-lime.

When quicklime is combined with water it changes to *calcium hydroxide*, commonly known as slaked lime, hydrated lime or often just 'lime'.

Lime can slowly absorb carbon dioxide from the air to form *calcium carbonate*. As this is chemically the same as the raw material, the whole process is often seen as a cycle, but in practice the carbonated lime which is finally achieved may be very different physically from the limestone or other original material.

For most building purposes lime is used as calcium hydroxide and the slow absorption of carbon dioxide to reform calcium carbonate is one of the ways in which it can set; this is known as carbonation. Care must be taken to encourage this reaction, for which practical details are given in the later chapters on limewashes, mortars and plasters.

2.2   Preparation

Lime burning

To manufacture lime, the raw material must be heated to at least a cherry-red heat, around 900°C, to allow the carbon dioxide gas to be driven off. This is nearly always done in a lime kiln and the process has been described in other publications from ITDG Publishing (Wingate, 1985).

The temperature regime as the material passes through a kiln will affect its *reactivity*, that is, the rate at which it will enter into chemical reactions. This will in turn affect the ability of the resultant quicklime to slake to a fine putty (or to a fine dry hydrate) and will affect the ability of the lime putty to react with carbon dioxide to achieve a good set by carbonation.

When wood is used as a fuel in lime kilns, the relatively low flame temperature, the long flames and the presence of steam all ensure a reactive lime. Similarly 'low' temperatures are achieved in the best modern kilns which are used to prepare the high-specification limes demanded for steel making. But when the kiln temperatures are higher, particularly in the later stages of lime burning, the pores in the quicklime close up and the material becomes less reactive.

Quicklime

The quicklime taken straight from the kiln is called *run of kiln quicklime*. This will be a mixture of materials which may include any of the following:

○ *Soft-burnt* quicklime which is the good (reactive) product.

○ *Under-burnt* quicklime which contains a residual core of unconverted carbonate. This is one source of the chalk or limestone which can often be seen in old mortar, where it acts as part of the aggregate, contributing to the porosity and aiding carbonation.

○ *Over-burnt* quicklime which is less reactive. It can spoil finished work by late hydration; the expansion during hydration can build up stresses within the mortar and consequent small explosions blow away the surface causing defects known as pitting and popping. When the over-burnt material is finely divided there can be a general expansion known as unsoundness. This destroys the bond between the mortar and its backing. Protect against these risks by using high specification quicklime, or by hand-picking lump lime, by sieving milk of lime or by using well matured lime putty.

○ *Hard-burnt* quicklime. This is deliberately made with a less reactive surface layer for convenience of handling, transport and storage.

○ Perhaps also some *ash and unburnt fuel*. These may be a source of harmful sulphate contamination, but on the other hand, the ash may also give a pozzolanic set to the lime, which is described later in this chapter.

The quicklime is significantly lighter than the limestone from which it has been produced. If the lump size is not too small the good, soft-burnt, material can be judged in the hand by its low density and open-textured surface. The over-burnt material feels denser and may have a sintered surface. Under-burnt material may also feel heavy because of its denser core. This method of checking quality is called hand-picking and it was once usual to read the term 'best hand-picked lump lime' in building specifications.

After hand-picking, any residue is known as small lime. In some places this has been used as a form of weak concrete for infill panels or for lime-ash floors. *Quicklime is caustic and hand-picking should not be carried out without wearing suitable protective clothing, especially gloves.*

Quicklime which is left in a moist atmosphere will degrade by air-slaking. A powdery surface develops on the lumps and, in time, the material falls entirely to a powdery mixture of calcium hydroxide and calcium carbonate. The speed of this decay depends on the humidity and temperature conditions, as well as on the reactivity of the lime. Under the worst circumstances it can take only a matter of a few hours. So if soft-burnt quicklime must be stored it should be in air-tight packaging. It is often better to slake the quicklime, straight away, at the lime works.

Slaking, dry hydrate and lime putty

A good, reactive quicklime will combine vigorously with cold water, breaking up, swelling considerably and generating a great deal of heat. For complete hydration it will combine with a certain proportion of water

Slaking into a lime pit

demanded by the chemical reaction. If somewhat more water than that is provided, the heat will drive off the excess water to leave a dry powder called dry hydrate of lime. This is usually just known as hydrated lime or bagged lime as it is often sold in paper sacks. In many countries this form of lime is readily available at builders' merchants.

The dry hydrate of an air lime can be used to improve the properties of cement–sand mixes, but it is unlikely to produce lime mortars or plasters which will carbonate well enough to give consistently good results. To ensure good results, the lime must be evenly burnt at a low temperature (around 900°C) and production, packaging, storage and delivery must be carefully controlled. For this reason it is best to use a lime putty run straight from quicklime. Clearly, hydraulic limes would not be sold as putties.

If a considerable excess of water is provided during the slaking, then the lime is run to a free-flowing milk of lime. This can be sieved to remove the larger particles of over-burnt and under-burnt material and discharged into a lime pit. The residue on the sieve should be discarded. In the pit, the suspended solids in the milk of lime settle out to form a cohesive mass called lime putty. Above this is clear liquid, a saturated solution of lime, called lime water. As the lime matures in the pit (or in suitable containers) the remaining fine particles of over-burnt lime can be given time to slake.

A well-matured lime will give a good defence against those defects which can spoil plasterwork, but the time required to mature the putty adequately will depend on the quality of the quicklime used and on how important it is to remove all risk of failure. For general use, in mortar one month is typical, and for plaster three months, but for the repair of historic churches in Denmark, local regulations state that lime putty must be at least five years old. Many of the other characteristics of a lime, such as water retentivity and plasticity, will also be improved by this maturing process.

Lime putties are often kept, at least for the first few weeks, in a pit in the ground. A porous lining allows excess moisture to drain away whilst the moisture in the ground prevents the putty from drying out. The same result is also achieved when the putty is stored in an ark, which is a wooden-sided structure above ground. This gives a firmer consistency than is achieved when the fresh putty is put straight away into watertight vessels; the firmer putty can produce a mortar which is less likely to show shrinkage cracks.

The slaking process is particularly dangerous and safety precautions must be taken to prevent the lime from splashing on to the skin or into the eyes. The person doing the slaking should wear waterproof clothing – boots, coat, hat – and cover the neck and mouth with cloth. Barrier cream should be used on the hands and wrists. Eyes should be protected with goggles and an ample supply of clean lukewarm water (that is, at around body temperature) must be kept to rinse lime splashes from the skin. An eye bath or suitable spray should be available to rinse out splashes from the eye. Eye rinsing should continue for twenty minutes and medical assistance should be sought. It is essential to have assistance available from someone nearby who is not carrying out the slaking. The slaking area should be free from obstructions and marked off with a barrier to keep other people away.

2.3 Hydraulic limes

Pure limes will not set under water, so for building in wet conditions including hydraulic engineering works – bridges, dams, harbours and locks – special materials are needed. These are also of importance for use in specific locations where conditions are often damp or wet, such as foundations and work below ground in damp soils, in drainage, in construction adjacent to rivers, and as an external render in damp climates, bathrooms and water storage tanks. Nowadays cement is usually used for such works, but before cement was available it was found that certain limes could set under water and these are known as hydraulic limes because of their suitability for that sort of work. The chalks and limestones from which they are made contain fine clay materials which, when appropriately fired in the kiln, combine with lime to form active compounds. These compounds can combine in water to give a chemical set which would be in addition to any set from the carbonation of the uncombined (or free) lime.

The most active of the possible clay constituents is soluble silica (SiO_2), but other contributions to the hydraulicity come from alumina (Al_2O_3) and from ferric oxide (Fe_2O_3) which gives a buff colour to many (but not all) of the hydraulic limes in their burnt and their set states. An indication of the likely hydraulicity can be obtained from a cementation index (Cowper, 1927; Boynton, 1980), which balances the significance of the components which may be found from chemical analysis of the limestone, giving weight to the most active ones. The notation used for this abbreviates SiO_2 to S, CaO to C, Al_2O_3 to A, Fe_2O_3 to F, and MgO to M:

$$\text{Cementation Index (C.I.)} = \frac{2.8(\%S) + 1.1(\%A) + 0.7(\%F)}{(\%C) + 1.4(\%M)}$$

The presence of these clay ingredients can be found by treating the limestone with dilute acid to dissolve away the carbonate. If the residue is a fine clay, with a greasy or unctuous feel, then the lime is likely to have hydraulic properties.

The hydraulic properties will depend not only on the constituents of the limestone but also on the firing temperatures. At high temperatures the lime begins to sinter and cannot slake unless it has been finely ground up. Where the proportions of clay are small the hydraulic set is minimal and the lime can also set in the normal way by carbonation. At the other extreme, where the proportion of clay is very high, there may not even be enough free lime to enable the lumps to break down on slaking, and these limes, called natural cements, must be finely ground before water is added. They will set very quickly giving high strength. In between those extremes there is a wide range of possible materials for which a classification was developed by the French engineer L.J. Vicat early in the nineteenth century. His system includes simple tests and indicates appropriate uses for the various limes. The descriptions which he suggested are still in common use and the table in Appendix 1 shows how they relate to the cementation index below.

Table 2.1: Cementation Index for various types of lime

Lime description	Cementation index (C.I.)	Active clay content in the limestone
Fat limes	close to zero	Very little clay
Slightly hydraulic limes	0.3 to 0.5	Around 8%
Moderately hydraulic limes	0.5 to 0.7	Around 15%
Eminently hydraulic limes	0.7 to 1.1	Around 25%
Natural cement	1.7	Up to 45%

13

Vicat also defines 'lean limes' in which the limestone contains a significant proportion of inert material. Many 'stone' limes fall into the 'lean' lime category but the description is also used for slightly hydraulic 'grey' limes. The burning of broken stone waste from quarrying could sometimes be an economic way to produce mortar locally.

Hydraulic lime mortars not only have this extra power of setting, but are usually stronger than non-hydraulic lime mortars. Thus they have often been used with the intention of giving durability to non-hydraulic construction works, but they can give rise to the same sorts of decay problems as mortars containing modern cements – undue stiffness and lower permeability which can allow soluble salts to cause damage to the masonry units, rather than to the more easily repaired joints.

Where feebly hydraulic limes were available, such as the grey stone limes in southern England, they were the first choice for masonry mortar. It is now recognized that a range of mortar strengths and qualities are necessary for differing situations. Ideally, if sufficient choice of lime is available, the best lime for any purpose can be selected. The purer (white or 'fat') air limes are the first choice for plastering. A table giving the chemical analysis of various limestones regularly used for producing hydraulic lime at the beginning of the twentieth century is given in Appendix 6.

2.4   Pozzolanic additives

Similar 'hydraulic' properties to these described above can be achieved by adding certain pozzolans to a fat or air-lime mortar. These materials contain very finely divided clay or similarly fine minerals which have at some time been subjected to great heat. Examples are certain volcanic ashes such as the original Pozzolana from near Naples in Italy, the fly ash known as PFA which is produced in power stations which burn pulverized coal, and brick dust prepared by crushing or grinding lightly-burnt clay bricks.

The reactivity of the pozzolans depends very much on their preparation and storage. For the best reaction the clays would be lightly burnt (say at 600°C) and be finely ground. Strongly pozzolanic mortars may, like mortars made from strong hydraulic limes, produce the decay mechanisms normally associated with cement-rich mortars.

A table listing artificial and natural pozzolans that have been used to promote a hydraulic set is given in Appendix 2.

2.5   Magnesian limes

The metallic element magnesium can form similar compounds to those of calcium, and although deposits of pure magnesium carbonate are very rare, the double compound of calcium carbonate and magnesium carbonate, called dolomite, is quite common. It is formed from calcium carbonate

14

rocks by the action of magnesium-rich brines. Where the conversion from calcium carbonate to dolomite is incomplete, which is very common, the dolomite occurs in rocks which still contain further calcium carbonate and these are called magnesian limestones. The magnesian limes formed from such limestones can be used for building work, but there is a problem to be overcome.

The magnesium carbonate converts to magnesium oxide (magnesia – the equivalent of quicklime) at a considerably lower temperature than that needed to convert the calcium carbonate to quicklime. When the lime is well burnt the magnesia thus tends to be over-burnt and can give rise to all the problems normally associated with late hydration. Thus special care is needed to slake this lime. One method is to slake under pressure in an autoclave; another is to store the lime putty for a long time. The usual advice is to follow local tradition and to be aware of the risks, but it should be stressed that where magnesian limes are used they have a very high reputation giving an early set and developing good strength.

3

Tools and equipment

3.1   Tools for lime

Only a very few simple tools are required to carry out most tasks involving
lime. The tools and equipment illustrated and described here are given as
reference to assist choice of the most appropriate tools. The craftsman is
likely to have his own favourites and starting with a limited number, possibly hand-made, may wish to add to these over the years.

Availability

Most tools now on the market are relatively inexpensive, machine-made
and readily available in many countries. They are also simple in form and
should not be difficult to manufacture locally. The following descriptions
set out the purpose of the tools generally, but the illustrations give priority
to traditional forms that may be simply made from wood or steel, as opposed to those that are mass produced.

Care and maintenance

Tools for plastering are constantly in contact with lime and coarse stuff, which
have abrasive, caustic, and vigorous setting properties. These materials tend to
adhere to the tools and cause them to corrode unless they are kept clean. The
tools that are in use need to be reasonably clean if good results are to be
obtained. Hardened plaster on tool edges will impair efficiency and make
clean, neat finishes almost impossible to achieve. Hardened gritty material set
on handles will soon cause sore hands. Both quality of finish and the life of the
tools can be improved by keeping tools fairly clean even while work is in
progress, and by cleaning all tools thoroughly at the end of the day.

Metal tools are best dried and wiped over with an oily rag to protect
against rust.

Wooden tools should be laid flat and kept out of the sun. This helps to
prevent the blades from warping, which is a tendency if they dry out too
quickly.

Selection

There are many builders' tools and a wide range of equipment used in
connection with lime. Good preparation of the material to be worked is
most important for successful results. This is common to all trades, crafts
and skills and therefore much of the plant and equipment described in this
chapter will be useful to all.

The setting-out tools described cover a broad range of simple aids to
accuracy. Some degree of setting out will be necessary whatever the task.

The degree of accuracy, however, will vary widely depending on local conditions and the standard of finish intended.

In areas where precise line and level are not required, or where irregular appearance is adequate, setting-out tools are of less importance. Without their use, a finished plaster surface will tend to follow the form of the background quite closely, however irregular it may be. This may produce an acceptable, and sometimes delightful, effect in the context of less formal and more irregular types of construction.

Plasterers, masons, painters and conservators tend to be the principal users of lime. The tools described are limited to those traditionally accepted for working with this material. Lime plastering techniques and the preparation and use of lime mortars are described fully but detailed descriptions of tools for each building trade are not the subject of this book. These have been well documented in other publications, a selected number of which are given in the Bibliography.

3.2   Plant and equipment

Although they are not craftsmen's tools, some plant and equipment has been included here as they will normally be necessary to carry out the whole process, particularly when sand is obtained locally and 'as dug'. In large building contracts some of the equipment described, such as scaffold, may be available from the general contractor, or employer. In smaller work, or where only plastering is involved, consideration needs to be given to what additional labourers' plant and equipment is required.

Slaking tanks, tubs and baths
Large containers for storing materials on site are always useful, particularly where a large volume of material has to be prepared. If ready-made containers are difficult to obtain, pits may be dug in the ground, and it is best if they are lined with any material that will help to keep the putty clean. Containers may also be made from barrels or drums cut in half. Alternatively they may be formed with waterproof sheet material such as polythene supported by stout framework. The containers will vary in size depending on use. In the main these will be for holding water, washing sand, slaking lime, storing lime putty and storing coarse stuff. Dustbins or empty oil drums with lids are ready-made containers that are useful for this purpose.

Buckets and shovels
These are items that can be put into constant use during all preparatory work. Due to the amount of wear they usually receive it is likely to be cost effective to ensure that they are of robust construction.

Screen
Ungraded sand, extracted from a convenient local source, will need to be screened to separate stones and any other oversize material. The screen is

Using a screen to separate gravel from sand

set up adjacent to the main storage area, and all sand is thrown through the screen to separate the good sand from larger aggregate which is unsuitable. A convenient size of screen is approximately 2m long by 1m wide with 150mm deep sides (6'6" × 3'3" × 6"). It is normally fixed at an angle of 45°. It may also be used for screening lime, although sieves are usually more appropriate. A suitable mesh size initially would be about 5mm, but for further details refer to Sections 5.3 and 6.4.

Sieves

The importance of sieving both sand and lime is described in the following chapter. Wire mesh sieves are made with a range of aperture sizes, allowing selection of the sand particle size to be made, depending on the quality of work and finish required. In addition they are most important for 'running' lime, that is, sifting out under-burnt and over-burnt particles and other unwanted material from milk of lime before it settles out as a putty.

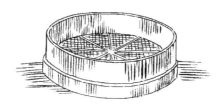

Sieve

Sand-washing equipment

In cases where the strongest renders, plasters or mortars are required, the sand must be clean. If mixed with earth or organic matter which coats the sand grains, the lime will not properly bind with it, and a weaker product will be the result. If the sand is found to be dirty after testing, described in Chapter 11, it may be cleaned by washing. A simple way to do this is to make a trough out of plain boards 2.5 to 3 metres (8' to 10') long. Put the sand in the trough to a height just below the outlet level. While gently stirring the sand, let a stream of water run through it from a hose, tap or spring. Allow the water to overflow at the lower end carrying away the particles of dirt, and the clean sand will remain (Verrall, 1931).

Sand washing

Larry

A larry is used for the thorough mixing of lime and sand to make either coarse stuff or fine stuff. It is also suitable for agitating quicklime in the water when it is being slaked.

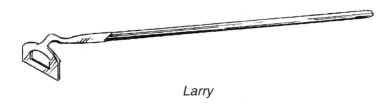

Larry

Drag or hair hook

This is similar to a rake, but with prongs set well apart for mixing hair with coarse stuff.

Drag or hair hook

Banker

This is a platform, usually made on site, for gauging large quantities of material with shovels. A convenient size is about 1.5m square, sometimes narrower in width to about 1.3m (5' × 4'). It is a considerable aid to mixing if the whole of the base can be made from one large flat continuous sheet without joints. On completion of work the banker may be removed and the floor left in a clean and undamaged condition.

Purpose-made bankers are now also made with galvanized steel sheet or formed plastic trays and baths.

Banker

Spot board

A spot board is a stout table top for holding plastering material. It may be made of heavy timber such as floorboards or thick plywood, or of steel. A convenient size is between 750mm and 1m square (2'6" to 3'3").

Spot board and stand

Scaffold

A safe working platform is normally essential to gain access to the higher levels of walls internally, to ceilings, and for all work at high level externally. Scaffold boards should be laid close together, fixed firmly and without traps such as unsupported ends overlapping scaffold poles. It is important and always worthwhile to consider carefully the method of erecting and using safe working scaffold, and all access arrangements.

Trestles

A simple method of working at high levels, particularly internally, is by standing on scaffold boards supported by trestles. Four-legged trestles are a convenient and safe method of support, and may be made up in timber or steel.

1. Trestle   2. Scaffold boards

Hop up

Hop up

A hop up is a simple but very useful piece of equipment, which enables the plasterer to gain sufficient height to work to the top of walls. Mostly used when working inside rooms close to the ceiling, it consists of three or four steps formed from planks or plywood boards light enough to be moved easily round the work area but sufficiently robust for the plasterer to stand on.

Stilts

Some plasterers can work effectively on ceilings by wearing stilts strapped to their legs below the knees.

3.3   Setting-out tools

Rules

Rules and straight edges are employed where large flat areas of plaster must be plumb and level. They are used for ruling off and straightening large areas of fair-faced work.

The floating rule is used for straightening the floating coat over large areas. A normal floating rule is between 2m and 2.5m long (6'6"–8'). Generally they may be varied in length to relate to the work in hand, and may be between 1.25m and 3.5m (4'–12'). The back edges may be tapered at the ends to reduce weight.

The feather-edge rule is used at internal angles and to roughly straighten two-coat work. It is sometimes used for floating the third (finishing) coat to an even surface before hand floating, scouring and trowelling. Aluminium rules and straight edges are now widely used as they are light and stable. Timber rules were used traditionally but they must be made from well-seasoned timber to reduce the tendency to warp.

Using a feather-edge rule for lime plaster ceiling patch repair (J. Orton working at Warwick Castle, 1995)

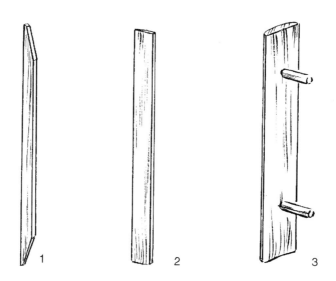

Rules: 1. Floating rule; 2. Feather-edge rule; 3. Darby

Ruling off with a darby after laying on plaster

The darby   is a variation of the feather-edge rule. It has the addition of two handles about 150mm long by 50mm diameter (6" × 2"), best fixed by screwing to the back of the blade at equal distance from each end. This is used for floating bays between screeds on walls and ceilings, and sometimes for floating the finishing coat to an even surface before hand floating, scouring and trowelling.

Squares

Squares are used to set up right angles. Set squares are triangular in form and may be made of wood or iron. They may be made in various sizes depending on the type of work in hand, but a convenient size for the majority of work is 300mm (12") on each square edge. Some incorporate small spirit levels which help in forming work plumb and level. Large squares of about 900mm (3') are used for large-scale work usually in connection with ceilings and screeding floors. A simple square may be made from the corner of a standard sheet of plywood.

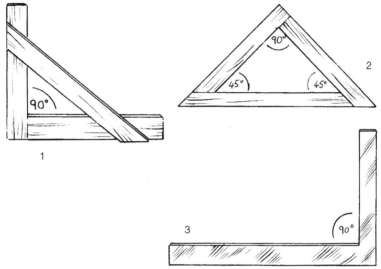

1. Wood square; 2. Set square; 3. Steel square

Chalk line and reel

Chalk lines are used for setting out long straight lines to work to on site. The line is a strong fine cord steeped in chalk and fixed on a reel. The line can be stretched and snapped on a ceiling or wall to leave a chalk mark for reference and setting out.

Chalk line and reel

Plumb bob

This is attached to a line, often a chalk line, and used for setting out verticals on the working surface. It is best made of a heavy metal such as lead. The heavier it is, the quicker it will settle in position, and the less it will be moved about by the wind.

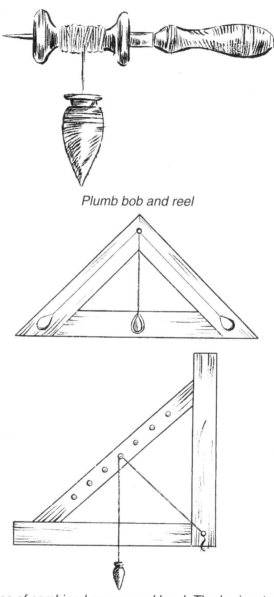

Plumb bob and reel

Two types of combined square and level. The horizontal level is established by use of the plumb bob

Combined square and level

Two traditional arrangements for obtaining level with square and plumb bob are illustrated opposite (Kemp, 1912; Orton, 1992).

Spirit level

The spirit level is used in conjunction with the plumb bob for setting out, to establish horizontal levels. It is often used in conjunction with the plumb bob, the square, and sometimes the compass for setting out new work.

Compass

Used mostly in connection with decorative work for describing arcs or circles during the course of setting out.

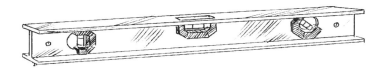

Spirit level

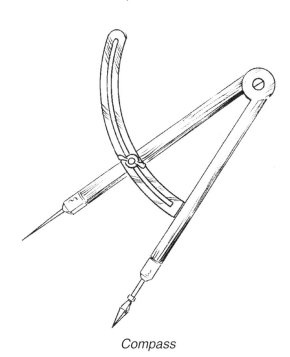

Compass

27

3.4 Plasterers' tools

Plasterers' hawk

Due to the advantages of lightness, these tools are mass-produced in plastics and aluminium. The traditional type is made of wood; often white pine, as it is a relatively lightweight timber and not liable to deform with wetting. Generally they are between 300mm and 350mm square (12" to 14").

Hawks are used for holding the coarse stuff with one hand whilst applying the plaster or render to the wall with a trowel or float in the other. The illustration shows a traditional wooden hawk and its component parts, to clarify the method of construction. It has a board about 15mm (⅝") thick. As a refinement to reduce weight, the four sides of the back may be chamfered from about 100mm (4") from the centre to leave the edges about 9mm (⅜") thick. A 9mm (⅜") dovetail groove 85mm (3½") wide and

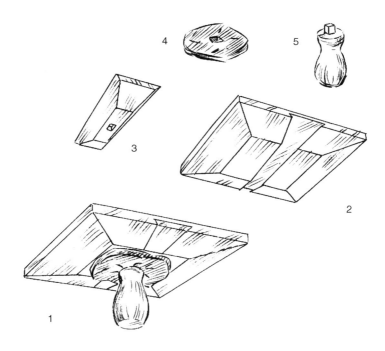

Plasterers' hawk: a traditional type made of wood
1. Assembled hawk;
2. Board; 3. Bar; 4. Cushion; 5. Handle

diminishing in width by about 5mm (¼"), is made in the centre of the board and across the grain of the wood. A bar that takes the handle is made to fit the groove.

Although wooden boards are usually made of softwood, there are advantages in using hardwood for the bar for greater strength. The handle may be of softwood, about 120mm (5") long and 35mm (1½") in diameter. A refinement of the handle is for it to be turned to produce a slight swell in the centre and a rounded knob at the end which makes it more comfortable and firm to hold. A leather or rubber cushion can be fitted on the handle to rest against the underside of the board to protect the hand.

Laying-on trowel

A laying-on trowel is used for spreading or laying on the plaster and for trowelling up where a smooth, steel-trowelled surface is required. It is about 280mm × 115mm (11" × 4½"). The plate is made of best well-tempered steel which is light and flexible. The handle is attached with either a single or double shank rivetted on to the plate.

Some craftsmen prefer to include at least two laying-on trowels in their kit of tools. One with a fairly stiff blade for applying first and second (render and floating) coats. The other with a thinner and springier blade reserved specifically for the third and finishing coat.

Laying-on trowel

Gauging trowel

A gauging trowel is used to add a small proportion of cement or gypsum to the coarse stuff on the hawk. It is also a useful tool for dealing with small quantities of material and for making good in awkward areas. It is often used for scraping down the other tools and equipment.

It is a steel-bladed trowel and can be of various sizes, but the most useful has a blade which is about 150mm (6") long and 75mm (3") wide at the heel or handle end, and tapers to a narrow point at the other end. It has a wooden handle fixed in place on the tang of the steel shank which is either rivetted or forged to the blade. The other most commonly used form of gauging trowel has a 200mm (8") bull-nosed blade.

1. Pointed gauging trowel; 2. Bull-nosed gauging trowel

Throwing trowel

The application of plaster using a hawk and laying on trowel is not universal. In some countries the traditional technique is to throw the material on with a large trowel, similar to but larger than the gauging trowel, about 125 to 150mm (5" to 6") wide at the heel reducing in width by 25mm (1") at the toe, which may be either cut square or rounded (bull-nosed).

Throwing trowel

Harling trowel

Wet dash, rough cast and harling are forms of thrown external render finishes for which a throwing trowel with curved blade is preferred. This is described as a harling trowel to distinguish it from the throwing trowel.

Harling trowel; also suitable for roughcast

Margin trowel

Margin trowel

This trowel is used for laying and polishing margins. It is made in many widths, the most useful being from 25mm (1") to 75mm (3").

Angle trowel or twitcher

This is used for working on internal angles. It is useful for difficult corners and enables two surfaces to be worked simultaneously. The edges of the blade are parallel and the end cut square. The front ends of the sides are cut back for ease of working in corners. The blade is about 90mm (3½") long and 65mm (2½") wide with a handle that is shorter than that of the gauging trowel.

Angle trowel or twitcher

Hand floats

Hand floats are usually made of softwood and are best in fine-grained pine or similar, if available. There is a range of hand floats for plastering and those used most frequently are given below.

Cross-grained float   This is used for 'scouring' or 'rubbing up' the finishing (third) coat which may be the last operation if a wood float finish is required. It might be followed by a steel trowel finish to give a harder smooth surface.

The cross-grained float is a wooden tool consisting of three principal parts – a blade, dovetail fixing, and handle. The blade is about 275mm × 112mm × 25mm (11" × 4½" × 1") and, as the name implies, has the grain of the wood running across the blade at right angles to its length. A hardwood bar is made to fit the dovetail groove, and the handle is fixed to the bar with screws. The bar strengthens the blade or 'sole' and helps to prevent it from warping.

Cross-grained float

Skimming float   The skimming float is used mainly for laying on the finishing (third) coat and is used where a float finish is required. It is also made of softwood, preferably pine, with the grain running along the length of the blade. It is similar in shape to a laying-on trowel and is usually about 300mm × 100mm × 12mm (12" × 4" × ½"). Constant use tends to wear the blades thin, but replacements can be fitted to the original handle.

Skimming float

Felt float   An efficient tool for scouring plain surfaces but with the disadvantage of not being able to work closely into internal angles as successfully as the cross-grained float. A range of textures and finishes may be achieved by covering a skimming float with soft materials such as felt, carpet, cloth, or even sponge. Whatever the material, it must be nailed securely to the edges of the blade or glued firmly to the face.

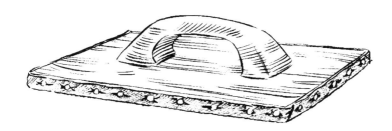

Felt float

Devil float   The devil float is used for removing any slight ridges or lumps that may have been left by the floating rule, and at the same time the nails in it scratch a key of the correct depth for good adhesion of the finishing (or third) coat. A deeper key would increase the probability of the scratch marks showing through on to the finished surface.

It is usually made from a worn out skimming float by driving a lath nail through each corner with the points projecting 3mm (⅛") from the face.

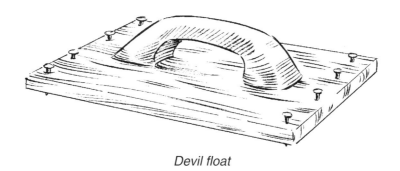

Devil float

Special wood floats

Special wood floats are used for finishing shaped work by rubbing up or finishing in shapes such as vee joints, mitres, raised bands and margins.

Special wood floats may be made in a wide variety of shapes to suit the profiles required for working up various designs and patterns in relief.

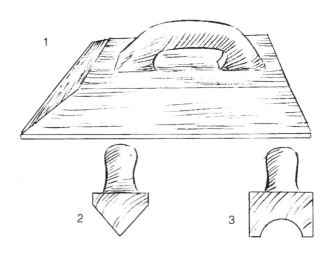

Special wood floats: 1. Float to reach under a projection; 2. Float for a vee joint – say for rusticated work; 3. Float for a raised band or bead

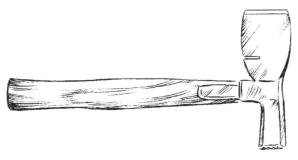

Lath hammer

Lath hammer

Also known as a plasterers' hammer, this is made with a steel head having one end in the form of a hatchet blade for cutting wood laths, and a slot for drawing out nails. The hammer head is usually serrated to prevent it slipping when the nails are being driven in. It may have a wooden handle fixed to the shoulder of the head. It is also used for general work, such as fixing other types of lath including expanded metal, and in any other work that requires nailing. It is used for nailing plumbed rules level, mould and template making, and cutting off occasional high spots from hard backgrounds.

Joint rules

These are used for forming joints, returns, and mitres to mouldings usually at internal corners and angles in all forms of plasterwork. Due to their shape, they are also useful for making good in positions difficult to reach with other tools.

Bevelled edge joint rule

Joint rule in use, Kedleston, 1994

There is a range of sizes of joint rule from 25mm (1") to 600mm (2') which is measured on the bevelled edge. They are made with width proportional to length varying from 35mm (1½") to over 100mm (4½").

They may be made of either rigid thin steel or hardwood. The long edge is bevelled if it is steel, and feathered in the case of hardwood. Wood joint rules should be of well-seasoned timber and are best cared for by the occasional treatment with linseed oil.

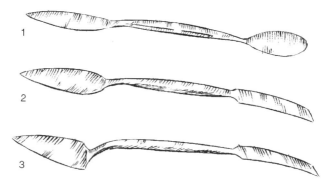

Various small tools
1. Round-ended leaf tool; 2. Square-ended leaf tool; 3. Trowel tool

36

Small tools

Small tools are useful for trimming and shaping and are used mostly in connection with modelling plaster enrichments. They are also very useful for other intricate work such as pointing mortar joints. They are normally made of well-tempered steel but similar versions may also be produced in hardwood.

Drags

Drags are used for scraping, or dragging, surfaces to make them generally flat, while at the same time leaving a rough surface as a key for the following

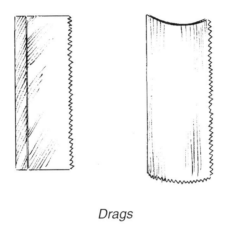

Drags

coats. They are also used for keying the back of cast items before fully set. The best material is thin steel plate, finished with toothed edges. They may be made in various sizes and shapes to suit the particular task in hand. They may be formed relatively simply from an old and discarded tenon saw about 150mm (6") long.

Scratchers

These are usually in the form of either a comb, wire, or lath scratcher, although a large stiff bristled brush may also be used. The comb scratcher is more often used in connection with keying the first and second coats of plasterwork, and the lath scratcher generally for keying render (first) coats on lath work. The wire scratcher is made of metal spikes fixed 12mm (½") apart into a wooden handle. The lath scratcher is made up of three to five laths each sharpened at the end to a point and spread out into a fan shape. One single sharpened lath may also be used (Millar, 1897).

Providing a key to render (first) coat with single lath scratcher, Zanzibar, 1989

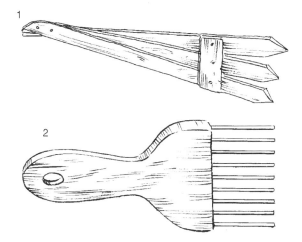

Scratchers: 1. Lath scratcher (for first coat); 2. Comb scratcher (for second coat)

Brushes

Stock brush This is one of the most important tools for plastering and rendering. Damping down dry areas is an essential part of the plastering process and is described in detail in the following chapters. A stock brush is used for damping the background and each plaster coat as necessary before applying the following coat. It is also used during the process of finishing the third or setting coat of lime plaster.

Stock brushes may also be used for cleaning off surplus material from the work area and plant, washing tools, and for applying limewash.

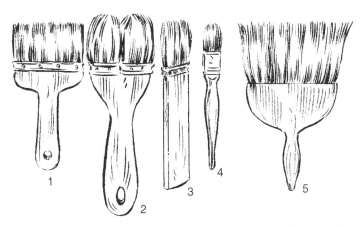

Brushes: 1. Flat stock brush; 2. Two knot stock brush; 3. Splash brush; 4. Tool brush; 5. Dusting brush

Splash brush   These are used in connection with preparing moulds for cast plasterwork and, as the name implies, are for splashing and brushing plaster into the mould.

Tool brush   This is the smallest of the plasterer's brushes and it is used for coating liquids such as oil, shellac, alum, grease, and other liquids on to moulds and tools. It is also used for dusting French chalk and for moulding small casts where a splash brush would be too large. It is also useful for washing off small items of work.

Bench brush, or dusting brush   This is used mostly in the plasterer's shop for dusting down and cleaning off moulds and work surfaces.

Files and rasps

These are used more in the maintenance of tools and equipment, and in modelled plasterwork than for plain plastering. They are made of steel and may be used for finishing running mould profiles, and for cleaning off small burrs or excess plaster from corners of moulds and casts.

Files are push fitted into hardwood handles which can be reused when the file is worn out. A metal ferrule prevents the wood from splitting.

Files and rasps

Chisel

Gouges and chisels

These are used for carving, cutting, and cleaning decorative plasterwork, and may be the same as, or very similar to, those used by joiners and wood carvers for timber work.

Spatterdash or tyrolean machine

Spatterdash, sometimes referred to as tyrolean finish, can be used to produce an attractive appearance, or it can be applied before plastering in
order to make a keyed surface for the plaster or render.

*Tyrolean machine: 1. Operating handle to rotate the flicker; 2. Rough or
fine adjustment*

Spatterdash is a wet, rich mix of hydraulic lime or cement and sand,
called a slurry. Sand and binder are mixed in the proportions of 1 : 1, 1 : 2 or
1 : 3. Slurry is thrown hard, or spattered, against the smooth block or concrete surface, and then allowed to harden. Throwing by hand, or harling,
will give better results due to the force with which the mix is applied.
Tyrolean machines are, however, in common use in many countries.

Care needs to be taken not to overload the machine with material. It is
better to use small quantities, refilled at frequent intervals. All of the slurry
must be used within one hour of the time it is mixed.

Do not set the flicker bar beyond the second notch when the machine is
new. Only when the bar wears out should it be set to a lower notch
(Winden, Vol. 2, 1986).

3.5 Masons' tools and additional equipment

Most plant, equipment and setting-out tools for various trades that work with lime, will be the same for all. These have been detailed in Sections 3.2 and 3.3. Many of the plasterers' tools described in Section 3.4 will also be of use for other trades. It would not be appropriate here to describe the full range of all tools used by every trade that works with lime. There are additional tools and plant, however, which are important for working lime-based materials and these are set out below.

Brick trowel

A steel-bladed trowel, also known as a laying trowel, for cutting, lifting and spreading mortar. It is one of the bricklayer's main tools and is made in a range of sizes to suit the individual craftsman, and with subtle variations incorporating regional preferences.

Sizes normally range from 250mm (10") to 325mm (13") long, some up to 375mm (15") for larger volumes of mortar.

Brick trowels are left- or right-handed with a hump or curve on the handed edge for cutting and trimming soft bricks.

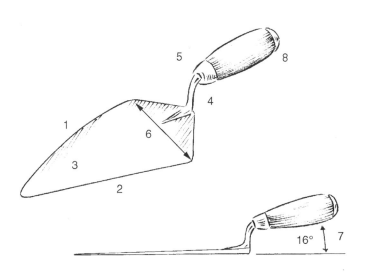

Brick trowel
1. Cutting or 'bolstered' edge; 2. Straight edge; 3. Blade (taper ground);
4. Tang; 5. Ferrule; 6. Shoulder or width; 7. Lift (usually 16°); 8. Handle

The wood used for the handle should be selected for qualities of resistance to impact, pliability, lightness, the ability to wear very smooth and not to splinter. Ash is one of the most suitable and answers all these requirements. Lynch (1994) deals with this subject in detail.

Line and pins

These are used to assist laying bricks and blocks to level between plumbed and levelled quoins. Lines are usually about 30m (100') long and must be strong and light.

A pin is inserted in a quoin mortar joint at one corner so that the line is level with the upper edge of the course. The line is fixed to the pin without using a knot so that it can easily be removed.

The line is stretched taut to prevent sagging and fixed to the corresponding pin at the bed joint in the opposite quoin. The line is set level with the top of the course to be built and the thickness of a trowel blade away from the wall face by using a sliver of wood or paper.

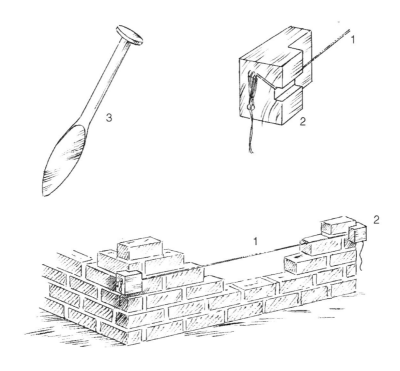

Line and pins: 1. Line; 2. Line and bobbin; 3. Line pin

An alternative to pins is the use of line bobbins. These are blocks best made of hardwood, cut to shape to grip the quoin corners by tension of the line. Sizes vary but 100mm × 50mm × 40mm (4" × 2" × 1⅝") is convenient. The line is stretched between opposite quoins and fixed to each bobbin. This is done by passing the line through a saw cut in each and wrapping it around screws projecting from the bobbin ends. For further reading, reference can be made to J. van Winden (1986) and G. Lynch (1994).

Brick hammer
Designed for rough cutting and trimming hard bricks and for axing soft bricks to size, the hammer is also used for tapping brick, block or stone to adjust them to plumb while the level is in position.

Club hammer or lump hammer
A general-purpose hammer, although it is primarily for use with a bolster. These are made in weights varying from 1kg to 3kg (2lb–7lb). The head is usually flat with chamfered corners of 'drop-forged' steel fixed to an ash or hickory handle.

Bolster
The bolster is used in conjunction with the club hammer for cutting bricks accurately. It is made as a single, shaped piece of steel, with flattened blade at one end and a handle at the other. The best bolsters are made by being drop stamped, spread under rollers, tempered, ground and polished. Blade widths vary from 50mm to 112mm (2"–5").

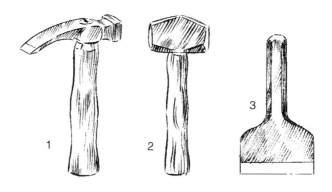

1. Brick hammer; 2. Club hammer; 3. Bolster

Pointing trowels

In addition to the small tools described in Section 3.4, special pointing and jointing tools are manufactured. Pointing trowels are of a similar shape to the brick or laying trowel, but smaller and without a cutting edge. They vary in size from 50mm to 150mm (2" to 6") long. Size is selected relative to the area and size of pointing mortar to be placed and compacted.

A very small pointing trowel called a dotter is used to make good the junction between the horizontal and vertical mortar joints in brickwork.

Finger trowel or margin trowel

This has a narrow long rectangular blade. Its length is from 150mm to 200mm (6"–8") overall and it is up to 25mm (1") wide. It is intended for pointing around frames and in narrow recesses although to ensure a well-fitted and compacted joint a traditional jointer or purpose-made pointing iron may give better results.

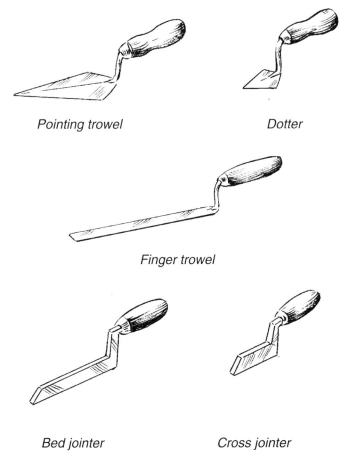

Pointing trowel   Dotter

Finger trowel

Bed jointer   Cross jointer

Traditional jointers

These used to be sold in pairs of bed jointer and cross jointer for compacting the horizontal (bed) and vertical (cross) joints in brickwork. Their principal use, in addition to compacting the joint was to give a finished profile such as a *bead, vee* or *tuck* to the face. Blades ranged from 2mm to 8mm (³⁄₃₂"–⁵⁄₁₆") in width.

Pointing irons

Purpose-made pointing tools are often made from waste material, preferably from steel. These can be fashioned by the craftsman himself to his own preferred sizes to suit his hand and technique. Basically a pointing iron comprises a cranked bar with ends flattened to the mortar joint width and the depth of crank arranged to keep knuckles clear of the wall face when compacting the mortar. A set of these can be built up over time at little expense to cover a range of mortar joint widths. The importance of good, solid and deep compaction of lime mortar joints cannot be overstressed. An experienced mason will value his own personal set of pointing tools.

Pointing iron

Mortar mills

Also known as roller pan mixers, mortar mills have two revolving cast iron or steel wheels, plus bottom and side scrapers to direct the material back into the line of the rollers. They sit in a wide shallow pan, which is normally filled only to a depth of 150–200mm (6–8") or so, the large volume being a function of the diameter of the pan. The rollers are adjustable in height, allowing the wheels to roll over the mix, with or without crushing the aggregate. Normally, for bedding purposes, the wheels should be set at approximately one quarter of the thickness of the bed joint; for instance, for 20mm joints, set the wheels at 5–6mm (or, for ½" joints, ⅛").

If finer material is required, it is possible to reduce the height of the rollers, allowing the larger pieces of aggregate to be ground down or crushed to the size required.

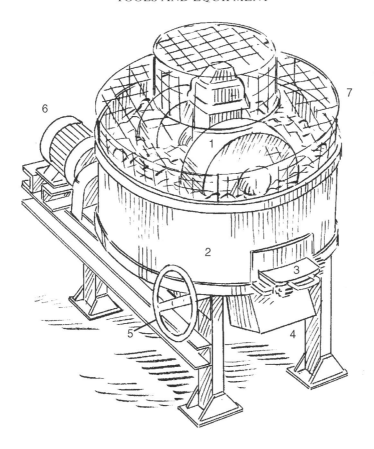

Motorized mortar mill
1. Rollers; 2. Pan; 3. Discharge gate; 4. Discharge chute; 5. Height adjustment; 6. Motor; 7. Guard

A mix of lime putty and sand in a mortar mill will produce a well-worked, complete mix in a matter of three or four minutes. One of the disadvantages of mortar mills is their low discharge height. They usually need to be set up on sleepers or dwarf walls to get a wheelbarrow under the discharge gate. This raises the height of the mixer, resulting in an increased loading height. Unfortunately, most mortar mills available at present are manufactured to deal with large volumes. The smallest, usually 200 litre capacity, is about twice the size of a standard 5:3½ cubic feet diesel or rotating-drum cement mixer.

If appropriate safety precautions are taken, a mortar mill can be used to prepare 'hot lime' mortar by mixing quicklime, sand and water.

A mortar mill can crush broken brick or tile in pozzolanic mortars and make it easy to reuse old lime mortar for repair works.

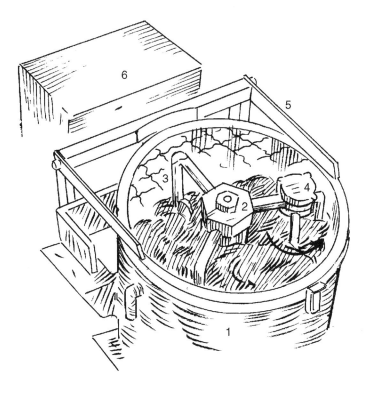

*Pan mixer: 1. Pan; 2. Rotor; 3. Scraper; 4. Rotating hooks; 5. Guard;
6. Motor*

Pan mixers

These also produce good even distribution of aggregates and binder although they do not crush aggregate or hydraulic lime residue. They are
similar in action to large bakery dough mixers, some have rotating hooks as
well as side, middle and bottom scrapers. Mixing times for lime mortars in
these machines depend very much on the mixer chosen, but it is usually
best to leave the mix turning for ten minutes or so.

Pan mixers are ideal for dry mixing of materials and then adding water.
When using them for lime mortars it is better to place the putty in the
mixer first, allow it to turn for two minutes or so, and then gradually add
the aggregate. As the material stiffens it may require the addition of small
amounts of water, whereas the mortar mill will not. In any event, the water
content for a building or pointing mix should be kept to the absolute
minimum.

If necessary, after the coarse stuff is mixed, it should be stored for a
period in a way that will allow any excess water used in the mixing to drain
away.

4

Limewashes

4.1   Uses and qualities

Limewashes are a family of paints which are particularly suitable for use on porous surfaces such as lime plaster, earth and stucco. More than any other paint, an unadulterated limewash allows surfaces to 'breathe', and this can increase the life of soft building materials which might otherwise be harmed if water was to become trapped behind impervious surface finishes.

Limewash was used very widely in many countries, but over the past fifty years has been largely displaced by modern synthetic paints which are simple to apply. When limewash is carefully made and applied it can be astonishingly beautiful and long lasting, but as it is such a low-cost paint it is sometimes made from poor materials or used too hastily. If prepared carelessly it will produce a powdery surface which may be just adequate on the farm, but is not suitable for houses or public buildings and gives little protection from rubbing or from rain. This poorly used limewash is sometimes described as 'whitewash' but that term has other meanings as well. In the past it was used interchangeably with the word limewash, but more recently it has been used to describe a paint made from chalk whiting bound with glue size.

Limewash helps to make rooms bright and hygienic and can be used with pigments to give soft colours or rich patterns. It gives a very matt finish which can mask blemishes in the wall surfaces. It dries and cures without giving off any fumes and it cannot contribute to the surface spread of flames.

Modern paints are said to be 'washable' and a good limewash is also washable, though a poorly applied limewash can easily be scrubbed off. Similarly, a poor limewash will rub off on clothing, although this is not a problem with good work. The difference is that a good limewash will have carbonated well after application to the wall and converted there to a continuous film of calcium carbonate. On the other hand, work with degraded materials or poor application, often too thick, will lack a cohesive structure.

Limewash is also used on the outside of buildings for decoration and protection. When it is brushed into any crevices on the surface it gives a smooth coating which, after an initial wetting, encourages an easy run-off of rainwater. At the same time the nature of this surface allows good, all-over evaporation which helps the wall to dry out. Limewash is unaffected by the ultra-violet rays in sunlight which destroy synthetic paints.

The regular application of a thin coat of limewash is a very old method of stone preservation which is particularly effective with limestones. In some areas it is the tradition to limewash whole villages every year and this contributes to the long life of the buildings as well as a cheerful feeling.

Because of its high pH value, limewash reduces the tendency of iron and steel to rust, but simple limewashes will not adhere well to smooth hard metallic surfaces and normal practice is to use an oil paint to keep the water away from the metal. However, limewash on paper is often included within the packaging of engineering goods to prevent rust and it may be possible to devise appropriate lime-based paint mixes for certain rust-inhibiting uses.

The principal limitation on the use of limewash is that considerable care is needed to get the best results. It is possible to modify the basic material in various ways to enhance certain properties such as the thickness of each coat, adhesion, abrasion resistance, water shedding or crevice filling, but the modified limewashes all have their own limitations.

4.2   Preparation of a basic limewash

Materials
Basic limewash is just a milky suspension of slaked lime (calcium hydroxide) in a saturated solution of limewater, but if this is to carbonate well it should be prepared from lime slaked directly from quicklime to a milk of lime or to a lime putty – not from a dry hydrate. For the best work, the particle sizes will be very fine and so quality can be compared by comparing the time taken for well-stirred mixes to settle out to putty and limewater. The less effective 'whitewashes' are sometimes made from dry hydrate and a binder such as size, but these can never achieve all the qualities of a good pure limewash.

Limewash from lime putty
The safest way to prepare limewash is to take a well-made lime putty which has not been allowed to deteriorate by drying out or by carbonation. Beat the putty to take out any stiffness and then gently add clean water, clean enough to drink, whisking it into the putty until the mix has the consistency of thin cream. Work this through a fine flour sieve to take out any gritty particles, as these would spoil the paint surface. At this stage any pigments should be added and this will be simpler if they have been premixed with hot water, shaken vigorously and allowed to stand. Add further water to give the consistency of milk – very much thinner than modern paints – and strain this through a muslin cloth or through the finest available sieve.

Limewash from quicklime
If a suitable putty is not available then an equally good limewash can be made using reactive quicklime, but this is a dangerous process. Wear protective clothing, goggles and rubber gloves; use a barrier cream on the wrists, neck and face; wear a cloth over the mouth and nose. Keep an

1. Premix pigment with water
2. Put some putty into a bucket and beat it
3. Add water and whisk it
4. Pass the creamy mixture through a sieve
5. Add the prepared pigment and mix in further water to a milky consistency
6. Sieve through the finest sieve or through muslin

Preparing limewash from lime putty

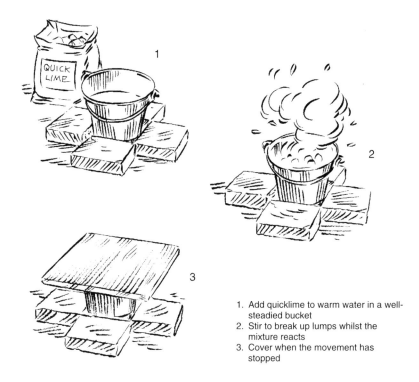

1. Add quicklime to warm water in a well-steadied bucket
2. Stir to break up lumps whilst the mixture reacts
3. Cover when the movement has stopped

Preparing a limewash from quicklime

eyebath and fresh water at hand and have a helper available to take you to the hospital! Keep onlookers well away.

Steady a large galvanized metal bucket between bricks or stones and half fill it with clean hot water. Add about one pint volume of reactive quicklime. What happens next will depend upon the reactivity of the quicklime, but the most reactive limes – which will give the best lime-washes – will very quickly begin to crumble in the water and generate a great deal of heat, enough to make the mix boil vigorously and splash out of the bucket. A lime with low reactivity may take a long time to break up and produce nothing more than a glub-glubbing noise or just crumble very slowly. In either case the mix must be stirred with a long-handled paddle to break up any caked material which may form on the bottom or sides of the bucket. If the mix becomes thicker than a thin cream then stir in more water. When the movements have stopped, even after repeated stirring, cover the bucket with a weighted-down lid or board and leave it to cool. This will produce a lime putty from which limewash can be made.

The basic limewash made from very pure lime will be startlingly white. Many limes contain slight impurities which soften the colour and those containing significant amounts of iron compounds can give warm cream colours which are very suitable for use without additional pigments.

4.3   Additives to the basic limewash

Colours

The basic limewash can carry a certain amount of pigment to give soft or medium-toned colours, but if large amounts of pigment are added then the limewash becomes less cohesive. Heavily pigmented washes will either need a binder or should be stabilized by repeated spraying with limewater.

Some pigments are destroyed by lime, but others – known as 'lime-fast' – are unaffected. A colour merchant will know which are which, and fortunately many of the lime-fast pigments are the cheapest ones. The most familiar of the lime-fast pigments are the metal oxides known as 'earth pigments' which either occur as natural earths or are prepared from natural earths by firing. These include yellow ochre, golden ochre, burnt ochre, raw sienna, burnt sienna, raw umber and burnt umber. Some manufactured pigments are also lime-fast and these include cobalt blue, smalt (a deep blue), emerald green, red oxide, Indian red, Venetian red, carmine lake, lemon yellow and cadmium yellow. Zinc white and lampblack are also lime-fast.

If it is not known whether a pigment is lime-fast then a simple experiment is advisable. Make up a small slab of lime mortar using lime putty and an aggregate of chalk or limestone. This could be in the form of render on a wall, or as a tablet. Paint the surface with the pigment mixed in water and paint some of the pigment on to a piece of paper. When the paper is dry, place it between the leaves of a book and after a few days compare the colour on the paper with that on the mortar. If there is any difference the pigment is not lime-fast.

If natural pigments are coarse they should be ground in a mill or with a pestle and mortar to assist the dispersion.

The pigment needs to be dispersed throughout the limewash and for this it is premixed with hot water to form a thin liquid which is allowed to stand. This is added to the limewash when the limewash is of a creamy thickness and the mixture is stirred for a long time. Accurate colour matching is almost impossible and it is important to make up a sufficient volume to complete the work. The colour of the liquid wash will always be very much darker than the dry colour and samples should be tried on paper which can quickly be dried in the sun or near a fire.

Binders

There are several types of binder which are sometimes added to limewashes: fats and oils, glues, gums and resins.

Tallow   Perhaps the most common is tallow, which is used to increase the water-shedding properties and, in rough work, make it harder for the lime-wash to rub off the wall. On the other hand tallowed limewashes do not allow such good 'breathing' and tallow has an unpleasant smell which may linger for many months. Tallowed limewashes are liable to support mould growth in damp conditions and so biocides such as formalin are sometimes added to the mix to counteract this problem.

Tallow is a clarified animal fat, especially from the hard fat around the kidneys. A lump of tallow should be shredded and added to a maximum of about ten times its volume of quicklime immediately before slaking. In the heat of the slaking reaction the tallow melts and some of it combines with the lime to form a soap. This allows the remainder to form an emulsion of tallow within the limewash.

When the tallowed limewash dries it can be impossible to apply further coats as they run off the wall just as water runs off a duck's back. Tallow should thus be used, if at all, only in the final coat of limewash. The presence of the tallow will reduce, or even eliminate, the chance of a good set of the limewash by carbonation. Tallowed limewashes should be used only where, for some reason, it is particularly difficult to achieve carbonation.

Lard and oils   Lard, a softer clarified animal fat, can also be used with quicklime in place of tallow. A similar effect can be achieved with lime-washes made from lime putty by using an oil. This may be added at the 'creamy' stage and dispersion would be helped by heating. Again, the lime forms a soapy material with some of the oil and this allows the remainder to emulsify. The usual oil for this is raw linseed oil, but other oils, including coconut oil or motor oil, may be just as effective.

Glue and size   Where dusting of the surface of a limewash is perceived as a problem, probably because of a lack of good workmanship or materials, then glue size is sometimes also added as a binder. Size is a fairly pure form of gelatinous animal glue or a comparable vegetable glue. It is used in proportions of around one part of size to 20 parts of lime putty. As with the tallow, the size completely changes the nature of a limewash, reducing its 'breathability', reducing the chance of correct carbonation and increasing the likelihood of supporting mould growths.

If there is no alternative but to use dry hydrated lime as the basis of a limewash then size should normally be used. In effect the mix is no more than a whitewash or distemper with very little contribution from the lime to the final performance.

Other glues may be tried in place of size and most water soluble glues are likely to give similar results. Even the modern PVA adhesives can be used and may be helpful where a limewash, albeit a heavily modified one, is required over difficult impervious backgrounds such as emulsion paint. In such cases there will be none of the advantages of breathability associated with good limewash.

When too much size or other glue is added, the surface will tend to curl and peel away. If too little is used the surface may be powdery. These additives are really helpful only with poor quality lime or where good workmanship is not expected.

Casein Skimmed milk or casein, which is a powder prepared from skimmed milk, can also be used in limewashes in much the same way as size. The milk or casein reacts with the lime to form calcium caseinate, which is a glue. This will have the same advantages and disadvantages as a limewash modified with size, but the surface appearance is likely to become marred by bubbles because of the lowered surface tension. Formaldehyde or some other preservative is essential if there is a possibility of moist conditions.

Gums and resins Gums and resins from tree exudations are used in varnishes, but water-soluble gums – such as those from acacia trees – may sometimes be used in limewashes. Strictly speaking, gums are water-soluble and resins are not, but the words are sometimes used loosely. When gums are used in limewash the properties are likely to be similar to those limewashes modified with size, but in every case trials would be essential.

Salts

When limewashes are used in historic buildings, it is unthinkable to introduce chloride salts, even in very small quantities, which might cause harm to the fabric of the masonry. However, it is well known that the addition of sodium chloride (common salt) or calcium chloride (crude commercial grade) can greatly assist the performance of a limewash. The salts act in two ways: they increase the solubility of the lime and they provide wetting and drying cycles which benefit the carbonation. The increased solubility means that the calcium hydroxide penetrates further into the surface for a better bond. The hygroscopic action, attracting moisture from the air, prevents rapid drying. On an internal wall this hygroscopic action would cause dampness to appear whenever the conditions are humid, but externally the salt would gradually wash off.

Alum is sometimes added to limewash mixes containing size or other glues where it is said to help the size to become more fluid. It has also been used with common salt limewashes although the reason is not clear, possibly because it has been generally believed to accelerate the set.

Mould inhibitors and disinfectants

Formaldehyde has already been mentioned as a mould inhibitor for use when glues, and particularly skimmed milk, are added to limewashes.

Formalin serves the same purpose, as may many other water-soluble mould inhibitors. Their action is not indefinite and even inside a building protection is unlikely beyond three years. Some have a strong smell which may take a long time to fade away.

When used externally, mould inhibitors are likely to rinse out quickly in wet conditions. If freedom from mould is important it would be better to avoid limewashes containing organic additives. In some climates the weather conditions readily produce green algae which dies to form a black slime and in such conditions the need for regular re-coating must be expected.

Where limewash is used in animal husbandry to disinfect the inside wall of, for example, cow-houses and poultry houses, the naturally disinfectant qualities of limewash can be enhanced with almost any water soluble disinfectants. These include flowers of sulphur, copper sulphate (to make Bordeaux mixture), crude carbolic acid or coal tar disinfectants.

Other additives
Sugar, like salt, greatly increases the solubility of lime and has sometimes been used to increase the penetration into porous surfaces. Soft soap has also been added, but, like skimmed milk, it is likely to cause bubbles when the wash is applied and these bubbles will spoil the finished surface.

Aggregates
In some countries it is customary to include fine aggregates with a lime-wash. These might be fine sands, silver sand or stone dust. This gives a considerable body to the mix and smooths over any surface blemishes. The aggregates can also contribute to the durability of the wash. On the other hand the heavy limewashes are harder to apply, and reduce the crispness of any surface details.

4.4 Applying limewash

Preparation
Producing a good material for limewashing is the easiest part of the operation to control, but the way in which it is used is every bit as important.

As slight variations in ingredients may cause very noticeable differences in appearance, it is important to mix all of the limewash for each coat as a single batch. If pigments are used, premixed as described above, the mixture must be stirred for a very long time; even the smallest agglomerations of pigment can form a noticeable streak on the surface as they are brushed out.

Sieve or strain with a very fine sieve or muslin cloth to remove all lumps, as dust and dirt will sit on the smallest specks of grit. The sieving also protects against blistering of any unslaked material.

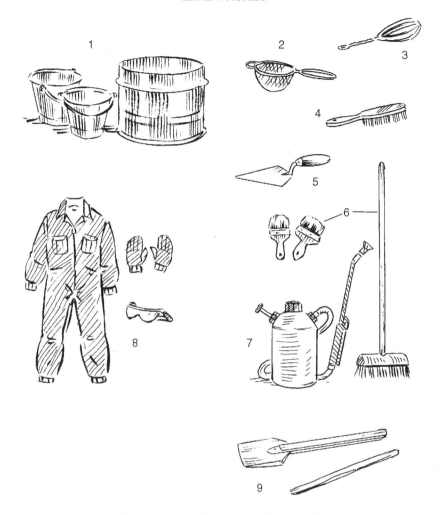

Tools and equipment for limewashing
1. Containers; 2. Sieve; 3. Whisk; 4. Stiff brush; 5. Small trowel;
6. Various brushes; 7. Spray; 8. Protective goggles, gloves and overalls;
9. Stirrers

The surfaces to be limewashed should be cleaned, free from dirt and grease. Damp them down with a hand pumped spray or by splashing from a brush until they are sufficiently wet that any further water would not soak in. However, the surface should not be running wet.

Application

Apply the limewash in very thin coats (unless it has aggregates) – no thicker than milk. When limewash from high-calcium limes is applied it will have no body at all and may look quite transparent, but as it dries and carbonates it builds up its body and colour. Use large brushes and paint quickly, always maintaining a wet edge. If the surface has been correctly dampened there will be no drag against the brush. Grass brushes are often used, but any brush with a rough textured surface to the bristles will work well. Never use limewash brushes for other paints as any residual lime in the stock can spoil their formulation. Thin limewashes may also be applied by spraying.

Keep the limewash stirred throughout the work so that the last brushful is as thin as the first. The best way to stir is with a caterer's balloon whisk in a round-bottomed bowl.

Do not let the work dry out quickly. In hot weather cover the work with damp sacking and polythene sheeting. If these are not available, keep damping down with a fine spray. Do not use limewash in direct sunlight or strong drying winds, as it will not carbonate if it dries too quickly.

Wait at least a day before applying the next coat. If the first coat has not had time to carbonate it may lift off as the next coat is applied. Dampen again before applying the next coat. The colour and body from the first coat may disappear when it is re-wetted, but it will return as the next coat dries.

The way in which the limewash dries will affect the colouring. If a wall has dense impervious stones set in soft porous mortar then the variations in suction between the stones and the mortar will mean that some parts of the wall dry more quickly than others. This may draw the pigments to the surface differentially and cause a pattern staining, concentrating the pigments at the damper areas. When the wall eventually dries fully the patterning will largely disappear, but there may still be some variations.

4.5 Performance standards and trial mixes

The ranges of possible materials and proportions are so wide that trial mixes will be essential in most cases. To judge the effectiveness of the trials it will be necessary to set out clear objectives which are appropriate to the circumstances. Some likely parameters are listed below.

Adhesion Can the limewash adhere to the particular background? Test by weathering trials or by scraping.
Cohesiveness Does the limewash resist dusting? Test by rubbing with fabric. Test again after natural weathering.
Colour match Accurate matching is very difficult without laboratory control of ingredients, but matching within limits can be achieved. Test when dried and after carbonation. Record precisely the quantities of ingredients to make up each batch, particularly the pigment to limewash ratio.

Colour fastness Are the pigments lime-fast and are they stable in sunlight? Test by comparison with lime-free samples and samples kept in darkness.

Weathering resistance Can the paint resist breakdown under the expected weather conditions? Trials would probably be long term, but cycles of wetting with running water and drying in sunlight could be arranged. Freeze/thaw trials could also be devised.

Splash resistance Where the limewash is to be used externally can the limewash resist the severe washing effect of splashing water?

Covering power Can the limewash conceal the expected range of variations in background colour? and how many coats would it take?

Mould resistance Does the mix support mould growth in the expected conditions of humidity?

Surface quality When applied as planned, does the limewash have an acceptably smooth surface, suitably free from bubbles or gritty particles?

Salts resistance If used in conditions of rising dampness, is the surface able to remain acceptably intact under attack from surface crystallization of salts?

5

Lime mortars

5.1 Definition of mortar

'Mortar is defined as any material in a plastic state which can be trowelled, becomes hard in place, and which is utilised for bedding and jointing' (Cowper 1927).

5.2 Performance

The word 'mortar' gives no indication of what the material is made of, but simply the job that it does. Although a mortar might be bound with clay, dung, gypsum or cement, this chapter will deal only with mortars which rely on lime for their binder. The mortars described have some similarities to the material used for internal and external plastering, but their requirements are rather different.

It is commonly supposed that the purpose of a mortar is to stick masonry units together, but this is only a minor part of the work to be done. The joints between the units should provide a cushion to spread the loads evenly, particularly with soft bricks and stones. They should act like a wick to draw moisture out of a wall and provide a good surface for evaporation. In this way they will take harmful soluble salts away from the masonry units and can act as a sacrificial material; the wall can then be repaired by the simple process of repointing the joints. For this to happen the set mortar must be softer, more porous and more permeable than the masonry units.

The simplest and most widely used lime mortar is known as common mortar, which is a mixture of about two or three parts sand or other fine

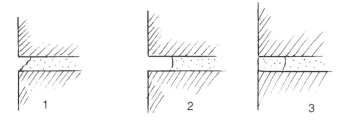

Sacrificial mortar joint: 1 and 2. Sacrificial decay of a soft joint, leaving the bricks undamaged; 3. The joint is eventually repointed

aggregate to one part of lime, perhaps in the form of lime putty. Needless to say there are a great many variations on even this simple mortar and its performance can vary from excellent to abysmal.

Much of the research into mortars has been carried out for military and civil engineers whose main aim has been to develop very strong mortars for fortifications and those that must resist constantly wet conditions and a severe environment. They were not concerned with the 'gentle' aspects which allow soft mortars to give exceptionally long life to buildings – in Norfolk many of the villages have a church in which parts of the flint walling are nearly a thousand years old, and these are all made with soft lime mortars. The military engineers unlocked the secrets of the hydraulic limes, the pozzolans and the natural cements. They developed the artificial (Portland) cements and they certainly made some very strong mortars! But for normal use a balance must be struck between strength, durability, availability and the general health and beauty of the buildings. An appropriate mortar must be used for each situation.

It has been found that mortars with higher compressive strengths generally also have higher tensile strength and, to some extent, adhesion. In engineered structures these all have their place, but in traditional, intuitive construction, the building forms are such that very little strength is required from their mortars. This is because their shape and thickness provide building forms which depend almost entirely on compressional stresses. In low buildings this is simple enough, but the gothic cathedrals of Europe are very large structures and often elegant, even though they were built with soft lime mortars.

There are many physical factors which tend to wear out a building, but the severest tests for the durability of a mortar are frosts and the crystallization of soluble salts such as those introduced by rising dampness or from Portland cement. In either case, ice crystals or salt crystals may form within the pores of the mortar. The way the mortar survives or fails depends on a balance of the strength of the mortar (to resist the forces of expansion within its pores) and the pore structure itself. When there is a suitable balance of very fine and larger pores, and predominantly larger pores linked to the fine pores, the crystallization stresses can be relieved. Remember, also, that what really matters is the survival of the wall itself and not just the survival of the mortar. A mortar with great strength may survive the testing conditions of salts or ice, but is more likely to cause damage to the masonry units (Torraca, 1988; Holmström, 1977).

Another way in which the softer mortars can contribute to long life is by tolerating the small deformations in a building. All buildings move, both from temperature changes and from variations in the firmness of the ground below their foundations. The soft lime mortars have self-healing properties; where a stiffer mortar might lead to just a few, relatively large, cracks – perhaps even breaking soft bricks – the soft mortar may deform

A Jointed with mortar which is too dense and insufficiently porous

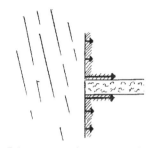

A1 Rain penetrates the masonry units in preference to the mortar joints

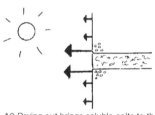

A2 Drying out brings soluble salts to the surface of the masonry units where they crystallize as the water evaporates

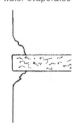

A3 The crystal growth breaks up the masonry units

B Jointed with soft and porous mortar

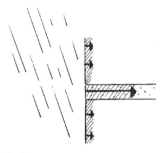

B1 Rain penetrates the mortar joints in preference to the masonry units

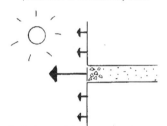

B2 Drying out brings soluble salts to the surface of the joint and less so to the surface of the masonry units

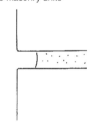

B3 Crystal growth breaks up the face of the joint, but this can be repaired in due course by repointing

Sections through hard (A) and soft (B) mortar joints

with many hundreds or thousands of very fine cracks. The free lime in the mortars can then, with the action of moisture, carbonate and crystallize to heal these fine cracks.

But the use of these soft mortars, made from pure or 'fat' (Class A) limes is far from straightforward. They set in two ways, firstly by simple drying when they lose their plasticity and then by the process called induration in which the lime becomes *carbonated*; part of the calcium hydroxide combines with carbon dioxide from the air, in the presence of moisture, to form a firm matrix of calcium carbonate.

There are various things which may be done to promote this carbonation, but it is nearly always a slow process – continuing for months or for many years – and it occurs from the air surface into the joints. Typically the process penetrates only 10mm to 12mm into the joint. This means that the greater part of the mortar remains uncarbonated and may, in particularly unfavourable conditions, dry out with no cohesive strength at all. Whilst the firm outside skin remains intact there is no problem in a compressive structure, but when, in time, the outer skin becomes eroded, the structure may lose strength. On the other hand it should be said that the process of induration may still continue as the outer skin erodes and there is usually a fair warning that remedial work is needed.

The normal requirement for inherent durability in a structure is for the inner parts of the structure to be stronger, or at least no weaker, than the surface parts. This is why the hydraulic limes and lime-pozzolan mixtures can be desirable, since they can achieve a set throughout the depth of a joint, in the absence of air. For particularly harsh conditions the strength of the eminently hydraulic limes (Class C3) may be needed, but in general, the weakest hydraulic limes (Class C1), and some Class B limes (see Appendix 10) can provide the necessary set without losing the advantages of a soft and porous mortar. Very similar mortars can be achieved when suitable pozzolans are used with fat limes.

The major part of most mortars will be the sands or aggregates and these will have a very considerable effect on the mortar quality, as will the methods of preparing and placing the mortar. The ease of use, termed the workability, will affect the quality of the work. For this the plastic qualities of a good lime putty are excellent. As with plastering, the ability to retain water against the suction of the backing will make the mortar easier to use and will help to achieve a good bonding to the units. The smoothness of good lime putty will enable a leaner mix to be used – that is one in which the lime can carry more sand.

One of the hardest things to describe in words is the way in which the softer mortars make such pleasant buildings, both beautiful and comfortable. The beauty must remain a subjective judgement, but the comfort is related to the way in which lime mortars, plasters and limewashes, respond to changes in moisture content. They are likely to absorb (and later transmit) any excess of moisture rather than to produce surface condensation. They will also give a softer acoustic.

5.3   Basic materials for mortar

Sands

The sand that is available locally will usually be more significant than any ideal specification. For best strength with any binder the sand should be well graded, that is, it should contain a wide range of particle sizes all equally well represented. More detail of this will be found in the chapters on plastering, but even without sieving and measurement, a dry sample held in the hand should be seen to have a wide range of particle sizes. The art of mortar making is to make the best use of the available materials and it is sometimes possible to blend two local sands, perhaps one from a pit and another from a river site, to get a suitable *particle size distribution*. For good mortar strength the sand should also be sharp, with angular particles that do not roll around easily when rubbed between the fingers. The wide-spread use of *soft* (not sharp) sands in modern work is to compensate for the appallingly bad workability when portland cement is used as a binder.

The arênes and psammites in France described by Vicat (1837) are special types of sand which have soluble silica impurities and may introduce a slight pozzolanic effect to a mortar. Lateritic sands also have a clay content which may be helpful. It is normal practice to rinse sands to remove any deleterious matter, including clays, and that will diminish or destroy the benefit. It is well worth conducting trials with unwashed samples of any sands of these types.

Porous aggregates

But, as we have already seen, strength is not everything! In some areas soft mortars are made using crushed limestone for the aggregate instead of sand. Apart from the softness of the aggregate this helps in two further ways. The freshly broken surfaces can 'seed' calcite crystal growth to bind the mortar. And the aggregates give a good pore structure which not only resists decay from frost and salt crystallization but also helps in the process of carbonation. Analysis shows that many good samples of old mortars contain aggregate-sized lumps of calcium hydroxide (Holmström, 1977). This may be from the crust and other agglomerations which can form in a lime pit or from mixing crushed quicklime with sand (hot lime) and such particles greatly improve a fat lime mortar. When this technique is used, the lime crust should be considered, for assessing proportions, as a part of the aggregate and not as part of the binder. This can explain the sur-prisingly rich mixes of 2 : 3 or even 1 : 1 'lime' and sand which are often found in the analysis of old mortars. Another way in which porous material can be included in a mortar is by adding the salvaged lime mortar from dismantled old buildings. This is most easily done when the mortar is mixed in a mill, but there are many examples to be seen in medieval work.

Crushed brick aggregate

A soft-burned brick (fired at below 950°C) is likely to be porous and when crushed for aggregate can assist the pore structure and durability of the mortar. If some of the brick dust particles are very finely crushed there is also likely to be a pozzolanic action. Some of the lime will combine with the brick dust to form a weak cement which will set throughout the joint (Teutonico *et al.*, 1994). This has been widely used in India, where a clay is fired especially for this purpose; the pozzolan is called *surkhi*.

Different classes of lime

The introductory chapter has explained the wide variety of limes which may be available and these have been summarized in chart form in Appendix 1. From previous sections of this chapter it is clear that each different type has its own beneficial properties. For work which will be subject to continuous wetting (harbour walls, bridge piers, water storage, drainage, substructures in damp ground and the like) an eminently hydraulic lime or strong lime–pozzolan mix must be used. For normal building work a grey lime (Class C1) is often a good compromise. Where the conditions are not too harsh, and where good building practices are used, the fat (Class A) limes can give very good results. Dolomitic limes (which contain magnesia as well as lime) are found to set well in mortars and provide good workability. This may possibly be because part of the magnesia remains unslaked during the preparation and can benefit the eventual setting.

Pozzolans

The range of natural and artificial pozzolans has also been described in the introductory chapter and detailed in Appendix 2. These will often be available as a substitute for naturally hydraulic limes and may be used in combination with hydraulic limes to increase their setting power or, perhaps, to regulate the quality of a mortar by careful blending. In choosing a pozzolan for use in mortar, take care not to use one which might introduce soluble salts which could harm the masonry. This is a particular risk with some of the fly ashes from power stations.

Water

Again, in order to keep down the soluble salts content and thus prolong the life of the masonry, the water used for mixing a mortar should be of a quality good enough for drinking. As military engineers have noted, it is possible to build with sea water, which has some short-term beneficial effects, but in the longer term there is likely to be damage both from the dampness induced by hygroscopic salts and from salt crystallization.

5.4 Additives

Cement

It is very common to use cement and lime together in mortars when they are both readily available. On the one hand the addition of small amounts of cement to a lime mortar can provide a quicker set – though at the risk of a loss of long-term durability by spoiling the pore structure and preventing carbonation (Teutonico *et al.*, 1994). On the other hand the addition of lime to a cement mortar greatly improves its workability and durability. However, this book is concerned with the use of *lime*, not cement, for building. Most benefits to a mortar which may be available from cement can also be achieved with suitable hydraulic limes or with pozzolan mixes.

It has been common practice to add varying proportions of cement to lime mortar mixes but this is not always advisable.

Research in Sweden and the UK (Teutonico *et al.*, 1994) has shown that the addition of a small amount of cement, that is less than 50% of the lime (i.e. mixed with proportions of cement less than in $1:2:9$ cement: lime : sand), tends to weaken the finished mortar rather than strengthen it. The cement, whilst giving an early set as intended, reduces the ability of the lime to carbonate and to develop a long-term gain in strength, for which the small amount of cement has not compensated. Mixes of this nature are prone to failure, particularly in extreme weather conditions.

Tallow and oil
These additives are not commonly used in mortars but can be helpful in particular circumstances. The tallow or oil can be combined into the mortar by adding it to the quicklime whilst it is slaked – just as for a comparable limewash. A tallowed mortar should have good (physical) flexibility and water resistance but will not have the usual benefits of high porosity and permeability. A case where this is particularly useful is in the flaunching around chimney pots, which can be subjected to a lot of vibration and to severe exposure. It should be noted that in humid conditions these mortars may support mould growth.

Sugar
Sugar will greatly increase the solubility of lime in water and this can help to create a strong set in a fat lime mortar. However, it alters the appearance of the mortar and, perhaps, the pore structure. There are usually other ways available to increase strength.

Proteins
Proteins introduced into a fat lime putty can assist the carbonation. The reason is not clear, but decomposition of the proteins may produce carbon dioxide throughout the depth of the joints to assist a thorough carbonation. They may also assist in air entrainment, which is described below. Many protein-rich materials have been used in the past including the use of the lime pits for disposing of animal carcasses. The effects of adding a number of the more common organic additives to lime are detailed in Section 4.3.

Air-entraining agents
As with cement mortars, there can be advantages if minute bubbles of air are entrained into the mortar during the mixing and beating. This may

assist carbonation of fat limes and improve the pore structure and hence improve the durability, although at the expense of strength. Air entrainment can assist the workability, unnecessary with fat limes but possibly helpful with lean limes (Class B) or certain hydraulic lime (Class C). Many of the more exotic additives such as egg and wort may have been used to entrain air, as were the alkali salts of various wood resins. There are modern proprietary air-entraining agents available and surfactants can reduce the surface tension of the water and thus produce bubbles.

Quicklime

The need to use lime mortars for the conservation of historic monuments, even in very difficult circumstances, has lead to an interest in the former use of 'hot lime' techniques. One of these involves adding powdered quicklime to the mortar mix immediately before placing it. This can generate a little heat within the mix and that will aid the setting in cold conditions. But curiously there is also a marked benefit even when dead-burned quicklime (from steel making) is used; a good first set is achieved in cold weather even though the dead-burned quicklime will not generate any heat.

Recent experience in Scotland (Masons Mortars, The Scottish Lime Centre), has shown that making mortar using the 'hot lime' technique appears to improve the binding qualities of coarse stuff.

5.5 Mortar preparation

Care in preparation

In medieval times the great building works in Europe were undertaken by teams who travelled, not just around a country, but across the continent. Their work was divided into separate trades, each under its own master (Saltzman, 1952). The preparation of mortar was one of these trades valued equally alongside stone masonry and carpentry. The master mortar-men would assess the locally available materials and blend and work them to suit the requirements of the particular building, judging the nature of the stones to be bonded, the climate and the particular part of the building. They arranged for their men to beat and chop the mortar to get the very best workability and economy of materials. All this is in very sharp contrast to the organization of a modern building site, where very little care and attention is taken in the preparation of mortar. We have come to expect the strength of cement binders to compensate for the use of poor aggregates and for poor workmanship, but to get the best out of lime, and the best out of masonry, this attitude is not acceptable.

Tools

Mortar can be mixed with simple hand tools using much time and effort for the best results, or with mills, as illustrated in Chapter 3, or high-speed

Medieval building construction showing preparation and use of lime mortar; illustrated in the medieval manuscript 'The Building of 12 Abbeys' by Girart de Roussillon (Coldstream, 1991) (Image source: Bilarchiv d. ÖNB)

Animal powered roller mill
1. Roller; 2. Mortar trough; 3. Pivot

mixers. The usual hand tools are the shovel and larry or hoe to mix and chop the mortar either on a board or in a shallow trough, perhaps with a flail or heavy pestle to beat it. This action does two things: it mobilizes the lime putty and spreads it all around the surface of each grain of sand or other aggregate; it also entrains a little air to form very fine bubbles. Lime putty becomes a colloidal gel which can become quite firm after long storage. The shearing action of chopping and beating completely changes this firm material into a smooth-flowing thin paste. For an exceptionally high specification, the engineer John Smeaton paid his workmen for a full day's labour to beat just two bushels (say 75 litres) of pozzolanic mortar, but that was an exceptional case. On the other hand it is not sufficient simply to turn the materials over together with a shovel. A common mistake is to add too much water to save time on the preparation. In most cases even a firm putty will contain enough water to prepare mortar from dry aggregates; too much water will lead to excessive shrinkage as the mortar dries out.

The simplest form of mill is a heavy roller, perhaps made of stone, running around a circular trench in the ground. The roller is restrained by a radial beam swivelling at the centre of the circle and can be drawn around by a horse, ox or donkey. This is the method used to prepare the lime-surkhi mortars where a very intimate mix is needed between the pozzolan and the lime. It also serves to crush the fired clay down to a suitable aggregate size and, when limestone aggregate is used, the mill can create the freshly broken surfaces which are reactive and promote crystal growth. The factory-made equivalent of this is the roller pan mill in which two cast iron rollers at either end of an axle either rotate around a ring shaped pan or else the pan rotates beneath the static axle. Earlier forms used steam engines for their power, but diesel or electric motors are now used. They could equally well be driven from the power take-off mechanism on a small tractor.

A small pug-mill

High speed pan mills have a stationary pan in which a set of beaters and scrapers revolve about a vertical axis, not unlike some forms of food mixer. In some countries, such as the UK, rotating drum cement mixers are often used; this is more cost effective than hand-work but the action of these mixers is not as effective as the other methods.

For large projects in the last century horse- or steam-powered pug mills were sometimes used for the mortar mixing. In these there is a vertical shaft with staggered and radiating iron blades which both chop the mortar and force it down through a close-fitting barrel of wood or iron. The mortar is then extruded out of the bottom of the casing, having benefited from the chopping action as well as a compression. Pug-mills are more usually found in brickworks for preparing the clay.

5.6   Mortar from non-hydraulic (Class A) quicklime

Lime putty is prepared as detailed in Chapter 2. It is important to ensure that the putty is of the correct consistency in order that proper proportions may be measured by volume before mixing with sand or aggregate. Methods of testing the consistency of lime putty are given in Chapter 11, pages 214 and 215.

A very common way to cut down on the labour of mixing mortars is to make use of some of the energy liberated by the slaking of quicklime. A hollow is formed in a heap of sand and the crushed quicklime is spread around the hollow and sprinkled with enough water for its complete slaking. The edge of the pile is then turned in to cover the quicklime with a thick layer of sand. This prevents rapid cooling as the putty is formed and the energy of the slaking forces at least some of the lime into close contact with the sand grains. Unless carefully burned lime is used it may be necessary to pass the mixture through a riddle to take out any lumps of seriously over-burnt or under-burnt material.

A variation of this is to break the quicklime into small pieces for accurate batching by volume and to mix this thoroughly, dry, with the sand in a pit in the ground. The slaking water is then added and the mortar is left to mature in the pit.

If the mortar is not stored for a very long period (years) there may be a risk of slight damage from pitting and popping, but this is not nearly as important in a bedding or pointing mortar as it would be in a plaster or render.

Before it is used, the mortar still needs to be beaten and chopped or put through a suitable mixer but not for as long as would otherwise be the case. Any pozzolanic additives are added at this stage.

5.7   Mortar from hydraulic (Class C) quicklime

Apart from the length of time for which the coarse stuff can be matured, slightly hydraulic limes (Class C1) can be treated in the same way as the fat limes. But when the stronger hydraulic limes are used, perhaps the most effective method of mixing is by introducing the quicklime and aggregates into a roller mill with enough water for slaking and mixing and grinding the constituents together. If this process is used, it is most important that the burning of the limestone has been well controlled and that there is no excessive residue. Excessive residue after slaking indicates that too much under-burnt and/or over-burnt lime is present which will weaken the mix. The small amount of heat generated (far less than from a fat lime) may assist in the setting of the mortar if it can be used immediately. The grinding action will reduce the risk of pitting and popping.

In many ways the bagged dry hydrates (from any class of lime) are easy to handle, but unless well burnt at a low temperature (900°C) and very freshly made they cannot match the quality produced by well-matured lime putty, or the careful use of quicklime. Bagged limes deteriorate by contact with moisture and air as well as with age, and packaging is not always date stamped. However, their performance is always greatly improved by allowing them to fatten up before use. The simplest way is to mix the dry hydrate, sand and water and leave this to stand for an absolute minimum of one day for a fat lime, but for as long as is practicable. When the more hydraulic limes of Class C2 or Class C3 are used their hydraulic properties are gradually lost during this storage and a balance must be struck between workability and setting power.

Hydraulic limes tend to be less permeable as they become more hydraulic. The degree of permeability of mortars made with Class C limes, however, is generally much greater than that of cement-based mortars.

The setting time of hydraulic lime mortar increases in proportion to a decrease in temperature and will be exceptionally slow in very cold conditions. If manufacturers do not provide guarantees of compressive strength, setting time and permeability it is advisable to carry out tests for these qualities before use. The more severe the climate and environmental conditions the more important these tests become. Speed of set is related to temperature, and frost before set will cause failure. This therefore needs to be taken into account and site conditions replicated when carrying out the tests. Methods of testing are detailed in Chapter 11.

5.8   Mix proportions

Whatever feels right probably is right. The best proportions will depend very much on the grading of the aggregates and the plasticity of the putty, but a starting point with good materials and sharp sands is about one part of putty to three of aggregate. If the aggregate is rounded (soft sand) or is not well graded or if the plasticity of the lime is less than good, the proportion of lime must be increased towards 1 : 2 or even richer. On the other hand, with particularly good materials, the lime can be reduced well below the 1 : 3 proportion.

The *richer* mixes, with extra binder, are more likely to produce shrinkage cracks unless the putty and sand are much drier than is usual – say by using a very mature putty, several years old. On the other hand they tend to give greater durability.

5.9   Application of mortar

Background

The masonry units should be cleaned of any dirt and dust and be well dampened, but not quite so damp that water can stand on the surface. For new works, the units can be dipped into a bucket of water well before use and again shortly, but not immediately, before they are laid. For repair works and repointing the background should be splashed with water several times in the hours preceding the repointing or building up. In new works the top of the previous day's work should be treated in the same way before building up. An alternative is to use a fine spray, as from a knapsack sprayer. The purpose of all this is to encourage slow drying and to reduce the suction against the mortar, which would tend to reduce the plasticity. However, a certain amount of suction is needed to ensure a good bond.

Pressing in

Physical pressure is needed to get the best bond between the mortar and backing. Units will be tapped into position for levelling and straightening in the normal way, but particular care should be taken to press in the joint faces. The usual tools for this are pointing irons, jointers, or a wooden stick. The easiest joint to form is thus a slightly recessed one which will form a sharp shadow line, but for best durability of the masonry as a whole, the joint should be brought up flush with the masonry units to give a smooth run-off for rainwater and to provide the best possible surface for evaporation from the joints. This conflict of needs is traditionally overcome by the separation of bedding work from pointing.

Pressing in mortar with a pointing iron

Pointing

After the units have been laid in the bedding mortar, the joints are pressed in and cut back to a depth equal to about the width of the joints or to a minimum of 10mm (⅜"), whichever is the greater. When the mortar has taken a set (and carbonated if it is a fat lime) the joint is then pointed up flush. The same mortar would normally be used for bedding and pointing, but this process allows the possibility of laying the units in, say, a stone lime or feebly hydraulic lime (Class C1) with a weak hydraulic set throughout the whole depth of the bedding and then pointing up with a fat lime. This should be able to carbonate through the depth of the pointing, but will retain all the benefits of maximum porosity and permeability which provide long-term protection for the masonry. The combination also matches a requirement for natural durability – that the facing should be weaker than the material at the heart of the joint.

Other advantages of separate pointing are that it is simpler to keep a consistent colour and style in the joints, particularly when many masons are working on one building.

Wide joints

Where the masonry units are unshaped rubble, or only irregularly-shaped blocks, the joints may need to be very wide. For this the mortar should include large aggregates, either as grit or preferably as a porous aggregate.

This will help to control the shrinkage, but shrinkage can further be reduced by pressing gallets or pinnings into the joints. These should preferably be of a material more porous and permeable than the masonry units, perhaps stone or chalk flakes or maybe pieces of broken tile. If they are placed carefully, they can make a strong and charming contribution to the appearance of the building.

Joint surfaces

The pressing in and working of the joints will tend to draw fine material, usually the lime, to the surface. This can seal off the joint and prevent the access of moisture and air needed to help the carbonation. When the joint surface has taken its first set this laitance should be removed with a stiff brush or by careful scraping. As well as helping the carbonation and future 'breathing' through the joint this will also enhance the appearance.

Removing laitance with a stiff brush

Protecting brickwork with a covering of sacks, sheets etc.

Moisture control

Not only is the initial wetting of the masonry units important, but the moisture control of the masonry for the first few days (or weeks in cold weather) is critical to successful work, particularly with the fatter limes. This is because the carbonation process can take place only at the margin of wet and dry material within the mortar. Slow drying also provides a protection from large shrinkage cracks and helps the formation of the larger pores. The work should be shaded from the sun and protected from strong winds with wet hessian or with tarpaulins or plastic sheeting. As the mortar dries out it should be re-dampened, preferably by spraying with a very fine mist. The fine droplets of the mist, with a higher surface area than larger drops splashed from a brush, may pick up carbon dioxide from the air to contribute to the carbonation. The length of time for which this degree of care is needed will depend on the weather conditions, on the pore structure and the porosity of the masonry units, but typically the mortar should be cherished for a week. With hydraulic mortars this is less critical, but they must still be protected from sudden drying and kept continuously moist for the same length of time.

Hydraulic mortars need to be kept moist for a different reason. Their set uses water in a chemical reaction, and so to achieve the design performance of the mortar, the joints must be kept moist for several days. In this case, the time for which the joints must be kept moist depends very much upon the hydraulic characteristics of the lime used.

5.10 Trial mixes

The need for trials

When a builder is working in his own area and with familiar materials the whole business of mortar preparation becomes second nature and, with ordinary care, success will be achieved every time. But with unfamiliar materials, whether the lime, the pozzolan, the aggregates or the masonry units, or with unfamiliar conditions – working in cold weather or at an unusual speed – it will be important to make trial mixes under carefully controlled conditions. The various processes described in this chapter all take time and although there is always pressure to hurry these trials, plenty of time must be allowed for them.

Trial proportions

The starting point, as described by Vitruvius (trans. 1960) two thousand years ago, would be a 1 : 3 binder to aggregate ratio if using a well-graded sharp sand, or down towards 1 : 2 with a rounded sand of poor particle size distribution. Vicat has suggested how a closer first guess for the correct ratio may be found by filling a measuring cylinder (or any other relatively tall container) brim full with the aggregate and measuring the proportion of water required to fill the aggregate without standing above it (Vicat, 1837). The volume of lime putty should not be less than the water absorbed. This is still a rough and ready procedure as the water will allow the sand to settle down to a smaller volume and the moisture content of the sand will obviously affect the test, but this will still provide a helpful starting point for trial mixes.

Detailed descriptions of testing methods are given in Chapter 11.

Properties to check
The trials should be used to establish:

○ the best proportions of the various ingredients
○ the effectiveness of any hydraulic limes or pozzolans
○ the colour
○ the texture
○ the carbonation achieved in the first weeks
○ strength achieved under site conditions, if this is critical
○ the optimum period between preparing coarse stuff and finally knocking up a hydraulic or pozzolanic mortar
○ time of set in air and under water.

Pore structure, though very important, is difficult to assess without laboratory equipment, although a rough guide to porosity and permeability can be established by speed and extent of water absorbtion by test specimens. Carbonation can be checked with *phenolphthalein indicator* or with various other vegetable dyes which are sensitive to the change of pH between calcium hydroxide and calcium carbonate.

Performance standards
These are detailed in Chapter 11 on testing and standards.

6

Plain lime plastering for interiors

6.1 Introduction

The word plastering has been used here in connection with all *internal* work. Similar materials used for *outside* work are dealt with in the next chapter and are referred to as external *render*. Traditionally the term 'rendering' was used to denote the first coat on solid walls. The term pricking up coat was used for the first coat on lath work.

Plastering is commonly understood to mean any process by which various surfaces of a building are coated with a smooth flowing ('plastic') material that eventually hardens. The plastered surface is often more suitable for the intended use of a building and more pleasing in appearance than the rougher structure, more hygienic and more suitable to receive decorative finishes. Lime plaster has fire-resisting properties, a valuable asset, particularly useful when selecting finishes for timber-framed and thatched buildings.

The cost of raw materials for lime plaster is low when compared with other plastering media. This allows the possibility of thick backing coats giving effective covering to poor backgrounds, covering up differences in levels and providing a substantially improved surface.

One of the advantages of using lime, rather than other binders, is that it is easy to apply. However, to achieve the most durable finish hard work is needed in the scouring of the finishing coat. This is achieved by firmly rubbing (scouring) the surface using a tight, circular motion and additional pressure on the float.

6.2 Tools

There is an old saying that applies to all trades including plastering, that 'a good workman is known by his tools'. Initially a few simple tools are required, and a good craftsman will eventually build up a varied assortment, whether bought or made by himself. The tools may be crude, but they must be effective for their purpose.

Implements for plain plastering comprise simple and inexpensive sieves or screens, shovel and larry. Hand-tools required are hawk, trowels, floats and plumb bob, straight edge, square, jointing and mitring tools, scratch, brushes, and plasterers' hammer for general work. Illustrations and detailed descriptions of these tools and their uses, are given in Chapter 3.

6.3 Backgrounds

Any walling material, provided it is structurally sound, stable, dry, and given a good key, is a suitable background for lime plaster. Surfaces subject

Indenting the earth surface

to damp may also be plastered if the correct techniques and materials are used. Damp conditions, however, are usually generated externally and this is covered in the following chapter, which deals with external renders.

Earth backgrounds

Adobe, clay lump, mud bricks, cob, pisé, tubali, stabilized earth, rammed earth, and compressed blocks will take lime plaster if a good background key is provided (Norton, 1986).

The earth surface to be plastered must be well compacted and dry, and the drying out may be very slow in some climates. A good key may be prepared in a number of ways, including the following.

○ Clay-rich soils may be stabilized with small quantities (5 to 6%) of powdered quicklime fresh from the kiln. Lime-stabilized earth daubs can be worked up to good plastering consistency which will set hard. This type of daub can be scratch keyed in the same way as plain lime plaster, described in Section 6.5 under first coat – solid walls, on page 91. It is important to use the appropriate safety precautions when handling quicklime, as described in Section 4.2.

○ Indent the surface with the point of a sharp tool without being concerned about spoiling the surface. Make all indentations close to each other and cut them in at random angles directed from the top to the bottom. Each hole should have a small check or cupped stop at the bottom which will assist retention and support of the plaster.

After fully indenting the wall, the surface should be well brushed with a soft natural bristle brush, to remove all loose particles and dust. If the surface remains loose and friable it should be stabilized prior to plastering. The degree to which this can be achieved depends to a large extent on the earth composition. After dampening, an application of either diluted limewash, joinery glue, or size will assist in fixing the dust and improving adhesion of the plaster. This application will also affect the suction and water absorption of the background, which may be adjusted and improved with experience.

78

○ On walls of adobe (earth bricks or blocks) mortar joints should be raked back to a depth of approximately 25mm (1"). The face of blocks should also be either grooved or indented, allowing the plaster to be anchored by this as well as the raked-out joints.

○ A key may be formed by projecting broken pottery, slate, or other hard inert material pushed into the face of the wall at close intervals during the course of construction. The broken tiles ought to be about 75mm (3") long, set into the wall to a depth of at least 50mm (2") to give adequate support, although the depth for a firm support will depend on the density of earth construction.

○ Wire as loops, straight lengths, mesh or chicken netting, can also form a key, providing it is tied back well. In brick and block construction it is a simple matter to turn the wire into mortar joints. In rammed earth, ties may be cast in during the course of ramming, or wire may be fixed by nailing.

○ Nails on their own, approximately 75mm (3") long and galvanized with wide flat heads, at 300mm (12") centres may be used when cost effective and practical in relation to other methods. The best way of providing a key with nails is to drive them in after the first coat of plaster has been applied and while it is soft. They are driven in flush with the undercoat and random spaced 300mm (12") apart to avoid defined plains along which the plaster might crack.

If this keying method is selected it is important to use metal that is non-ferrous, galvanized or coated to prevent rust. Ordinary untreated nails and wire will rust, which will eventually damage the plaster and cause loss of key, particularly where moist or damp conditions are prevalent.

Stone, bricks, concrete block, and other solid walling backgrounds

There are two possible approaches – either to plaster directly on to the masonry or to batten and lath out the walls to give a dry lining, which is described in the next section.

If the masonry is suitably porous the plaster will adhere well to its surface provided that the surface has been carefully dampened first. If it is not porous, the joints should be raked out and if the units are large, smooth and dense their faces may need to be hacked back or treated with a bonding agent such as PVA or SBR. Coarse stuff forcibly thrown or spattered on to the surface and allowed to dry thoroughly is another method of improving the key.

Prior to plastering all solid backgrounds it is important that they are allowed to dry out for a sufficient period after construction in order that initial drying shrinkage is complete. However, a small amount of 'construction moisture' is advantageous in that the body of the wall holding moisture safeguards the newly applied plaster against drying out too rapidly. The background should then be moistened with clean water before application of the plaster. If this is not done, differential movement between the background and the plaster, due to rapid moisture absorption from the wet plaster to the dry wall, will cause cracking and possible failure of finished work.

Lathing

Lathing is generally the most suitable background for plastering timber-framed structures and for providing a homogeneous and continuous finish to walls that are not solid. The laths are fixed to wood joists, studding or battens to form a foundation for plaster finishes on structural frames, partition walls, and ceilings. Laths may also be fixed so that they form inclined or curved surfaces.

Solid walls may be battened out to receive laths. Battens may vary in size but the optimum dimensions are 50–65mm (2–2½") wide by 15–25mm (⅝–1") thick, fixed vertically at 300–350mm (12–14") centres, to receive the laths. Battens may be nailed or screwed to the wall with plugs which may be wood, fibre or plastic, except where chimney flues occur, in which case they should be secured by iron ties driven or bedded into the joints.

Walls likely to be damp should be battened, as the clear air space between the masonry and the lathing helps to keep the plaster dry. Battens should be isolated from the wall with an inert damp-proof material such as plastic washers, slate or any non-ferrous metal. The air space between the

Sawn lath attached to soffit of spiral staircase with timber bead mould to external angle; Warwick Castle 1996

back of the lath and face of the wall should be well ventilated at top and bottom, and the ventilation holes covered with flyscreen mesh.

Reed, wattle, wicker work, slate strips, wire mesh, expanded metal, and stainless steel mesh are alternative materials to wood that may be used for lathing.

○ *Wood lath*   Laths of straight-grained wood, either split or sawn, will give an excellent background, these are best set out as shown overleaf.

Among the best timbers for lathing are oak, sweet chestnut, hazel, red Baltic fir, American fir, spruce, deal, and Scots pine.

Laths are stronger if they are prepared by splitting (riving) down straight grain rather than by being sawn. The most practical and cost-effective method will need to be judged locally. Optimum lath size is 25 to 32mm (1"–1¼") wide by 5 to 6mm (¼") thick in 900 to 1500mm (3'–4'6") lengths.

Soaking wood laths in lime water before fixing will assist slow drying out of the plaster and give a stronger key.

Laths are fixed parallel to one another, and approximately 10mm (⅜") (little-finger thickness) apart so that the intervals afford a key for the plaster. Each lath is fixed by nailing through wherever it crosses a joist or batten. The moist plaster passes between the laths, forming protuberances or nibs at the back which harden and form what is known as the 'key'. The nibs must protrude far enough through the lath that gravity acts on them causing them to slump downwards, curl over the lath below and in this way grip well. This prevents the plaster falling away from the laths and keeps it firmly in position (see illustration below). The ends of the laths must not overlap one another and should be set with a 3mm (⅛") gap between ends to allow for swelling when wet. Where laths cross the supporting timbers no nibs will be formed and so special steps must be taken when lathing over wide support surfaces.

○ *Counter lathing*   All framing timbers over 75mm (3") wide should have fillets or double laths nailed along the centre, and the facing laths nailed to them. This is known as counter lathing to give a better key. Counter lathing is also necessary where plaster has to be applied close to a flat surface, such as round columns and beams.

In the same way, if ceiling or floor joists are of wood, a narrow fillet or batten may be nailed on the underside of each to receive the laths, again to keep interruption of the plaster key to the minimum as shown above.

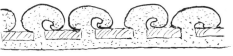

Moist plaster forming nibs at back of laths

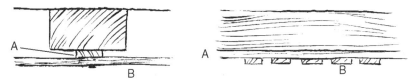

Counter lathing. A: Counter lath; B: Lath

○ *Setting out wood lath* A break joint should occur every ten to twelve laths as shown below. The thickest laths should be used for ceilings.

The danger of fixings rusting and the rust showing on the surface can be avoided by using non-ferrous or galvanized nails.

Brandering for ceilings is the term used for running battens at right angles to joists before lathing. Brandering is set out at 300–350mm centres (12–14") as for battens.

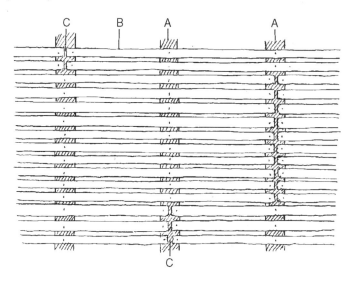

Lathing for walls and ceilings
A: Floor joists or partition studs or brandering battens set at 300–350mm (12"–14") centres; B: Laths; C: Break-joints approximately every 12 laths and staggered three times

○ *Reed* Strong reed, well-fixed, with laths at right angles to the reed, nailed to wood studding behind, was common in the past and may give adequate support. Alternatively, reeds may be nailed individually with fly-nails or bound with cord. Both reed and straw have traditionally been used as a lathing key for plaster. Considerable pressure, however, has to be applied to ensure that the lime is forced between the reeds to form an adequate key.

○ *Wire netting and metal lathing* Wire netting, securely stapled to battens or joists, can be an economic method and it is fire resistant. Care must be taken, however, to ensure adequate firm fixings and a sufficiently fine mesh to enable a sound key to be formed.

A disadvantage of metal lathing is its tendency to rust. It may be protected by dipping in bituminous paint, by giving it an impervious coating or galvanizing before use.

A further disadvantage of all forms of metal lathing for lime plaster is its inability to retain moisture. The plaster will therefore dry faster than on wood lath. Care must be taken to prevent rapid drying out. This applies to both sides of the plasterwork. The backing plaster key is particularly vulnerable when the space behind is very well ventilated.

It is advisable to avoid mixing different metals used for laths and fixings. Some metal combinations can set up electrolytic action which can lead to salt contamination and breakdown of the plaster.

○ *Expanded metal lathing* There are numerous proprietary systems of expanded metal lathing, many of which incorporate special features such as arrangements for rapid fixing.

Difficulties may arise in plastering on the lighter types of expanded metal as it tends to distort with the weight of the plaster and pressure of application. This may give a wavy appearance and cracks over the fixing lines. Metal lathing should not, therefore, be treated as a rigid background. In order to overcome this some proprietary types have been developed with ribs which give a considerably improved performance in terms of firm background and key.

○ *Stainless steel lath* Stainless steel mesh and stainless steel lath have also been developed and are effective. They are, however, relatively expensive and not always readily available.

6.4 Materials for lime plastering

Wealth may encase walls and ceilings in decorative woods and marbles, but for the mass of mankind lime plaster must continue to be the simplest, most sanitary, least costly, and most enduring finish for homes. The health of the majority of mankind is therefore largely dependent upon the material used in its mixture, and the principles which shall actuate its employment. For all kinds of lime plastering it is of the utmost importance that the lime should be thoroughly slaked and mixed with the proper amount of good and clean sand, hair, and water, and the whole thoroughly incorporated and tempered, and allowed to mature before using. Success largely depends upon the care bestowed on the materials and the way they are manipulated.

W. Millar, master plasterer and modeller, London (1897).

Lime putty

Lime putty from fat-rich limes of over 95% calcium and magnesium oxide (CaO + MgO) is suitable for internal plastering. Lean chalk-stone limes, and feebly hydraulic limes may also be used provided care is taken with their preparation, as detailed in Chapter 2. It is essential that the putty lime is prepared immediately after burning. Quicklime should not be left longer than three days at maximum before being run to putty. Ideally it should be run to putty as it leaves the kiln.

It is essential that air does not reach the lime prior to use, and a simple way to achieve this is to keep it covered with water in a storage tank or pit. Alternatively, it may be kept in airtight containers.

Sand

The quality of sand or fine aggregate is of primary importance for the production of good coarse stuff and setting stuff. Sand is formed of particles of rocks, often containing quartz, produced by the action of rain, temperature change, wind, wave and frost. Basically it has been formed by the weathering or erosion of exposed rock. This weathering may occur in different forms anywhere in the world, making 'sand' the most widely distributed substance in nature.

The best sands are pit, river and washed sea sands. They may be tested for impurities as detailed in Chapter 11. These impurities may be organic matter, loam, clay, silt, and salts. If the total of these exceeds 6%, either the sand should be washed before use or an alternative found. Sea sand should always be washed with fresh water to free it from its heavy saline content.

The presence of salt may encourage plaster to retain moisture and cause efflorescence in white blotches on the surface. Good sand for lime plaster should be hard, sharp, gritty, and clean. It should always be washed and graded for the best quality work. For coarse stuff and the first plaster coats it should not be too fine. Good sand for plasterwork may be rubbed between the hands without soiling them.

Best results will be obtained if all sand is first sieved through a mesh of the following maximum size:

○ Internal lime undercoats – aperture size 5mm (³⁄₁₆")
○ Internal lime finishing coats – aperture size 1.18mm

For the finest finished three-coat work, a sand particle size below 800 microns is recommended for the fine stuff, mixed with lime putty which has passed through a 600 micron (¹⁄₃₂") sieve.

Table 6.1 compares the different standards for the most commonly used sieve sizes for plastering and gives the appropriate range of particle size for each of the plaster coats.

The closer to an even grading of sand particle size, the better the mix. In practice no sand has completely even grading and very good results can be obtained where there is an increased proportion of particles at the middle to lower end of the range. The quality of various local sand deposits may be checked for even grading to some extent by eye, but more accurately by particle size analysis (sieve analysis). Test sieves with the aperture sizes shown in Table 6.1 are suitable.

Table 6.1: Sands for internal plaster

Aggregate particle size		Nearest equivalent standard mesh size			
Optimum particle size per coat	Aperture size BS 410–1969	Tyler mesh size	ASTM Standard E 11.70 USA		DIN Standard DIN 4188
	5.00mm	³⁄₁₆"	No. 4	4.76mm	4.00mm
	2.36mm	no. 7 mesh	No. 8	2.38mm	2.00mm
	1.18mm	no. 14 mesh	No. 16	1.19mm	1.18mm
	1.00mm	no. 16 mesh	No. 18	1.00mm	1.00mm
	0.85mm	no. 18 mesh	No. 20	850 microns	0.80mm
	0.60mm	no. 25 mesh	No. 30	600 microns	0.63mm
	0.30mm	no. 52 mesh	No. 50	300 microns	0.25mm
	0.15mm	no. 100 mesh	No. 100	150 microns	0.125mm

(Left margin brackets indicate: FIRST COAT, SECOND COAT, THIRD COAT ranges)

A mesh and particle size conversion table is given in Appendix 3.

The various national standards give precise limits of quantities to be retained on each sieve. National standards specifying and describing tests for sand are listed in Appendix 4. For practical purposes, when the test is carried out it can be seen that the closer to an even quantity of sand retained on each sieve the closer the sand is to having a broad particle size distribution.

Material below 60 microns (0.06mm), regarded as silt, probably containing other impurities, is best excluded by washing and sieving if possible. As a general rule up to 6% silt can be tolerated without undue harm to the finished work. A simple sediment test for determining the quantity of silt in a sand is given in Section 11.4 of Chapter 11.

Alternatives to sand

Many of the inert 'soils' used for earth structures, well-known in areas of South America and Africa and usually referred to as red soil, murram, or laterite, can be satisfactory substitutes. The critical factors are an absence of (or minimal) clay content, and freedom from organic matter and silt.

These sandy soils formed from weathered rock have particle size gradations that vary greatly. Although different in composition, a wide range of laterite types may be found in close proximity to one another. A simple sieve analysis will establish particle size distribution, enabling the most suitable to be selected as an alternative to sand if this is not available.

Various hard inert waste materials, provided they fall within the particle size limits given in Table 6.1, may be considered. These include stone dust or chippings, crushed brick, tile, gravel, stone or slag, volcanic ash, flyash and pozzolans. Experiments with lime-stabilized lignite flyash are detailed by Baradan (1993).

Fibres

Traditionally in the western hemisphere ox, cow, or goat hair has been added to the first, and occasionally second, coat of lime plaster to reduce cracking and strengthen the finished work. Deer, yak and llama hair can also be used. Some alternatives are Manila hemp, sisal and jute fibre. Hair and fibres should be clean, free of grease and strong but not coarse. The first coating on lath needs more hair than for a solid background.

All forms of fibre are best cut into lengths of from 35 to 90mm (1½" to 3½") long prior to mixing in with the coarse stuff. It is best to use haired stuff immediately after adding hair to the coarse stuff mix. If a large quantity of haired stuff is made up and stored it should be used within one month of preparation. Action of calcium hydroxide (lime in its wet state) is likely to dissolve the hair over a longer period.

Coarse stuff

Coarse stuff is prepared for the first coat of lime plaster. For internal work it is usually composed of lime putty slaked and sieved from well burnt fat lime or chalk (Class A, shown in the classification of building limes, Appendix 1), mixed with sand and hair. The usual proportions are 1 of lime to 3 of sand, but the proportion of sand may be reduced to 2.5 times the putty. This will be judged by the plasterer using his or her experience in relation to the type of background and the materials available. The quality of sand ranging between soft and sharp will also affect optimum mix proportions. Round-grained or 'soft' sand is detrimental if not blended or incorporated with some angular grained or 'sharp' sand.

Thorough mixing, including chopping and ramming, is important for ease of workability, to assist even curing, and for final strength. It should be mixed continuously until the whole mass is uniform in colour and consistency. 'Knocking up' should be done at the beginning of each work session and as often as is necessary.

The hair is sprinkled into the mix and distributed with the hair hook, or larry. It should be gradually and evenly teased in to give good distribution without balling into tufts or lumps. The coarse stuff is larried up until the required amount, roughly 0.5kg (1lb) of hair to 100 litres (3 cubic feet) of coarse stuff is well mixed in. A simple method of measurement is two handfuls of hair per barrow of coarse stuff. A test to check whether there are sufficient fibres in the mix is to take a trowel full of coarse stuff and count the hairs dangling off the edge. Some recommend about 25 to 30 but once again there is no substitute for experience of local materials and conditions to determine the optimum for best results. Millar (1897) advises one hair every ¹⁄₁₆" round the perimeter of the trowel after it has been dipped into the mix and tapped.

The mixture may be kept wet in an airtight container indefinitely before adding hair or fibre. Once hair is added, however, it should be used within one month. It is essential that coarse stuff is kept moist at all times prior to use and that no part is allowed to dry out. Storage in watertight containers or a covered pit is recommended. Workability and setting qualities improve with the age of the coarse stuff and storage for a minimum of two weeks with a good lime putty is generally accepted good practice.

Setting or skimming stuff (also known as fine stuff)

The best finishing coats for plain lime plastering are composed of fine washed sand and lime putty. The mix should be stored in a container that can be covered over and kept free from dirt and dust. The finishing coat mix is variable depending on the type required, but for standard work anticipating a paint finish, mixes ranging from 1 : 1 to 1 : 2 of lime : sand are common. This range may, however, be extended to between 1 lime to 3 sand and 3 lime to 1 sand; once again trial mixes with local material are advised.

Some sands, being very fine, make it too fatty, and fine shrinkage cracks will appear. If this is the case a better graded sand should be found, or at least more, and preferably slightly coarser, aggregate should be added to the mix. The optimum sizes of sand grains are detailed earlier in this section. Silver sand below 300 microns is preferred by some for skimming stuff in high quality work. A small amount of white hair may be added to improve strength, but this is seldom necessary.

Retarders, accelerators and hardeners

Variations to workability, speed of set and finish may be achieved by gauging with small quantities of various additives, although with good

Retarders	**Accelerators**	**Hardeners**
(For lime only)	Calcium chloride	Crushed shells
Glue size	(CaCl$_2$)	Pulverized soapstone
Oils	Gypsum	(talc)
Sugar, dissolved in	Alum	Marble dust
beer or vinegar	Borax	Bone ash
	Pozzolans	Forge ashes or furnace
(For material gauged	Bone ash	cinders
with gypsum)		Granite dust or chippings
Keratin	**Bonding agents**	Alum
Sodium citrate	Sugar	Sugar (jaggery)
	Molasses	Molasses
Air entrainers	PVA – polyvinyl	Pozzolans
Chalk and limestone	acetate	Rye flour
particles	Acrylic emulsions	Oils
Broken brick and tile	White of eggs	SBR
Beer	Styrene-butadiene	Gauging with lime water
Charcoal	rubber (SBR)	Dextrin (Verrall, 1931)
Ash residue		

workmanship this should not normally be necessary. Finishes that need to resist damp conditions are detailed in the following chapter.

Clearly small-scale trials are always advisable when experimenting with new materials or mixes. The additives listed above are recorded as having been used in the past. If any of these materials are available locally, experimental trials to produce special mixes may prove worthwhile. Various other traditional additives are given, together with methods of application for differing requirements, in Chapters 4, 7 and 8.

6.5 Plain lime plaster application

The good workability of lime plaster is associated with its ability to retain water against suction of the background. This reduces the tendency of plaster to dry out too quickly while it is being worked, and ensures that sufficient water remains in the mix for complete hydration and hardening. Hardening depends in part on slow drying out to be fully effective.

It used to be common practice to slake quicklime, possibly first crushing it, and then to mix it with wet sand as a method of preparing coarse stuff for mortar. This method does not safeguard against under-burnt or over-burnt limestone being incorporated in the mix, and is therefore not recommended for plaster. If incorrectly burnt lime particles are incorporated in the finished plaster they are likely to be subject to delayed slaking over weeks or months or sometimes even years. This can cause unsightly pitting and popping of the surface, and sometimes complete failure. Coarse stuff and setting stuff should be prepared with putty lime produced as described in Chapter 2.

Plain lime plastering may be carried out in one, two or three coats. Three-coat work is of the highest standard. Two-coat work is for secondary areas. One-coat work is a low-cost finish, and can be completed with a stock brush after scouring.

The methods of plaster application are given in detail after these general descriptions.

One-coat work

This consists of a layer of coarse stuff of a uniform thickness, up to about 18mm (¾"), spread over solid background or lath to achieve a smooth and even surface. The plaster should be stiff enough to hold together, but sufficiently soft to be pressed between laths to form a key or adhere to the roughened surface of a solid background. This is the cheapest kind of plastering even when scoured twice and is markedly inferior to two- and three-coat work.

One-coat work is probably easier to apply and more likely to be successful on solid walls. It is seldom used on lathing.

Methods of finishing one-coat work include use of the sponge float, carpet float, felt float and bag rubbing with a ball of hessian sacking. It is suitable for undulating surfaces on rough random stone walling which, although irregular, can produce a soft and delightful appearance.

One-and-a-half-coat work

Sometimes termed 'coat-and-a-half'. This is a first coat of coarse stuff from 6mm (¼") to 15mm (⅝") thick which is allowed to firm up partially but not harden fully. After scouring the surface is scratched with a coarse broom, and immediately following this a thin coat of very fat coarse stuff is applied. This mixture is produced by adding extra lime to the coarse stuff. This is levelled with a darby and then trowelled and brushed. It is important that the second application is laid while the first is still green (see Glossary). The sequence allows the coats to combine well together by allowing the backing coat to shrink and stabilize whilst allowing an easier working of the surface to achieve a reasonable finish.

Two-coat work

This is still relatively cheap and inferior to three-coat work.

○ *First coat* The first coat of about 15mm (⅝") thickness is applied to the lathing or solid wall after any necessary dubbing out as described above, and roughly straightened with a feather edge rule or darby. The surface is scoured once on solid background. Following this it is roughed over by scratching it with a birch broom or devil float to form a key for the second coat.

○ *Second coat* The second coat is composed of a thin layer of 'setting stuff' or 'fine stuff' and is trowelled on after the first layer has hardened. If the first coat has become very dry it must be moistened well before the second coat is applied to avoid shrinking, cracking and failure of the finishing coat. After trowelling on the second coat of 2–3mm (⅛") in thickness, it is brushed first wet, and then later with a damp brush the last time before it finally hardens. It can be scoured if a well-consolidated surface is required.

Three-coat work

This method of plain lime plastering would be expected for the more important rooms of all good buildings, although areas of lesser importance in the same building might sometimes receive two-coat work. Three-coat work is a technique that creates the best straight, smooth, strong, and sanitary surfaces on walls and ceilings.

The traditional description of three-coat work was render, float, and set. Over the course of time a range of different descriptions and terminology for lime plaster coats and materials have developed to the stage where

Table 6.2: Recommended mix proportions for three-coat work

| Coat | Recommended mix proportions | | Thickness | |
	Lime	Sand	(mm)	(inches)
1st	1	2½–3	6–16	¼–⅝"
2nd	1	3	13–16	½–⅝"
3rd	from 1 to 3	from 3 to 1	3–5	⅛–³⁄₁₆"

there are now so many they may cause confusion. To avoid this, therefore, the terms given here are restricted to plaster coats, described as *'first'*, *'second'* and *'third'* in order of application.

Application in detail

○ *First coat – lath work*   Wood and reed lath backgrounds should be well wetted the day before, and again two hours before work proceeds. The extent of wetting depends to a large degree upon climate. It may be necessary in hot dry conditions to damp the lath immediately before application of the first coat. The constant principle is that at no time should the lath be so dry that it will absorb moisture rapidly from the first coat when it is applied.

Against this, however, too much water on the background immediately prior to plastering will make it impossible to keep the plaster in position. If the wall becomes dry in patches, these areas should be damped again to ensure uniform adhesion. Plastering should be done in the shade and this is particularly important in tropical climates.

Laying and spreading the first coat of coarse stuff on walls and ceilings forms a foundation for the subsequent two coats. The hair in the coarse stuff helps to provide a strong binding key, particularly on lathing. Before applying the first coat the coarse stuff may be tested by taking up some on the point of a trowel. If it is adequately haired and mixed, the stuff should cling to the trowel when held upside down, and the hairs should be evenly distributed. It should be stiff enough to hold up when laid, but sufficiently plastic to squeeze easily through gaps between the laths. It is important that the coarse stuff is of the proper consistency, otherwise it will fail soon after being applied.

Using the steel laying trowel, the coarse stuff is laid across the lath in a diagonal direction. Each trowelful is spread steadily and firmly, joining up each time with the previous area laid, working from the 'heel' of the trowel. When first coating a ceiling, a forward push from the shoulder will usually be found to be more effective and less tiring than drawing the trowel towards the body. Laying on to partition walls is best done using a series of upward movements commencing with areas near the top of the wall and progressing downwards. It is essential to apply sufficient pressure to force the plaster into intimate contact with the background.

After a period of approximately one hour to let the work 'steady up', the surface is scratched using a three-pronged lath scratcher, or a single pointed lath (which is slower but gives a better job), the scratch marks are made diagonally to the laths at an angle of 45°, about 25mm (1") apart. Scratches are crossed in both directions leaving a lattice of diamond shaped scratch marks. Sufficient pressure should be applied to cut into the work but not enough to reach the surface of the supporting laths or remove the hair.

When first-coating ceilings, laying the stuff diagonally, and overlapping each trowelful helps to retain the stuff in its place, which otherwise is apt to drop. The stuff should be laid on with a full-sized laying trowel using sufficient pressure to force it between the laths. The stuff should be laid to as close a uniform thickness as possible. This should be between 10 and 15mm (⅜ to ⅝"). A thickness of 13mm (½") gives the best results, depending on aggregate size.

○ *First coat – solid walls* Following preparation of a solid wall background, as described in Section 6.3, it should be swept down with a stiff broom and well wetted systematically in advance, to allow deep, even penetration and to control the suction (but not to kill it altogether). Any holes or deep parts should have been 'dubbed out' previously and allowed to dry. A slightly stiffer mix can be used for this. By throwing the material in with the 'toe' of the laying trowel a more effective bond is achieved than by spreading it. Any larger wads of plaster should be plugged with carefully selected pinnings of brick, tile or stone to counteract shrinkage.

The first coat on a solid wall is a slightly softer mix than for lath work. It is simply spread over the wall with a steel laying trowel and scratched as for lath work, but without the delay after application. The scratching or keying should never be done carelessly, nor be regarded as an unimportant detail.

It is important not to miss the scratching key anywhere, especially round door or window openings, where there may be jarring or vibration. The stability of succeeding coats depends on this key. A trowel must not be used as a scratch tool as it is too sharp and narrow and would be detrimental to the strength of the coat and the key.

○ *Second coat* The first coat must be given time to dry out thoroughly before the second coat is applied. Any dust should be swept off the surface and the first coat lightly damped down with clean water. In hot dry conditions it is important to ensure the first coat does not dry out too quickly. To effect this, it should be covered with damp sacking or other sheet material, and kept moist for preferably no less than seven days. The colder the climate the slower the set. In continuous very cold (near freezing) conditions the set may take a month or more and needs to be judged by trials and experience. Frost in plaster that has not set is likely to cause it to fail.

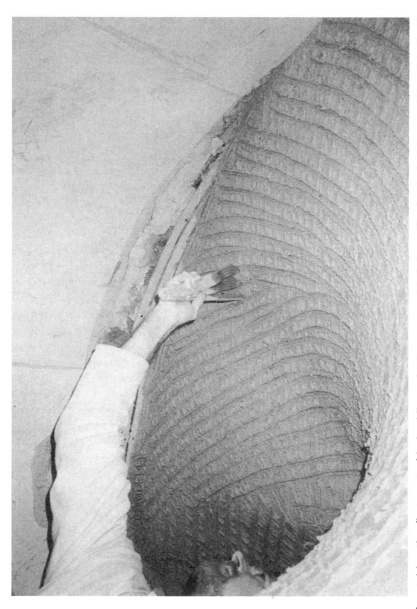

Scratching the first coat of haired lime plaster on wood lath to soffit of spiral staircase, Warwick Castle

Laying on the second coat

For the best work, plaster 'dots' are applied and then plumbed and levelled to form 'screeds'. These screeds are brought to a true face with long 'floating rules'. When the screeds have hardened sufficiently, the spaces between are filled with coarse stuff, applied with a trowel. The plaster is levelled off with wooden floating rules, the ends bearing on the screeds until a perfectly straight surface is obtained. The wooden floating rule helps to compact the material during the action of 'ruling in'.

Further consolidation is then achieved by 'scouring'. Once the work has stood long enough to give a firm surface, but not so long as to allow it to become dry, it should be well scoured over with a wooden hand float. This should be done twice on the day of application and once the next day, if necessary.

Scouring must be done vigorously, efficiently and evenly, as the quality of finished work depends on it. If scouring is done too early the plaster will be broken up, weakened, and moved to a new shape. Scouring too late will damage the surface. If the work becomes too dry too

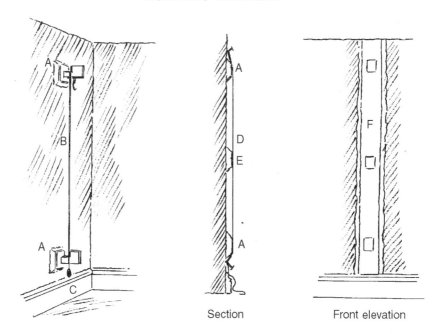

Section   Front elevation

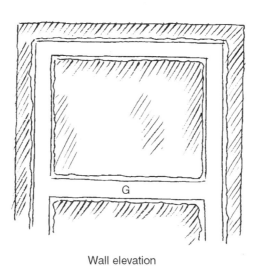

Wall elevation

Method of preparing levelling screeds prior to plastering
A: Plaster dot; B: Plumb line; C: Plumb bob; D: Tight line; E: Intermediate
dots set to line; F: Plaster screed flush with dots; G: Vertical and
horizontal screeds to wall

Using a floating rule between screeds

quickly, crazing and cracks will rapidly appear. Some crazing is to be expected during the course of drying out, and the purpose of scouring is to re-seal and consolidate the surface. If the work does become too dry, water may be sprinkled on with a brush to assist the circular rubbing action of the float.

A 'devil float', a wooden float with thin wire nails projecting through the corners about 3mm (⅛") beyond the sole of the float, is then passed over the surface to form a key for the third and finishing coat. The devil float should be worked in a close circular motion to leave a series of close and irregular indents to give a sound and uniform key.

○ *Third coat*   The lime : sand proportions of the setting stuff for the third coat vary depending on the finish required. The richest mix would be 3 of putty to 1 of sand and the leanest mix 1 of putty to 3 of sand. The mix used depends on the desired hardness and the type of finished surface suitable for the area plastered. For standard work, with a trowel finish, lime-sand mixes between 1 : 1 and 1 : 2 are common.

Lime-sand mixes of 1 : 2 or even 1 : 3 are used for textured surfaces with a wood float. A great deal depends on the type of sand selected. The harder and sharper the sand, the more lime will be required for

Using a devil float

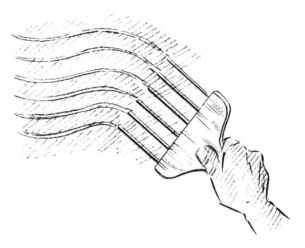

Comb scratching the second coat; comb used instead of a devil float on small and moulded areas

workability. Trials with available materials are advisable to provide samples for selection before deciding on the final mix. For best results fine sharp sand should be selected or sieved for the finishing coat. 'Silver sand' is a common term for this type of sand in the UK.

The surface of the second coat must be first damped down early and thoroughly with water to control the suction. Setting stuff should not be applied until the second coat is quite firm and nearly dry, to allow for any contraction that may take place. For the very best work, setting stuff for the third coat is applied in three successive layers, with time between for the work to 'steady up'.

The first layer is skimmed over as tightly as possible with the steel-laying trowel, or skimming float if preferred. The next layer is laid on with a wooden skimming float in the opposite direction to the first. This can then be 'ruled in' with a wooden feather edge rule, if straightness is critical. The third layer is applied in the same direction as the first again, and as tight as possible with a steel trowel.

The method of application by alternating the use of the trowel and float for each layer by first using the steel trowel, then the wood float and finishing with the steel trowel again is the recognized way to obtain the best finish in high quality work. Excellent results with a wood float only

Skimming on the first layer of the third and finishing coat

may be achieved if a textured finish is required. When the work is firm enough it is well scoured once, or sometimes twice, with a cross-grained float.

Good scouring compacts and consolidates the surface. Water is used more sparingly for the final scouring, using only as much as is necessary to moisten the surface and allow the float to work freely. This scouring is continued until a dense, even and close-grained surface is obtained ready for 'trowelling up'.

The work is trowelled up using a steel trowel and a broad flat stock brush. Water is sprinkled or brushed on to the surface, followed directly by the trowel. This is done two or three times, always in opposite directions. The trowel will make a ringing sound, rising in pitch as the hardness increases. Trowelling the finishing coat is best carried out with a half-worn trowel called a 'polisher', the edges of which should be perfectly straight and parallel.

When the surface is hard enough the whole of the work is gone over with a stock brush three times, in opposite directions. The first two times the brush should be lightly wet and the third semi-dry.

This should produce a very fine and beautiful surface, which may be left undecorated as the final finish. Once again, as for the previous coats, final strength will be greatly increased if it dries out slowly. If it is to be decorated it will take limewash very well, and when fully dry accepts virtually any other form of applied decoration with appropriate sealers. Limewash tends to take to a polished finishing coat best after it has hardened up but whilst it is still green.

6.6 Texture and finishes

The final texture and quality of finish depends in the main on the materials and tools used as well as workmanship. Different finishes having various surface textures are possible. These are obtained by using a range of techniques.

○ A rough open-grained texture may be achieved by a fairly rough wooden float followed by a sponge-faced float.
○ Scouring with a good cross-grained wood float on its own leaves a pleasing dense open-grained finish.
○ A plastic float and well-scoured surface leaves a more polished homogeneous appearance.
○ Scouring and finishing quickly and vigorously with a steel trowel and water will close the grain on any surface giving a more dense and smooth effect.
○ After scouring by polishing hard with a steel trowel whilst continually flicking on lime water, a dense, glass-like finish can be achieved. The

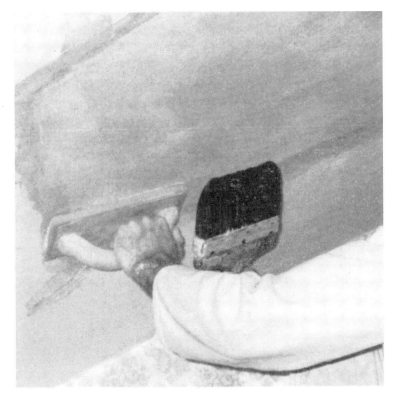

Finishing with stock brush and sponge float

degree of density and smoothness being in direct proportion to the extent of hard polishing carried out.

○ A final skimming coat, 3mm (⅛") thick, of one part lime putty to one part silver sand may be finished by passing over with a wet stock brush in one hand while following immediately with the steel trowel in the other to give a completed surface. This is an adequate low-cost finish for less important areas. (Constantinides, 1992; Young, 1991)

6.7   Ceilings

Levelling ceilings

In best quality work a level line is necessary prior to applying plaster to ceiling laths. A line should be first carried round the wall at an easily workable position down from a starting point on the ceiling, say 300mm (12"). A straight edge is levelled against the wall, and the wall marked at each end. After levelling around the room against walls has been completed a datum line is drawn round, or snapped with a chalk line, from which ceiling levels are set out (see illustrations overleaf).

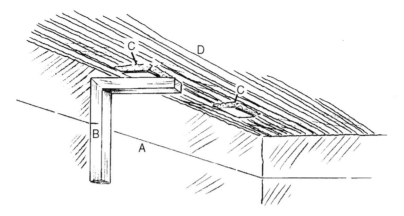

Setting out dots for level ceiling screeds
A: Horizontal setting out line marked on wall; B: Set square marked at
distance required from setting out line (A) to finished surface of ceiling
plaster (underside of C); C: Plaster dot on ceiling; D: Ceiling background
or lath

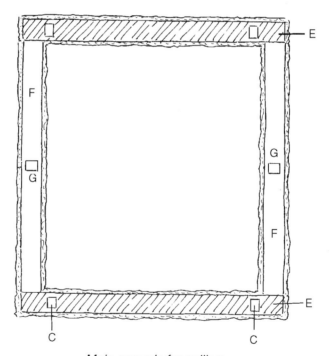

Main screeds for ceiling
E: Screeds run first between dots; F: Cross screeds run second between
first two screeds and levelled on dots G

Ceiling dots

A set square is used for working off the wall datum line to transfer the finished ceiling level to ceiling dots. The set square is marked at the level line at the lowest part of the ceiling allowing for its full finished thickness. Plaster dots are then put on to the ceiling at suitable intervals for a 3m (10') floating rule. This may be smaller, but the fewer dots the better.

Bedding the dots

A small amount of coarse stuff is placed on a short (100mm, 4") length of lath on the ceiling to form dots in the positions shown in the upper figure opposite. The material is pressed in with a square until the dots go in far enough for the square to meet the level line. Four screeds are then formed in a similar manner to those described for the second coat for walls in Section 6.5. Dots and screeds are kept away from the corners to allow for the working of the floating rule.

Cross screeds

After the main screeds have been formed, cross screeds are required to fill in the remaining part of the ceiling. Screeds should always be formed the long way of the ceiling and be as few as possible. They are usually put in 1.8m (6') apart, which is a convenient space for a bay. It is best to work in pairs for this, with the bays being filled by one person laying on the material with a trowel, whilst the other rules it off with a floating rule, feather edge or darby. All plasterwork then proceeds in a similar manner to that described for walls.

6.8   Gauging with gypsum or plaster of Paris

Perfectly good finishes may be achieved for internal work by using lime on its own but for ease of working and speed of set small quantities of gypsum, if available, may be added to the finishing coats. It has often been used in conjunction with lime plaster due to its rapid hardening properties. The use of gypsum plaster on its own is described in detail by Coburn, Dudley and Spence (1989).

The addition of a small quantity of gypsum to lime plaster has the effect of reducing the normal shrinkage whilst drying out by accelerating the set. This reduces the amount of labourious handwork (scouring) necessary to give a perfect finish with a lightly sanded lime putty. The exact proportion of gypsum added depends greatly on local conditions and on the individual judgement of the experienced craftsman. The amount is therefore usually determined by the setting time required which is learnt by previous experience or carrying out trials.

Gypsum should not be used where there is the possibility of damp or moist conditions as it is highly absorbent and will break down when wet.

Gypsum has been used extensively for decorative interiors in the past. It is a material ideally suited to casting moulds and enrichments for ornamental plasterwork.

The table in Appendix 9 is based on BS CP 211 and gives a guide to the quantity of gypsum to be gauged with lime plaster for varying backgrounds.

7

External renders and thrown finishes

7.1 Introduction

A well-designed and well-executed external render is expected to be durable, of attractive appearance, and to make a major contribution to the general weatherproofing of the structure to which it is applied.

The choice of materials, texture, colour, and decoration of a building's finishes will be influenced by functional requirements, building design, climate, location, and the availability of local resources. Regional history, culture, and tradition may also be influential in the choice. One of the greatest attributes of lime-based finishes is their versatility. In addition to practical use they are eminently suited to providing a medium for both individual expression and the continuation of cultural tradition by the application of decoration in both colour and relief. This chapter is concerned with the more practical aspects of plain finishes whilst Chapter 8 outlines a range of decorative plasterwork techniques.

Durability depends upon many factors including detailing, the bond between render and background, the degree of exposure, composition of the mix, and the standard of workmanship.

Detailing

A lime-based render is not designed to act as a dense impervious water barrier. Experience has shown that attempts, with ordinary Portland cement, to provide render which will not permit water penetration often fail due to its rigidity and tendency to crack. Water running down the face enters the render and background through these cracks and cannot easily escape. The trapped moisture is then the cause of further, and accelerating, deterioration putting the rest of the building fabric at risk.

The more porous lime renders allow moisture to evaporate and the building to breathe (Hughes, 1986). A guiding principle for detailing should therefore be that moisture *will* penetrate the render to some extent before being driven off by evaporation. Damp-proof membranes and flashings may be provided to protect exposed and vulnerable junctions. Areas requiring attention, for example, are built-in timbers, particularly roof and floor joist bearing ends.

Close attention needs to be given to all rainwater, waste and soil drainage. If maintenance is to be kept to a minimum it is essential to provide adequate drainage from all gutters, downpipes, and waste pipes, to ensure that there is no accumulation of water on or adjacent to the building. In very wet climates elements such as sills and eaves should project well

Lime harling carried out by T. Meek Associates to exterior wall of Brodie Castle, property of the National Trust for Scotland, 1996

beyond the face of the wall and be provided with ample drip grooves to ensure that water is thrown clear of the wall face.

Bonding

Preparation of the various backgrounds that may be rendered is the same as that for plastering internal walls, and has been described in detail in Section 6.3. Porous and rough surfaces will need little preparation but to ensure a good bond between render and a hard, smooth background material, the surface will need more attention to provide an adequate key.

Exposure

Exposure to adverse environmental conditions may be reduced in a number of ways, thus helping to decrease maintenance, and the demand for very high levels of workmanship and materials. Careful siting and orientation to take advantage of the protection of local features and buildings may help to lessen exposure to the elements. Extending roof overhangs, forming verandas, and constructing balconies, are other ways of giving additional protection to the walls as well as providing shade.

Composition of the mix

Attention to the quality of materials for exterior rendering is no less important than previously described for internal plastering. Unlike internal plastering, however, the majority of external renders take advantage of the weathering characteristics of textured surfaces. A textured surface tends to shed water running down the face, and distribute it giving a more evenly weathered appearance. A far greater range of materials has been used for external renders than internal plasters because of the special requirements in damp conditions. Materials for external render are detailed below in Section 7.4.

Workmanship

If good durability is to be achieved the standard of workmanship is as important as that for internal plastering, described in the previous chapter.

7.2 Tools

The majority of tools for external work can be the same as those used for internal plastering. In addition to these, for some external finishes such as roughcast, harling, and selected aggregate dashings, a hand scoop or dashing trowel may be used. A finely textured sprayed finish may be achieved by the use of a hand-held and operated 'tyrolean' spray machine. Although ease of operation makes this a popular tool, a more durable finish is possible by hand throwing, due to the ability to dash, or throw, coarse material on to the surface with greater force.

Plant and equipment

Independent scaffolding is preferable to that tied into the wall face. It is hard to fill and make good putlog-holes so that they cannot be seen. When the holes are filled and rendered it is extremely difficult to prevent differential shrinkage on drying and consequent cracking of the finish at these points. If making the scaffold fully independent is not possible, it is preferable to tie it back through window and door openings, parapets and roof structure or brace with raking shores, to keep putlog-holes to the minimum consistent with safety. Scaffold boards need to be kept well back from the wall face, about 300mm (12"), to allow an even finish without showing joints in the render at scaffold lift positions.

7.3 Backgrounds

Backgrounds should be prepared as described for lime plaster. The range of materials used for external walling which also act as background for external render, are extensive. External lime-based renders may be applied to wattle, lath, earth, stone, brick, block and many other less common materials, such as simmons rope (entwined straw rope) used with hazel poles in Scotland.

Generally, backgrounds may be classified under four main types.

○ *Weak resilient material* Wattle, lath, and lightweight slabs are often set within a separate structural framework. Although these panels are of adequate strength when rendered, there is little restraint to the expansion or contraction of render as moisture content varies when drying out. There is therefore an advantage in keeping the panels relatively small.
○ *Moderately weak porous materials* Earth structures, blocks incorporating lightweight aggregates, and the softer types of bricks. Renders on these should not be stronger than the background.
○ *Moderately strong but porous materials* Lightly fired clay and concrete bricks and blocks, rough masonry, and rubble work are suitable for taking strong render coats which should be well keyed.
○ *Dense, strong smooth materials* The harder bricks, blocks and stonework are more usual for exterior than interior walls. One of the most common methods of providing a key is to hack the surface with a small pick-axe or scutch hammer. Other ways of obtaining a key are to rake out mortar joints or to apply a splatterdash coat of strong render, provided it is allowed to dry out slowly and thoroughly before applying the first render coat.

Bricks containing excessive amounts of soluble sulphates are not a good base for rendering where there is likely to be persistent dampness. A method of testing for the quantity of soluble sulphate present is given in Chapter 11.

7.4 Materials

The basic materials for external render are the same as those for internal plastering but there are many variations and additions which have been developed over centuries to improve performance and weathering, and to withstand damp conditions.

Lime putty and sand, usually with the addition of hair, remain the principal ingredients for making coarse stuff but slightly coarser sands are used for the finishing coats to give a more textured surface.

Class A lime renders will stand well provided they are skilfully prepared and applied to building fabric that has the opportunity to dry out regularly.

Problems can occur when there are continuously wet conditions, however, and various methods have been developed to overcome these.

○ Limewash shelter coats incorporating additives with watershedding properties can be applied. These may play a dual role by also improving appearance due to their own colouring, or when pigments are added.
○ The use of artificial hydraulic lime: incorporating a pozzolan into the mix imparts hydraulic properties to the render.
○ Using natural hydraulic limes.

Limewash shelter coats

Additional protection to external render may be given by the application of limewash shelter coats or paints, described in Chapter 4. Limewash is an effective, and low-cost treatment that will enhance the building and improve weathering. It is, however, a relatively short-term solution. Limewash has traditionally been applied on a fairly frequent basis; every few years, if not annually.

Excellent watershedding properties for limewash are obtained by the addition of organic oils, although it has been shown that these biodegrade over time. Linseed oil has frequently been used in Europe. There is no harm in experimenting with readily available local oils, such as castor oil or coconut oil, which has been tried in Zanzibar, or whale and fish oils in Brazil, or the juice of the boiled empty locust bean tree pod used in Ghana. The latter is also referred to as ground creeper *cucurbitaceae* (Spence and Cook, 1982).

An extensive range of additives has been used with limewash in the past, many of which are described in Chapter 4. Regional variations in climate and locally available materials indicate that the best economic approach is likely to make use of resources particular to that region. Experiments to test locally available materials on separate trial panels is recommended before commencing with the main work.

There are many ways to improve the weathering of external lime renders, but it should be borne in mind that these methods have been developed over centuries, often to deal with a wide variety of differing climate conditions. In practice, for one locality, it is necessary only to establish a limited number of solutions which are durable over time. Provided suitable local materials are available, little further investigation should be required other than to develop the skills and workmanship needed in their application. In many areas severe climate involving continuous damp or freezing temperatures may not occur, in which case a simple two-line instruction from the 1928 edition of *Specification* (Architectural Press, 1928) is relevant. This states:

'Fat lime may be used for external plastering and will stand well, but care is required in its use'.

Pozzolanic additives

The setting action of natural hydraulic limes can be imitated by mixing fat limes or lean limes (Classes A and B, Appendix 1) with additives know as pozzolans. These can be divided into two groups, one natural and the other artificial.

The natural pozzolans are mostly of volcanic origin, but also include diatomaceous earths. The artificial pozzolans are mainly produced by heating natural materials such as clays and shales, and some siliceous rocks.

The chemical constituents common to most hydraulic limes and pozzolans are various forms of silica, alumina and iron. In general terms, the combination of being subjected to heat, and reduced to microscopic particle size (of the order of 75 microns or below), assists these reactive elements to combine with lime at ordinary temperatures in the presence of water. Calcium silicates and aluminates are the principal stable insoluble compounds formed which possess cementing properties. Magnesium and iron oxides, also often present in hydraulic limes, assist the formation of compounds and improve the set. Calcium silicate and calcium aluminate hydrates develop into a gelatinous amorphous material and a network of fibrous crystals which is considered the main cause of hardening.

Extensive use and experimentation with pozzolans in the eighteenth and nineteenth centuries to improve a hydraulic set led to detailed research and development of artificial hydraulic limes, and the eventual production of Portland cement. The range of pozzolans available worldwide is extensive. They are used regularly in combination with fat limes, and are an excellent substitute when hydraulic limes are not readily available. A list giving examples of natural and artificial pozzolans is set out in Appendix 2.

For further reading on hydraulic limes and pozzolanic additives see Wingate (c. 1990) and Hill, Holmes and Mather (1992).

Hydraulic limes

The ability of hydraulic limes to set under water was widely known before the introduction of Portland cement. Hydraulic limes were specified for buildings where there would be damp conditions, especially below ground, and in river works. They were also commonly used for external renders in the nineteenth century, particularly in areas where this type of lime was readily available. The use of hydraulic building lime, however, has steadily declined, almost to the point of extinction in many countries, since the advent of Portland cement.

Some geological research may be necessary to determine whether hydraulic lime is available locally or close enough to make transport viable. Relatively simple methods of burning and slaking hydraulic limes, in a similar way to burning and slaking fat limes, are possible, although if hydraulic lime putty is produced it must be mixed and used without delay before setting takes place. Hydraulic lime : sand external render mixes were usually prepared in the proportions of 1 : 1, 1 : 1½, 1 : 2 or 2 : 5 lime to sand ratio. In the British Isles these were termed common stucco. An indication of the setting times and other properties of the wide range of hydraulic limes is given in the proposed Classification of Building Limes tabled in Appendix 1.

The length of time hydraulic putty lime is left standing before use is critical. Set can take anything from two to over 20 days depending upon extent of hydraulicity. If the silica and alumina are in the process of combining with lime to form stable compounds, the longer this is allowed to continue undisturbed, the better the final set. The longer the putty stands before being knocked up and reworked, the less of the hydraulic property will be available, although workability will be improved. It is possible that there will be some limes that prove to be the exception to this rule. Recent experience in Scotland (Scottish Lime Centre) has shown that workability and the speed of set, although probably not final strength, may be improved by allowing some hydraulic limes to mature as putty or coarse stuff for days or even weeks before being finally 'knocked up' for use.

If the hydraulic properties are to be fully utilized it is therefore best to use the lime immediately after slaking. Conversely, it is known that keeping a putty lime under water before use improves working qualities. In practice, therefore, a compromise is reached, and the putty lime is matured for a relatively short period, for instance, overnight or for one or two days, and some sacrifice of the hydraulic property is made in order to obtain a more workable mix. Due to speed of set this is not possible for the eminently hydraulic limes which must be converted to dry hydrate, or left as quicklime, as these are the only practical forms in which such materials can be prepared for storage and transport.

Table 7.1: Aggregate particle size for external rendering

Optimum particle size per coat	British Standard aperture	Equivalent standards			DIN Standard maximum % to pass	% weight passing sieve
		BS Tyler mesh size	ASTM Standard mesh size			
5.00mm	³⁄₁₆"	No. 4	4.760mm		4mm	100
2.36mm	no. 7	No. 8	2.380mm		2mm	90–100
1.18mm	no. 14	No. 16	1.190mm		1mm – 85%	70–100
0.60mm	no. 25	No. 30	0.600mm		0.5mm – 60%	40–80
0.30mm	no. 52	No. 50	0.300mm		0.25mm – 25%	5–40
0.15mm	no. 100	No. 100	0.150mm		0.125mm	0–10

FIRST COAT / SECOND COAT / THIRD COAT

The fine texture of hydraulic lime is superior to that of other artificial cements, and gives plasticity to the fresh mix. The coarse stuff becomes pliant and easy to use. It will adhere well to a wide range of surfaces, and assures a strong bond with the other materials. The work carried out, once cured, does not break down in damp conditions (Cathedral Works Organisation, 1992).

Sands

Sands should be clean, sharp and hard to withstand weathering. They should preferably be slightly coarser than those used for internal plaster-work. The British, American and German standards for sand particle size distribution recommended for external render are shown in Table 7.1.

7.5 External lime render, mixes and application

The lime-based external finishes, and renders described in this section are:

○ plain render or 'London stuccos', known traditionally in England as common, rough, trowelled, and bastard
○ dry dash (pebble dash)
○ wet dash (rough cast and harling)
○ traditional Indian renders
○ lime gauging daub and earth finishes

Plain render

Four kinds of plain lime-based renders were traditionally used in London and the south of England. They were also widely used in many areas of the world before the introduction of Portland cement. For ease of reference, London stuccos have convenient descriptions (Millar, 1897) and these have been used here: common, rough, trowelled and bastard. The basic materials, with some variations, are the same as those described for internal lime plastering three-coat work, and application of the first two coats is similar. The principal differences are the introduction of pozzolans or the use of hydraulic limes for exposed situations. There is a wide range of alternative finishing coats. The names given here for convenience are traditional, although they have fallen out of use during the course of the last century due to major changes brought about by gauging with Portland cement.

○ *Common stucco* All classes of limes may be used for this render, although generally it appears that in the UK in the nineteenth century Class B or C limes (Appendix 1) were preferred. The more severe the exposure to damp and cold conditions the greater the advantage of using hydraulic lime. References to hydraulic or grey stone lime frequently occur for common stucco work in nineteenth and early twentieth century specifications. A small proportion of hair was also included in the mix for first and second coats, and occasionally for the finishing coat.

The recommended mix proportions are given in Table 7.2. Where possible and where continuous damp or severe exposure was not a factor, limes from classes A, B and C1 would be chosen.

Variation in the thickness of the finishing (3rd) coat is due to choice of sand. Coarser sand is more durable.

R.F.B. Grundy (1930) recommended plain rendering using blue lias (Class C2 or C3 moderately or eminently hydraulic lime) for severe exposures to be applied in two coats, as given in Table 7.3.

A further variation using stone lime (Class B or C1) given by W. Verrall is to use a mix of 2 grey stone lime to 3 sand for the finishing coat (Corkhill, 1931 and Verrall, 1931).

Table 7.2: Plain render – common stucco mix proportions

| Coat | Recommended mix proportions | | Thickness | |
	Lime	Sand	(mm)	(inches)
1st	2	4 or 5	9 – 16	$^3/_8$–$^5/_8$
2nd	2	5	9	$^3/_8$
3rd	1	3	3–9	$^1/_8$–$^3/_8$

Table 7.3: Plain render with hydraulic lime

| Coat | Recommended mix proportions | | Thickness | |
	Lime	Sand	(mm)	(inches)
1st	1½	3 or 4	6–19	$^1/_4$–$^3/_4$
2nd	1½	1½–2	3–6	$^1/_8$–$^1/_4$

○ *Rough stucco* This term is applied to render that is intended to imitate stone ashlar. The traditional finishing coat was 3 parts washed sharp sand and 2 parts grey lime putty. A flat surface is important and this is normally levelled with a straight edge. It is well-scoured with a wood float and finished with a 'felt float' (a wood or steel float covered with felt, carpet, or sponge) in order to enhance the texture. The surface was lined out with shallow grooves in the position of mortar joints to represent ashlar masonry. The finish was stained to represent the colour of stone by mixing ochres and other pigments with diluted sulphuric acid to achieve the tints required. Small areas of the coloured work were prepared and dried for selection before proceeding with the final tinting.

○ *Trowelled stucco* An external render prepared specifically to receive a paint finish. Millar recommends the use of chalk lime putty (class A fat lime) for the finishing coat mixed in the ratio of 2 : 2½–3, lime to sand. The sand should be sharp and washed but not as fine as that for internal plasterwork. A floating rule is used to achieve an even and flat surface. This is scoured with a wood float, first without water, then a further three times with a steel trowel, with water if necessary, and continued until an extremely hard surface is obtained. Finishing is by brushing off with a soft damp brush thoroughly in all directions. The initial gloss disappears as the surface dries out, and leaves a good finish for painting after preparation with an appropriate primer. (Millar, 1897)

○ *Bastard stucco*   Similar to trowelled stucco but not of such a high quality and requiring less work. The render is of the same mix but has two coats and is scoured only once. This is suitable for undulating surfaces where a flat level finish is not necessary. A felt float may be used to complete the work as this method is more suited to dealing with undulations than using a float with a hard edge. A bag-rubbed finish is another alternative for uneven surfaces. This is achieved by bunching a hessian bag or similar cloth into a ball which is used to rub down the surface after it has firmed up but before it is fully dry, to give a textured and irregular finish.

7.6   Thrown finishes

Dry-dash

Other terms for this are pebble-dash or spar-dash. Mixes and the thickness of coats are as for plain render, with the exception that a minimum of 12.5mm (½") thickness is given to the last, or third, coat for dashing.

Suitable dry dash material includes coarse grit, gravel, felspar, stone, pebbles, flints and hard limestone or granite chippings which is flung against the last coat. All dashings should cover the whole surface evenly and each piece of aggregate should be at least half embedded in the soft render behind.

The dashings are selected aggregate normally averaging 9mm. They should be thoroughly washed and screened through minimum 6mm and maximum 12.5mm mesh.

The aggregate is held in a bucket, or purpose-made shallow box and thrown with a throwing or harling trowel as illustrated on pages 30 and 31. Care should be taken to obtain a wide and even spread of dashings to give a uniform appearance to the finish. When this has been completed, any uncovered parts may be filled by hand, and as an option the whole surface can also be gently pressed flat with a trowel, or wood float.

The operation is best achieved by two men working together, one laying on the last render coat, whilst the other follows immediately behind with the dashing.

This finish has the advantage of shedding water well in conditions of severe exposure. Some traditional specifications, for work in cold climates, recommend that hydraulic limes, either natural or artificial, are used and that they should be hot. That is, crushed quicklime straight from the kiln is mixed with the sand and water to make up the coarse stuff for the last coat. The hot lime method can be successful if the limestone is carefully burnt by a skilled lime burner, best hand-picked lump lime is used, and the slaking process is completed immediately before application. It is not recommended for those without experience in the use of lime (Caxton House Editorial, 1908).

Wet dash – rough cast

In wet dash processes the final coat, or coats, are of coarse aggregate mixed with a wet lime binder. The technique used in England is called 'rough cast' where the dash coat is applied over a multi-layer render. This is one of the most durable forms of render and has often been used as an external finish.

The method of application frequently specified for rough cast in England in the early twentieth century depended upon the final coat to give its durability and individual character. It is composed of a coarse material similar to that for dry dashing, such as shingle, crushed stone, gravel, felspar, or possibly broken pottery. It should preferably be washed and then mixed with hydraulic lime and sharp sand in the ratio of 2 lime to 3 sand. Water is added to the coarse stuff and gravel to bring it to a semi-fluid consistency.

Wood lath on timber frame (Photographs supplied by Rory Young)

Lime: sand render on wood lath for external rough-cast finish

Finish of lime:sand rough cast applied to keyed render coat

Completed lime rough cast to external timber-framed wall,
Gloucester Street, Cirencester, 1990, by Rory Young

Table 7.4: Rough cast mix proportions

Coat	Recommended mix proportions		Thickness	
	Lime	Sand	(mm)	(inches)
1st	1	2	9	⅜
2nd	1	2½	9	⅜
3rd	1	2½	13	½
Dash coat	1	1½		

The first coat is a haired lime coarse stuff, the second the same materials but well scoured and keyed. While the finishing, or third coat of render is wet, the gravel slurry, often with pigment included, is thrown on from a dashing trowel. This is followed immediately with a stock brush dipped in the wet dash to lightly brush down the surface for a uniform colour and texture.

Wet dash – harling

In Scotland external wet dash lime mortar coatings are known as 'harling' and are generally applied as a series of two or three thin cast coats, without underlying trowel-applied render coats. The technique involves careful preparation of the masonry surface, prior to application of the actual harling coats, by means of packing and pinning out (also known as galleting) with the small off-cuts of masonry waste from rough squaring of the stones, small pieces of broken clay tile, permeable sandstone and so on, set in lime mortar. The objective of the technique is to create a sound, level surface to receive the harling, which can then be applied in very thin consistent layers. The process is a masonry technique rather than a plastering technique and, in the case of severely undulating surfaces, may involve the construction of horizontally bedded masonry on a small scale within the deepest hollows.

This technique is particularly suited to masonry walling constructed of rounded, or field, boulders where the recesses between the boulders require to be built out to a level plane before a mortar coating can be applied at a consistent thickness. The backing mortar must be well cured before application of the harling coats. Provided it is well executed, this is one of the most durable forms of render and has been used extensively where exposure to the elements is severe. It has a good record of lasting well in these conditions and is a common finish in Scotland.

Methods of applying harling vary according to local custom, as do its composition and the size and type of aggregate used. In Scottish practice the mortar used for harling is frequently the same mix as is used for the construction generally, comprising coarse sharp sand, up to 6mm, and lime putty in a ratio of around 1 part lime to 2.5 parts sand. Other materials, such as shell sand, are frequently incorporated in the harling mix (Meek, 1996).

Lime harling by Tim Meek Associates to house in Inverness, Scotland, 1995

There are various references to the use of hot lime in the preparation of harling and rough cast. If the kiln is close to the site and burning has been well controlled, or 'best hand picked lump lime' is used, it may be crushed. The resulting quicklime grit or powder is mixed with wet sand to slake to coarse stuff and harling material. This hot lime technique was favoured in cold and wet climates. It is more suitable for mortar. Any poor material in the quicklime will not be detected, although if the lime has been well burnt this is less critical where a coarse and very rough thrown finish is intended.

(Rivington, 1899; Gwilt, 1894; Caxton House Editorial, 1928; Grundy, 1930; Ashurst and Ashurst, 1988a; Jaggard and Drury, 1946; Millar, 1897).

7.7   Traditional Indian renders

One- and two-coat stucco

One- and two-coat work are described for Indian plastering by Millar. The one-coat work is composed of 1 part shell lime and 2 parts clean river sand. This is well mixed and beaten up into coarse stuff and allowed to stand. Immediately prior to use it is knocked up again with the inclusion of jaggery water (water with coarse sugar), mixed in the proportions of ½lb (225g) jaggery to one gallon (4.5 litres) of water. The mortar is then laid on as for one-coat work and scoured with a wood float. While it is being scoured the face of the work is sprinkled with a thin shell lime limewash. Scouring with a hand float is continued until a smooth face is obtained, and the total thickness is about half an inch (12mm).

Madras Chunam

This is described by Captain J.T. Smith in a note to his translation of Vicat (1837).

The celebrated Madras Chunam is a stucco laid on in three coats, the first a common mixture of shell-lime, and sand, tempered with jaghery water (water of jaghery, a coarse very brown sugar, which is derived from the cocoa tree), and about ½ inch thick; the second, of a finer description, made with sifted shell-lime and white fine sand, which is also sifted to free it from pebbles or foreign matter; and this coat, as well as the third, is applied without jaghery, which is omitted on account of its colour, and its frequently containing deliquescent salts. The third and last coat which receives the polish, is prepared with great care; the purest and whitest shells being selected for it, and none but the white sand of the finest description, and of that a very small proportion is used, varying from one-fourth to one-sixth. The ingredients of the third coat (as well as the second also, sometimes) are ground with a roller on a granite bed to a perfectly smooth uniform paste, which should have the feel and appearance of white cream.

In about every bushel [36 litres] of this paste are mixed the whites of ten or a dozen eggs, half a pound [225g] of ghee (which is butter clarified by melting over a slow fire), and a quart of tyre (which is sour curd fresh prepared), to which some add powdered balapong (or soap-stone) from a ¼ to ½ lb [112 to 225g] which is said to improve the polish.

Each master bricklayer has generally a recipe of his own, which he boasts of as superior to all others. The essential ingredients, in addition to the lime and sand, seem to be the albumen (the white of the eggs), and the oily matter of the clarified butter, for which oil is sometimes substituted.

The last coat is laid on exceedingly thin, and before the second is dry; it dries speedily, and is afterwards rubbed with the smooth surface of a piece of the soap-stone (steatite), or agate, to produce the polish, an operation which is sometimes continued for many hours, after which it is necessary to wipe it from time to time with a soft napkin, to remove the water which continues to exude from it for a day or two after completion.

Indian stucco

Millar (1897) details Indian plastering sixty years later than Captain Smith, and describes the same ingredients for Madras Chunam. This indicates that it was well regarded, and has been a regularly used high quality finish for generations. Similar mixes, but with different names, have been used regularly in other parts of India. In Rajasthan for example it is known as Arayash. One ingredient of note is the steatite, or soapstone, pulverized to a fine powder. Soapstone occurs in many parts of the world. If available locally, it may well be worth experimenting with its addition to the mix. As a surface treatment it will assist in achieving a high polish if this is desired, and produces a fine surface for painting. It will improve hardness and is non-absorbent and so will accept light washing.

Madras plaster

The Indian Standard Code of Practice for application of lime plaster finishes, Indian Standard 2394–1984, specifies Madras plaster. This is a special plaster finish applied in three or more coats to obtain a high quality smooth polished surface in places where lime from shells and fine sand are available. It is similar, to but less complex than, the Madras Chunam described by Captain Smith.

First coat   The first coat of lime plaster is applied to the wall as set out under first coat of plain render in section 7.5 above. This is allowed to set for two to four days and the surface scratched thoroughly in diagonal lines crossing each other. The plaster is kept constantly watered till it is nearly set and then the second and third coats are applied.

Second coat   One coat, about 5mm thick, of the specified mix set out below is applied and brought to an exact level surface with long wooden floats or, where required, with curved moulds. The surface of the undercoat is watered, if necessary, before applying this coat.

Mix for Madras Plaster second coat

	Parts by volume
Shell lime (Slaked)	12
Fine white sand	9
Powdered marble	1

The sand is ground very fine. The marble is also ground fine and sifted through muslin. The materials are mixed with water and kept in a heap, well wetted for two days.

Third coat   The same mix as used for the second coat is ground on flat stone slabs with stone rollers to the consistency of fine river mud and applied to a thickness of about 2mm over the second coat, which is wetted beforehand.

The surface of the third coat is polished first with two trowels and then with very hard smooth stones. While the polishing operation is in progress soapstone powder contained in muslin bags is dusted on the surface. The operation is continued until a high smooth polish is obtained.

Curing   Curing (by damping) is started 24 hours after finishing the plaster. The plaster must be kept wet for a period of seven days, and suitably protected from external damage during this period. The dates of plaster must be legibly marked on the various sections of the walls so that the curing for the specified period can be monitored.

7.8 Lime gauging, daub and earth finishes

Mixes for daub and probably pargetting often include slurried cow dung as an additional binding and setting agent. One traditional mix is in the proportions of 4 parts lime to 1 part dung. The use of a cow dung additive to lime mixes was widespread in England as it has excellent setting properties (Innocent, 1916). The addition of cow dung slurry helped to strengthen and waterproof the mix. It also provided an initial set, tackiness, and reinforcement to give flexibility, porosity, and gradual hardness. Various other lime render mixes incorporating slurried cow dung are recorded such as 4 : 1 : 1 lime putty : sharp sand : slurried cow dung plus chopped straw (Fiddler, 1992; Ashurst, 1977; Innocent, 1916).

Thorough preparation when incorporating cow dung slurry into the mix is essential, long periods of mixing and beating coarse stuff being normal procedure before application.

Lime putty mixed with cow dung slurry is still used for parging chimney flues, and in historic building repairs, due to its strong, tenacious, and resilient qualities. The proportion of cow dung varies from that previously stated, with up to 3 parts cow dung to 1 part lime putty. The incorporation of cow dung into mortar and render mixes to improve binding and water shedding properties has been, and to some extent still is, used world-wide.

The term 'daub' covers a very broad range of mixes, the lime content of which ranges from the high proportions of lime putty described above to nil. Regional variations of daub mixes are extensive enough for some to say that there will be as many types of daubs as there are daubers. Daubs are applied to wattle and lath panels, various forms of interwoven sticks, rods and thin tree growth sometimes coppiced for the purpose. Daub mixes may contain a variety of materials, the most common being earth with a clay content, cow dung, silt, sand, chopped straw, aggregate of small stones or pebbles, and sometimes, but not always, lime.

In parts of the world where local lime is regularly produced on a small scale, it is normal to add lime to daub mixes that have a high clay content. At the Weald and Downland Museum UK, the clay sub-soil was used for daubing on wattle panels in the proportions 2 lime : 1 earth : 1 sand : 3 chalk granules.

Limewash, perhaps mixed with some sand and other additives, is used for finishing clay lump, either directly or more often over an earth-based render. Dorset soil walls are repaired with lime and cob mixed with straw and often finished with limewash tinted with earth pigments. Local chalk has been burned for the quicklime.

For wychert, a chalk cob walling technique used in Buckinghamshire, UK, weak lime plaster mixes in the order of 1 lime : 6 sand have been used for first render coats. Subsequent coats and a limewash would usually incorporate oil or pozzolanic additives to improve weathering (Wright, 1991).

Lime : soil renders are suitable for lime or cement stabilized earth backgrounds, in proportions between 1 : 5 and 1 : 10 and are improved by adding 1 part brick dust. A suggested initial trial render for use with stabilized earth is 1 lime : 2 pozzolan : 9 sand (Norton, 1986). If this is not strong enough an alternative test panel of 1 lime : 1 pozzolan : 6 sand could be prepared for comparison and trials.

In many cases the durability of a soil render may be improved by the admixture of lime. There are various factors which will affect the results, including the type of minerals in the clay and the proportion of clay in the soil. A rich clay content, perhaps 10% or more, would be good and suitable soils might be modified with between 5 and 10% of lime (BQSF, 1974).

7.9   Gauging with Portland cement

Portland cement is regularly included in lime-sand mixes for renders where Portland cement is relatively inexpensive and easily available. Its ease of application and quick set, together with initial weather resistance, has encouraged over-use, often to the exclusion of lime. The disadvantages of too hard a render have been described in the introduction to this chapter. If natural or artificial pozzolans, or hydraulic limes are available, there is little advantage in adding small proportions of cement. The addition of too much Portland cement to renders applied to weak backgrounds is likely to lead to early failure. It is not advisable to add cement to mixes for buildings originally constructed with lime-based mortars and renders because this makes them too hard, impervious and inflexible. In cases where it is considered both feasible and necessary to gauge with Portland cement the commonly used mixes are shown in Table 7.5.

Table 7.5: Proportions for lime-sand-cement renders

Lime	Cement	Sand	Comment
3	1	12	It has been shown that this low proportion of cement to lime ratio does not provide durable renders and is not recommended.
2	1	9	This mix is not advisable in severe climates without strict supervision for careful batching and thorough mixing. Generally satisfactory for use on weak backgrounds provided mixing is well supervised and it is not subject to severe ambient conditions. Wet and freezing conditions before set will cause failure.
1	1	6	Usually a reliable strong mix, but too strong for soft and weak backgrounds.

The principle that the finishing coats should be no stronger than the backing coats applies as for other renders.

There is a strong case against adding small quantities of cement to lime mixes as detailed in section 5.4 in the chapter on mortars (Ashurst *et al.*, 1988a, Teutonico *et al.*, 1994; Holmström, 1977).

7.10   Identification of faults

The majority of defects in new render and plaster may usually be attributed to one or more of the following causes.

1. unstable or poorly keyed background.
2. the use of poor materials.
3. method of preparing materials.
4. method of application.
5. lack of aftercare.
6. exceptionally severe weather during or immediately following application.

Background

Faults

Cracking

Various ways in which the background may be prepared are described in Section 6.3. As the background is the surface of the structure that supports the plaster finish, any movement in the structure is likely to be reflected in the plaster in the form of cracks. Structural movement can occur for other reasons than simply inadequate foundations or insufficient bracing. One of the most common is movement between differing materials such as timber, brick, stone, or metal. Differences in moisture absorption or thermal expansion as well as separate support produces a tendency for the two materials to expand and contract independently of each other. Cracking of the plaster over this movement line is the result.

Undersized structural members giving rise to deflection in floors, ceilings and walls can be another source of cracking. Well-haired plaster will help to reduce cracking from slight movement. Vibration of the structure may be caused during the course of construction. This, when the plaster or render has not fully set, is a time when it is at its most vulnerable. Care to avoid heavy impact (positioning of beams or trusses etc.) or vibration (hammering in nails for example) should be taken when rendering is in progress and for several weeks afterwards while it is curing.

An inadequately prepared key will allow the following coat to separate and bulge or fall away. Laths spaced too close together, too far apart or on flat surfaces without counter lathing may cause the first coat to separate from the backing.

Faults
Bulging and separation from backing

Poor materials

Selection of suitable materials is described in Section 7.4.

Crazing, powdering, general weakness

Sand which is not sharp and has small rounded grains is termed soft. Too much soft sand in the mix, whilst making the material easier to work, will lead to crazing and cracking, or possibly powdering of the finished work. Soft sand will reduce the strength of the render substantially. Silt and topsoil in the sand will produce faults that are similar but more pronounced.

A range of coarse and fine sand grain sizes will provide a stronger material. If the sand grains are too uniform in size a weaker material will result leading to the possibility of cracking or crazing.

Cracking, crazing

The presence of salt in sand, water, or the backing, will, although unlikely to reduce strength, cause efflorescence or white blotches of salt crystals on the surface. This can often build up to wispy clumps that have the appearance of very fine cotton wool. The presence of salt also tends to induce dampness by attracting moisture from the air.

Efflorescence, induced damp patches

Hair or fibres in the mix provide a tensile strength to the key and to the render whilst dry. They help to reduce cracking whilst drying out and curing.

Breakdown due to vibration or impact

If hair is omitted the render may still stand well on firm and very well prepared solid backgrounds. A substantially improved key, however, particularly on lath, will be obtained by the addition of hair or fibre. A strengthened key will help to withstand cracking due to slight movement or vibration on soffits, below floors or on reveals adjacent to doors. If hair is omitted this may cause a weakness, breakdown and possibly separation from the backing.

Separation from backing

Lime preparation is described in Chapter 2. Lime needs to be fresh, well burnt, and well slaked. The binding power of the lime is due to re-absorption of carbon dioxide from the air to re-form calcium carbonate, and the formation of calcium carbonate crystals (calcite), both of which increase hardness. Hydraulic limes harden additionally due to the chemical reaction between calcium hydroxide and active clay. Exposed to air a lime mortar mix carbonates from the

Lack of binding power. General weakness

surface inwards at a steady, although decreasing rate. This will vary depending on ambient conditions but can be over 5mm in the first week. The surface of freshly burnt lime will carbonate in a similar way. Generally, therefore, the longer quicklime and hydrated lime are exposed to the air before use the greater the reduction in binding power and the weaker the finished work. *Faults*

If limestone is over-burnt, late hydration may take place in the centre of small particles surrounded with over-burnt material. Precautions against this happening are: Defects in the plaster due to late hydration

○ to ensure the lime is well burnt by good supervision at the kiln
○ to sieve out all larger particles when slaking (i.e. 0.6mm or more in diameter) or to use air separation for dry hydrate
○ to store putty under water for long enough (normally over three months) to ensure all late hydration takes place before use.

If these precautions are not taken and particles of over-burnt lime are included in the mix, late hydration will cause the particles to expand in the finished work. Failure may then occur in a number of ways:

○ General expansion of finely divided over-burnt material causes unsoundness in the plaster as a whole. Expansion of the entire coating will lead to the plaster shearing away from its backing. This results in bulging and the creation of voids behind the surface. Bulging and loss of key
○ Larger over-burnt particles subject to late slaking may expand suddenly, forcing out a cone-shaped section of surface plaster. Sometimes the expansion will be slower and may cause a slight swelling in isolated areas before damaging the surface or blowing. Pitting and popping

This will leave the plaster with hollows and sometimes small lumps, or in severe cases larger areas of failure, and is known as pitting and popping.

Poor preparation of materials

Lime putty should be of the correct consistency and not too wet for preparing coarse or fine stuff. Tests for consistency are given in Chapter 11. If the lime putty is too wet then the binding power is reduced. Render with too high a water content is likely to develop shrinkage cracks, generally weakening the finished work. Ramming, as well Poor binding and cracking

124

as mixing thoroughly, is an important part of preparing good coarse stuff as workability will be improved without adding water.

Faults

Storing coarse stuff made with fat lime and sand, provided it is well covered and kept continuously moist, helps the lime to encapsulate all aggregate particles improving mix consistency and final strength of the render. A minimum of two weeks standing time for the coarse stuff is recommended.

Inconsistent strength and weaker finished work

Poor method of application

In addition to the importance of providing a good key to the background, the absorption (or suction) of water from the mix should be controlled. Moist conditions assist a slower curing process and improve the eventual strength. If the background is not damped down or, if this is not possible, at least partially sealed, rapid absorption of all water from the mix into the background may result in failure of the key and separation of the first (backing) coat.

Separation from the background

For the same reason as above it is important to provide a good key and damp down each coat before applying subsequent coats. Separation or slumping may also occur if one coat is applied to an excessive thickness.

Separation of coats or slumping

Compaction of each coat either by throwing on, hard scouring, or both, is a major contribution to final strength. This is particularly important for the finishing coat, which can be applied and scoured in three layers to achieve the most durable results. A very light application without compaction may result in a friable surface liable to craze easily or crumble with little resistance to abrasion.

Crazing and weakness of the surface

Similar defects may arise if too much water has been added to the mix.

Lack of aftercare

Carbonation and chemical reactions that give final strength take place best in moist and warm conditions that dry out slowly. The setting and curing of hydraulic and non-hydraulic mixes is slowed progressively to zero the closer temperatures are to freezing. When humidity and moisture content are exceptionally high non-hydraulic mixes will not carbonate. During the work and following completion it is therefore essential to ensure ambient conditions, i.e. temperature, humidity, moisture content and air movement, are not extreme. The work should be shaded from direct sunshine and sheltered from continuous rain.

Lack of curing

Work carried out without protection in temperatures close to, or below, freezing is likely to suffer from frost damage. Any lime mixes which have not developed strength by curing and have not dried out sufficiently are also at risk from frost.

Work allowed to dry out too rapidly will not have time to carbonate well, or develop chemical reactions to provide sufficient binding power.

Non-hydraulic lime, and possibly some slightly hydraulic lime mixes, kept continuously wet or extremely damp for a long period after completion of the work may not fully carbonate. They are likely to fail before sufficient hardening takes place.

Faults

Frost damage, crumbling or flaking

Lack of binding power, crumbling, powdering

Softness, lack of strength and poor binding properties

8

Decorative plasterwork

8.1 Introduction

Plastering with lime and other plastic materials has been used as a medium of decorative expression throughout the world. It is not unusual to find instances where plaster ornament pre-dates written history. Decorative plasterwork in itself is one of the most visually descriptive records of the artistic, cultural and economic development of the society in which it has been produced. Examples range worldwide covering countries and places as varied as:

Pyrghi, Greece where Xisto, a sgraffito technique, is used for decorating façades today as it has been from before the seventeenth century (Oliver, 1975).

Lamu, Kenya, the one surviving city of more than 30 independent city states that flourished on the East African coast from the 13th century is renowned for the extensive carved plaster decorations in many houses and mosques (Siravo and Pulver, 1986).

West African buildings of the Hausa in northern Nigeria are decorated on their façades and internally with signs and symbols in deep relief moulding (Dethier *et al.*, 1982).

The rich and exciting history of Zanzibar's past is vividly recorded in the decorative plasterwork of the many public and domestic buildings in the historic Stone Town capital (Holmes and Wingate, 1992).

Chinese ornamental plaster modelled *in situ* by hand, Arabian, Persian, Italian, French, Russian and English decorative plasterwork among others abounds from centres of excellence to the most humble dwellings (Millar, 1897).

A brief description is given here to introduce and illustrate the potential of lime-based plaster as a decorative medium. Each section of this chapter outlines some of the most common decorative types and sets out the main techniques. Any further information should be sought from the specialist publications given in the References and bibliography.

8.2 Run mouldings

The description 'run mouldings' refers to projecting embellishments of a uniform profile over their whole length. They are built out from a plaster face by moving (running) a template along temporary timber runners, or the wall surface. The work is built up in several stages.

Run mouldings are usually positioned at the extremities of walls, and at the edge of openings. They are applied externally and internally, and are a feature that has both a practical and an aesthetic purpose.

*Diapered plaster panelling in the Alhambra, Spain, thirteenth century
(source: Millar, 1897)*

Running an external cornice at Kedleston Hall, Sulphur Bath House, 1994

In external work cornices are run as horizontal moulded projections often at the eaves, or at the head of parapet walls, usually immediately below coping stone level. 'Corbelled coping stone' according to the Oxford Dictionary is the Greek description from which the word cornice has been derived.

The external cornice illustrates a practical use of the run moulding. Its form may be a simple cantilever, or a series of cantilevers positioned at the wall head. This arrangement supports the roof covering above, enabling it to project further. The detail enables water to be thrown off the roof clear of the wall face below, thus protecting it generally as well as from heavy weathering at a vulnerable junction.

An internal cornice is an ornamental moulding applied to the upper part of the wall at or near its junction with the ceiling.

The application and detailing of mouldings has a long tradition of carefully considered design to emphasize and enhance a building's features and proportions. As plaster is a plastic material it can be formed into run mouldings with the aid of templates called running moulds. These may be designed simply for basic shapes to strengthen and improve details at changes of plane. They may also be developed to many levels of complexity for decorative effect, almost without limit. This variety of application and design has been well recorded for over 3000 years, often influenced by the Greek classical orders and proportions.

Cornice mouldings may be as simple as a bead or a cove, or may be very elaborate with a series of shapes one above another, enriched with separately moulded and cast ornaments. However simple or intricate, they may be formed with a running mould on site, or run on the workshop bench. The procedure for forming run cornices varies with their complexity and whether they are run internally or externally. The principal technique is, however, relatively consistent. The description below is confined to running an internal cornice round the top of a plastered wall adjacent to the ceiling.

For a cornice run *in situ* the first operation is to form the running mould or template. This is cut accurately to the chosen profile of the intended cornice. Soft sheet metal, such as zinc, is the best material for this, although it should be possible to use a range of other materials provided they lend themselves to being carefully cut out to the desired profile, and are tough enough to withstand pressure of the plaster whilst in use without deforming, cracking or wearing out. The profile or template is fixed to a timber support and the whole construction is known as a 'running mould'. The process of assembly is termed 'horsing up'.

A simple and inexpensive way to run small mouldings is with a thumb mould. This may be made in wood only, including the profile. If the ceiling and wall surfaces are reasonably true these may be used to guide the mould without the aid of running rules or rails.

There are two principal means of forming background support. Internally, for large cornices, the most common is to prepare cornice brackets of

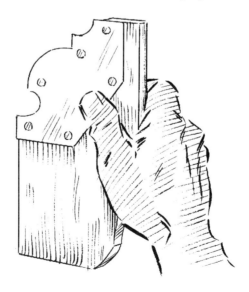

Thumb mould

130

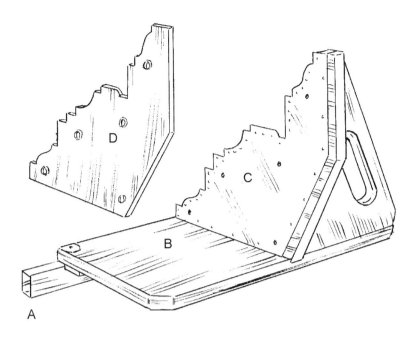

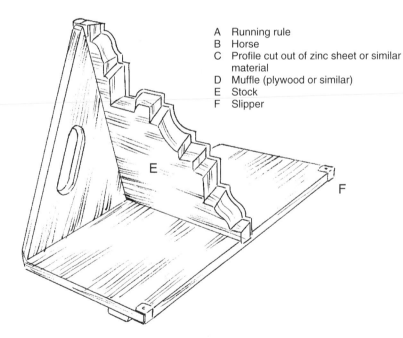

A   Running rule
B   Horse
C   Profile cut out of zinc sheet or similar
     material
D   Muffle (plywood or similar)
E   Stock
F   Slipper

A running mould

timber fixed to the wall on which to nail laths. These are set out in a similar way to those described for ceilings in Chapter 6, Section 6.3. Alternatively, and for use externally, brick, block, tile or stone, may be corbelled out or supported on brackets or spikes, to form the projecting background on which to run the render or stucco.

The second coat of wall plaster must be perfectly straight when mouldings are intended. When the second coat has been completed to both wall and ceiling, the running mould is placed at either end of the ceiling adjacent to each wall. It is set out plumb and square in its true position for the intended cornice. This is to carry out the final marking of the cornice position at each end. A chalk line is then snapped through from end to end. A piece of charcoal, burnt stick or pencil, will mark better than a chalk line on light-coloured screeds.

The running mould will be moved along running rules. These are made of planed timber about 50–65mm (2–2½") wide and 12mm (½") thick and the top edge, on which the mould will slide, may be greased. They are aligned so that the nib of the running mould will follow the chalk line on the ceiling. The rules may be fixed with dabs of gauged putty but it is safer to nail or screw them to the timber studs supporting the lath and plaster or into masonry joints.

Master plasterer J. Orton using a comb scratcher to give key to second coat of lime plaster on ceiling cornice at Kedleston Hall, Derbyshire, 1996

An interior cornice run moulding completed by Colin Baggs at Warwick Castle, April 1994

The running mould is fitted out with a series of muffles which allow the profile to be built up in stages. Each muffle has a profile which would shape a coat of render or plaster about 12mm (½") thick. The final coat would be approximately 3mm (⅛") thick and would be formed by the zinc profile. The other muffles may be made of any suitable board material.

Coarse stuff for the first coat of the cornice should be extra haired and very well scratched to give a strong foundation for the following coats. A typical method of working is to first cover the cornice brackets and then rough out the whole cornice length. The coarse stuff is put on with a large gauging trowel, or with a laying trowel, following the general form of the mouldings. The running mould with the appropriate muffle is offered up to the running rules and run across the length during this process to ensure adequate clearance from the coarse stuff.

The coarse stuff is then allowed to dry and harden as for the first coat lath work described in Section 6.5.

Succeeding coats of lime plaster are put on to follow the general form of the mouldings. This operation is normally carried out by at least two men with one man to run the mould, whilst the other steadily supplies additional

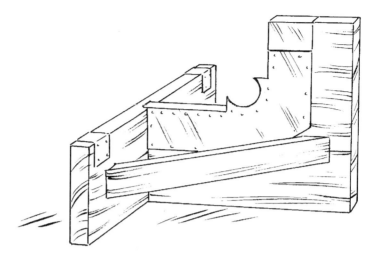

Running mould for a staff bead

material and lays on to fill out all parts of the moulding. The man running the mould will also feed and fill out the moulding with any stuff that gathers on the side of the running mould. Small mouldings of about 250–300mm (10–12") girth can be run and fed by one man whilst his partner is laying on.

The final coat is run at the end of the operation. It may be similar in composition to the third or final coat described in Chapter 6. For internal work only, it is common to gauge with gypsum, if available, at 2 lime putty to 1 gypsum for the final coat. The addition of gypsum improves speed of set and sharpness of detail. Mouldings can, however, be run successfully in lime : sand mixes only if the fine stuff is carefully selected and prepared.

After completion of the run lengths, mitres are made good by hand with the aid of joint rules and small tools, an operation that requires considerable skill. Finally, the running rules are taken down after all the mouldings have been completed and then their fixing positions are made good.

Running moulds are also used for forming staff beads. These have been developed to improve and strengthen external angles. The rounded profile eliminates the need to form sharp corners which, in plaster, are vulnerable to impact damage. Staff beads may also be formed in hardwood or other materials to give added strength to exterior angles. Proprietary metal angle beads for external corners are now mass-produced in many countries.

8.3   Cast moulds

The craft of casting plaster moulds, like most lime plaster techniques, is ancient and has developed over centuries. A range of modern materials has been designed to make the process faster, easier and more precise.

Flexible gelatine moulds and advanced gypsums are examples of materials used increasingly from the mid nineteenth century. The basic concept, however, remains unchanged and this is that by making a model or pattern or using an original piece of ornament it is possible to re-cast the original form, including all its details, in plaster. Once a good mould is made, plaster casts may be taken as many times as required, for as long as the mould remains sound.

The technique is used in many ways including casting small repeats such as enrichments to cornices. Moulds may be taken from original work *in situ*, or from specially made models in the workshop.

Gypsum plaster or 'plaster of Paris', when available, is the easiest material for casting moulds, and is normally used for this purpose today. If gypsum is not available, lime mixes can be used but need to be much drier for moulding in order to set. Lime with a very low water content, rammed into rigid moulds made of wood or burnt clay is the basic technique required for forming cast moulds without gypsum. Wooden moulds carved in reverse can be used for this purpose and were once common. Gypsum moulding techniques are described below as an introduction to the method of producing decorative plaster ornament. This is often used in conjunction with lime plaster decorative work, such as run cornices discussed in the previous section.

Models or 'patterns' may be made of wood, dry clay, plaster, or any other material that lends itself to being sculpted, moulded or carved. The more flexible the mould material the more intricate the shape that can be copied, thus the popularity of modern cold-pour silicone rubbers. The traditional mould material based on beeswax and resin, however, can be used for producing a wide range of forms that retain sharpness and detail.

Preparation of a model (or pattern) for casting is the first step. Following careful cleaning it needs to be sealed to prevent absorption from the mould material. Whatever the sealant, whether size, shellac, or paint, it needs to be fine and applied carefully to avoid loss of detail. Its purpose is only to ensure a complete seal and to do this two or even three coats may be necessary, each coat being allowed to dry before application of the next.

Finally a light coat of fine grease or oil is applied with a soft brush to prevent adhesion of new mould material to the model. Prior to wax moulding the model should be dipped in water.

Cold-pour silicone rubber for preparing flexible moulds may be obtained from various manufacturers, although these are mostly based in North America and Europe. If a more readily available local material is required the traditional technique is to prepare moulding wax from a mixture of 1 part pure bees wax with between 1 and 2 parts powdered resin (for resin, see Glossary). This will be satisfactory for models that are not undercut. To prepare the moulding wax dissolve the mixture over a gentle fire. It is important not to overheat and to ensure the wax does not boil, which would make the mould become too brittle. Between 5 and 20% tallow may be added to the wax to improve its richness, if needed. A good way of uniformly dissolving the wax is to use a double container, the outer one holding hot water. The wax will have reached the correct temperature for pouring when it has cooled just sufficiently to enable a wet finger to be dipped into it comfortably.

An open mould box may be formed out of clay, plaster slabs, or wood. The model is placed on the moulding board and bedded down on a plaster dab to prevent movement. A 12mm (½") thick clay 'fence' is cut out from a sheet of clay to form the sides for a clay mould box. These should be a minimum of 18mm (¾") higher than the highest part of the model. They are cut to length and fixed on edge round the outside to contain the liquid wax. Any weak points can be reinforced or buttressed with additional clay. The inner surfaces are then smoothed lightly with a very small quantity of water on the fingers to prevent them sticking to the wax.

The faces of the model and inside of the moulding box should be cleaned and prepared by lightly brushing over with clean water before pouring the wax. This should be poured on to the lowest part starting at one end. The wax must be poured in a steady stream to flow unbroken over all parts of the model. If there is a break in pouring a crack will form at this point. The method of pouring starting from the bottom helps to force air upwards and reduces the chance of air pockets, or bubbles forming.

The wax is allowed to cool and when a skin forms cold water sprinkled on will speed the cooling process. The fences are then carefully removed.

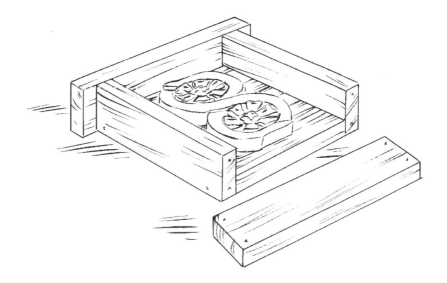

An open mould box with model

The mould and model are gently placed into cold water which will allow them to separate easily.

The new mould needs to be seasoned before it is used for casting. This is done by washing out in clean water and applying a thin film of soft soap with a fine brush.

Plaster for casting is best gauged with gypsum if available, but, if not, hydraulic lime mixed with finely sieved sand or other fine aggregate will be adequate for bolder and the less intricate designs that are not poured. These are mixed drier and pressed hard, or rammed into rigid moulds. Experiments with other additives available, to arrive at a stiff casting plaster consistency, may well prove worthwhile.

The fine and creamy casting plaster is brushed over the surfaces of the wax mould with a fine brush. The remains of the plaster are then immediately poured on and pressed in with a brush or gauging trowel. The upper surface is finished, or struck off, flush to the back of the mould. The back of the cast is then keyed ready for fixing.

To release the cast after the plaster has set the mould is placed in warm water for about five minutes until the wax is sufficiently flexible. The mould

Completed lime plaster cast moulds by Simon Swan, 1996

is then gently eased to release the cast. Thin casts may be strengthened by inserting reed, cane, wood or wire in the plaster before it sets.

Slower setting materials, such as hydraulic limes and pozzolanic cements, may be used in a similar manner providing the moulds are adapted to cater for the different techniques of pressing and compacting (or even vibrating) as opposed to gently pouring in a cast. Generally for slower setting materials the mould must be of robust construction. If a wet pour technique is used with slower setting materials shrinkage is likely. In most climates several days' curing will be required before sufficient set has taken place to safely de-mould.

For restoration work a fat lime putty has been dried out to a 'leather' hardness and beaten into robust moulds (Constantinides, 1992). Some of the best results can be achieved with reverse moulds carved out of timber, although the skill required to make these moulds takes time to develop.

8.4   Pargeting

The term *pargeting* is usually used to describe decoration on external plastered walls where designs are formed by raised or indented patterns in

Pargeting to front elevation of a house, Clare, Suffolk (Bankart, 1908)

138

*Hausa merchant's house, Nigeria. Note the similarity to the technique
used in Clare, Suffolk (opposite) although this is not lime plaster
(photograph by David Buxton from Oliver, 1975)*

the plaster finish. The technique can be found in many parts of the world
although the materials used vary with local availability and tradition.

The art of pargeting is 'sculpture in low relief' and the best results depend
on both artistic sensibility and able craftsmanship. It is a finish that depends
on freehand skills. Mechanical design and hard straight lines are seldom
employed in traditional work. The three-dimensional modelling gains in
effect with a play of sunlight and shadows cast from above or the side.

Ornamental patterns are formed in relief by the use of wooden stamps,
rollers, or by modelling *in situ*. These techniques produce indentations or
raised lines on the surface and become an integral part of the building to
which they are applied.

Traditionally in England lime plasters for pargeting were reinforced with
dung, finely chopped hay, straw, or hair reinforcement. Hair is still used in
the first and second coats today. Bankart (1908) quoted Professor Lethaby
as saying,

The old material was well washed, beaten, stirred and tested so carefully, and for so long a time, that, when laid, it was as tough as leather.

The render is normally applied with a wood float but a steel trowel may be used for smoother finishes. It is important to use the minimum amount of water which may be achieved by very thorough chopping and ramming of the coarse stuff. First and second coats may be the same as for the plain render. The lime to sand mix for the third or finishing coat varies between 1 : 1 and 3 : 4 lime : sand. In continuously wet weather, and damp locations, hydraulic lime is recommended. Short chopped hair, or other fibre not more than 50mm (2") long, should be incorporated at a rate of roughly 0.5kg (1lb), of hair to every cubic metre (cu. yard) of coarse stuff mix.

As with all other renders it is essential to avoid too rapid drying out which is likely to cause initial movement and cracking. Faces exposed to the sun or wind should be covered with hessian, or similar cloth and kept damp for a minimum of two weeks.

No limewash application should be made until the work has thoroughly dried out, and this could well be between six weeks and two months from initial rendering, depending on climate (Stenning, Richards and Carpenter, 1982; Carpenter, 1983).

8.5   Modelling stucco *in situ*

Lime stucco has been used at various periods in the past for decorative modelling and design in relief. The hand-modelled lime stucco process was popular for highly decorative work up to the beginning of the twentieth century. It is a method of enriching a plaster surface with raised and modelled lines and forms for pleasure of the decorative effect. The shapes may be inspired by nature and draw on the natural qualities of the material.

In situ decorative modelling that makes use of local plastering materials can be found throughout the world.

Modelling *in situ* is normally approached by the craftsman as a source of interest and delight. It can be an elaborate but relatively inexpensive form of decoration as the cost of materials is not high, although labour costs vary in the extreme from one country to another.

The overall form and main lines of the principal panels, borders and frames are decided first. These forms may be located and set out with the setting-out tools described in Chapter 3.

The design may be applied direct to the wall or ceiling surface, but for the most exacting design, full size cartoons are set out on paper. Once the drawn work is finalized the pattern can be traced or pounced through to the plaster surface and then roughly drawn out again with pencil, charcoal or chalk.

Any coves, angles, frames or beads involved in the design are fixed or moulded *in situ* first.

Small ornaments may be modelled, moulded and cast separately as detailed in Section 8.3 on cast moulds. These repetitive enrichments can be fixed at regular intervals to form additional decorative effects.

Some techniques use stamps to produce the principal ornament *in situ*, with the rest worked up by hand. Repetitive patterns may be made by pressing moulds on to the stucco composition while it is still soft. The most delicate and ornate work associated with modelling however, is usually carried out by skilled craftsmen or artists entirely by hand using the metal or wood modelling tools described in Chapter 3.

The stucco composition needs to be a fine mouldable putty, somewhat resembling modellers' clay in texture and consistency. This is achieved by using extremely fine (Class A) lime putty well matured and sieved through fine muslin. Many recipes have been given and the most common ingredients for good results are a mixture of this putty with marble dust at a ratio of between 1 : 1 and 1 : 2 lime : marble dust. Alternatives to the marble dust are very fine brick dust, fine sand, and dust from dense limestone. It is important to mix these ingredients thoroughly with as little water as possible to arrive at the right consistency.

The putty may be altered to change the speed of set and workability in various ways if the ingredients are available. Gauging with gypsum for internal work, the addition of glue size, rye dough, and other additives detailed in Section 6.4 have all been recorded as successful in the past. It is clearly advisable to carry out trials with locally available materials before beginning the main work. Hydraulic lime, artificial or natural, should be used for exterior work, particularly in wet climates, or where very wet conditions are likely to persist.

The plaster ground should be well wetted and scored before stucco is applied. Wetting the background whilst modelling is in progress is clearly not practical, and therefore care needs to be exercised in planning the extent of work.

Heavy projections should be strengthened by fixing *armatures* (see Glossary) to reinforce the stucco. These supports may be nails, or screws driven through backing plaster into the background or framing behind. Additional support can be provided by tying tarred twine, or wire to the nail heads. If metal armatures are chosen these should be non-ferrous for external work.

The principal forms of the decoration are blocked out first – often with a coarser mix without finishing the detailed modelling. These are then followed by the thinner ornament and final surfaces which are best finished in one continuous operation.

The heavier parts of the decoration are then finally sculpted and modelled in stages relative to their size, the quantity of stucco prepared and the speed at which it sets.

Modelling stucco in situ *at Prior Park, 1994 (photo:* The Independent*)*

Successful free-hand modelling was completed at Prior Park, Bath, in 1994 using a mix of 1 lime putty : 2 marble dust, gauged with rabbit skin glue size and gypsum.

Free-hand modelling in lime stucco was used and developed extensively in Europe from before the sixteenth century. Simple recipes similar to the one above are usually adequate. They were developed to a fine art by the beginning of the twentieth century and knowledge of other methods and ingredients used may be of value when formulating a local mix. A well-respected and recognized standard text on decorative plasterwork was written by George P. Bankart (1908) who gives the following recipe for stucco:

The lime is fat lime about 9 years old.
This is first dried, then crushed, and put through a very fine sieve: then mixed dry in the proportion of:

2 lime : 1 part marble dust : 1 part rye flour : 1 part kaolin (china clay).

1 part plaster of Paris is added to 3 of the above mixture to prevent cracking. Thoroughly mix in a dry state. In making up for use, form a ring of the dry mixture on a slab.

Two solutions are used.

'A' solution: composed of ½lb of marshmallow root, *althoea officinalis radix*, to 1 gallon of water.

'B' solution: ½lb gum acacia (gum arabic) to 1 quart of water.

Take three parts of 'A' to 1 part of 'B' and mix up into the powdered material until it takes a consistency of dough, or paste, or plumber's putty; work and pulverize (sic) it thoroughly with a trowel and wooden mantel, until thoroughly pliable, smooth, fat, and clear working. Allow to stand for a day and retrowel thoroughly before use. It can be kept soft for a week in a wet cloth; but it is better made up fresh, and used thinly, and newly made.

8.6 Depeter

The first three coats are prepared in the same way as for dry dash and rough cast detailed in the previous chapter. The third coat is given an even and uniform texture by a gentle levelling of the surface with a hand float.

Small pieces of stones, broken flint, pottery, spar, glass, sea shells,

The southern Sotho people from the former Eastern Free State of South Africa slake lime for decoration of their houses and use rich colours for varied designs in depeter (photograph by James Walton from Oliver, 1975)

marble, or other hard decorative stones are selected and cleaned. While the third coat is still soft, these pieces are pressed in by hand.

Ornamental patterns in colour and texture, margins, bands, or other designs may be worked in, and otherwise blank surfaces enriched. (Caxton House Editorial, 1928; Grundy, 1930; Millar, 1897).

8.7 Carved and diapered plaster

In Lamu on the east coast of Africa, mentioned in the introduction to this chapter, carved plaster is a traditional form of decoration. This method of ornament is applied extensively to the older buildings, and follows an established order in each house. Evidence suggests that the sequence of elaborately decorated spaces is connected with special, probably religious, ceremonies or rituals.

Decorative friezes below cornices are formed in carved plaster. Carved plaster designs form architraves around archways and niches. Lime plastered walls are decorated with carved and moulded panels.

The most flamboyantly decorated room of a house on Lamu is the Ndani. The greater part of its principal wall is filled by a multi-tiered complex of

Mihrab of the ruined Shangani mosque, Zanzibar, with remarkable carved plaster enrichment

niches and carved decoration called Zidaka. The carved panelling, and recessed niches of the Zidaka are the focal point of the room and are used to display items of value (Siravo and Pulver, 1986).

Carved decorative work in the region is much in evidence and carving as a craft is widely practised there today, although chiefly reserved for decorative work on timber ornaments and furniture. The carved timber architraves and doors of Zanzibar are typical examples of the richly carved decoration so popular in this area.

The lime putty or stucco used for carving was derived from the coral rag stone, or in some cases cowrie shells. Finely sieved sand or finely crushed shell could be used as aggregate. As in other parts of the world, additional local ingredients to improve the adhesive qualities and slow setting for a fine putty were probably incorporated. These were likely to have been vegetable or fish oils. It is also possible that volcanic dust, or brick dust may have been added as a pozzolan. Firm evidence of traditional organic additives is extremely difficult to obtain as they degrade with age. Analysis of stuccos from Zanzibar show mixes ranging from neat lime to 1 lime to 2 aggregate for selected stucco samples taken from various buildings.

In situ carved plaster was popular in the architecture of Paris up to the beginning of the twentieth century, particularly for the entrance halls of large mansions. Finely ground lime was mixed with coarse gypsum as a base material. This was kneaded in the hands in small quantities with very little water added and worked up like bakers' dough to form a putty. This kills the initial set of the gypsum but produces a pliable substance suitable for carving once it is set.

The plaster was then thrown, or dashed, on to the background until it was roughly level. It was allowed to dry partially and whilst in this pliable state some areas were levelled further with drags. The ornamental parts were given a much thicker application and then carved like soft stone. After the work was fully dried it was completed by rubbing down with fine sandstone. The end result was hard and durable (Millar, 1897).

Decorative Spanish and Moorish plasterwork known as Diaper is carved plaster in flat relief. The Moors made beautiful use of plaster which is well illustrated on the plaster panelling of the thirteenth century Alhambra in Spain shown on page 128.

Tracery patterns carved in low relief, are frequently repeated and produce a regular diaper which was very popular in the fourteenth and fifteenth centuries.

It is generally thought that diaper work was set out with a template cut to the pattern. The flat plaster of the ground was then cut or carved back. This left the original design as a flat shape on the plaster face between, and proud of, the incised carving.

Incised patterns cut into plaster are a common form of decoration on many Spanish buildings up to the nineteenth century.

8.8   Sgraffito

Sgraffito is a word of Italian origin and means 'scratched'. The term was once applied to scratched or incised decorations on potter's clay whilst soft. It is now employed for decoration scratched or incised in plaster before it has set. It may be used for both external and internal decoration.

Eugenia Politis (1975) writes of the Xisto technique employed for decorating buildings in Pyrghi, Greece. Xisto means scratched surface. This is a single technique which produces delightful and intricate patterns that are applied to the façades of many houses in the town.

Traditionally a black beach sand was used in the base render mixes. Sand and lime are both well sieved. The finishing coat is prepared by gradually adding the binder, traditionally lime, in small quantities at a time whilst knocking up. The amount of binder is increased slowly until a proportion of 2 binder to 3 sand is reached and the mixture has the consistency of thick cream. The mortar is well scoured whilst wet to encourage the lime to the surface. The surface is allowed to stiffen for two or three hours and is then painted with several coats of white or coloured distemper.

Xisto decoration to house in Pyrghi (photo: Terry McKenna)

Sgraffito frieze in two colours (source: Millar, 1897)

Designs are set out using straight edge, nail and stretched thread. Geometric patterns are drawn out by the craftsman using compass, rule and nail. The top surface within the design is then scratched away exposing the dark mortar underneath.

Each coat may be coloured by careful choice of aggregates or with earth pigments which have been described in Section 4.3.

Mr Heywood Sumner is quoted in several books (Millar, 1897; Bankart, 1908) on the subject and records his considerable experience of sgraffito at the end of the nineteenth century as follows. He made his coarse (first) coat with cement and sand to be durable in damp conditions. A good hydraulic lime could be used as an alternative to the cement. The surface of the coarse coat should be well roughened to give a good key, and it should stand some days to thoroughly set before laying the finishing coat.

When sufficiently set, fix your cartoon (pattern) in its destined position with nails; pounce through the pricked outline; remove the cartoon; replace the nails in the register holes; mark in with chalk spaces for the different colours, as indicated by the pounced impression on the coarse coat; lay the several colours of the colour coat according to the design, as shown by the chalk outline; take care that in doing so the register nails are not displaced; roughen the face in order to make a good key for the final coat.

147

When set, follow on with the final surface coat (uncoloured lime plaster), only laying as much as can be cut and cleaned up in a day. When this is sufficiently steady, fix up the cartoon in its register position; pounce through the pricked outline; remove the cartoon; and cut the design in the surface coat before it sets; then, if the register is correct, cut through to different colours according to the design, and in the course of the few days the work should set as hard and as homogeneous as stone, and as damp-proof as the nature of things permits.

When cleaning up the ground colour which may be exposed, care should be taken to obtain a similar quantity of surface all through the work, so as to get a broad effect of deliberate and calculated contrast between the trowelled surface of the final coat and the scraped surface of the colour coat. The manner of design should be founded upon a frank acceptance of line and upon simple contrasts of light against dark or dark against light.

The colour coat is laid 3mm (⅛") thick, and for external work fine stuff would be composed of 3 selenitic or eminently hydraulic lime to 2 silver sand. Silver sand being washed cleaned sharp sand passing a 600µm or 0.6mm sieve.

The top coats are scratched away where required, leaving the colour necessary for the design. The backing must be perfectly hard and must be set before subsequent coats are applied. When colours are used, the bottom coat should be pricked up before the application of further coats. Only small areas should be worked on and each patch should be finished before continuing to the next.

In some modern sgraffito techniques, areas of design are masked out with tape, and the coloured material worked up to the tape. When setting is complete, the tape is removed and new tape placed over the completed work so that fresh colours may be applied to the plain areas. For this method the backing must be firm and hard (Stagg and Pegg, 1984; Millar, 1897; Kemp, 1912).

8.9   Italian stuccos

Recent research into Italian lime stuccos and plasters has been carried out in England by N. Harvey and demonstrated by J.R. Orton (Hill, Holmes and Mather, 1992). Italian lime stucco and render mixes prepared by Mr Orton were exhibited at the International Seminar for Lime and Alternative Cements at Stoneleigh in 1991 and are detailed below. At this seminar, the coloured marmorino was formed on wood lath; the remaining stuccos were built up on clay tiles to represent a wall.

Coloured marmorino (Venetian)

Used in Italy internally and externally for coloured walls and ceilings in the sixteenth to nineteenth centuries. More usual in Venice than in the rest of mainland Italy. *Note* All are based on fat lime (non-hydraulic) and more suitable for use in Mediterranean climates than northern Europe.

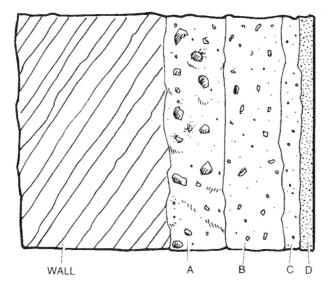

WALL   A   B   C D

Section showing the build-up of coats for plain marmorino; other Italian stuccos are built up in a similar manner
A: Arricio, the first rough coat of plaster; B: Intonaco I, the levelling coat of plaster; C: Intonaco II, the first setting coat; D: Marmorino, the smooth marble plaster coat

- ○ *Arricio* (first coat)
  3 – coarse crushed terracotta, 8 mesh
  1 – slaked lime putty, 20 mesh
- ○ *Intonaco I* (second coat)
  1 – moderately crushed terracotta, 12 mesh
  ½ – sharp washed sand
  1 – slaked lime putty, 20 mesh
- ○ *Intonaco II* (third coat)
  1 – fine washed sand
  1 – slaked lime putty, 40 mesh
- ○ *Marmorino* (fourth coat)
  1 – fine marble dust, 50–60 mesh
  1 – fine slaked lime putty, 40 mesh
  Desired colour, (natural earth pigments)
- ○ *Decoration* (fifth coat)
  as marmorino one or more coats

Plain marmorino (Roman)

Harder than pozzolan stucco, finished with a steel trowel and scoured and polished very hard over a day.

149

○ *Arricio* (first coat)
   3 – coarse sharp washed sand
   ½ – crushed brick
   1 – slaked lime putty, 20 mesh
○ *Intonaco I* (second coat)
   3 – sharp washed sand
   1 – slaked lime putty, 20 mesh
○ *Intonaco II* (third coat)
   2 – fine washed sand, 20 mesh
   1 – slaked lime putty, 40 mesh
○ *Marmorino* (fourth coat)
   2 – fine marble dust
   1 – fine slaked lime putty, 40 mesh

Plain intonaco (Roman)

Italian version of common stucco described in Section 7.5.

○ *Arricio* (first coat)
   3 – coarse sharp washed sand
   ½ – crushed brick
   1 – slaked lime putty, 20 mesh
○ *Intonaco I* (second coat)
   3 – sharp washed sand, 12 mesh
   1 – slaked lime putty, 20 mesh
○ *Intonaco II* (third coat)
   2 – fine washed sand, 20 mesh
   1 – slaked lime putty, 40 mesh
○ *Limewash Finish*
   Lime Putty, 100 mesh with skimmed milk and pigments.
   The skimmed milk in this sample was not effective as a binder.

A pozzolan stucco (artificial; Roman)

○ *Arricio* (first coat)
   2 – coarse sharp washed sand
   1 – crushed Moler brick dust
   1 – slaked lime putty, 20 mesh
○ *Intonaco I* (second coat)
   3 – pozzolan (coarse to fine crushed Moler brick)
   1 – slaked lime putty, 20 mesh
○ *Intonaco II* (third coat)
   2 – pozzolan (moderate to fine crushed brick) 30 mesh
   1 – slaked lime putty, 40 mesh

Ancient Roman stucco
Trial specification for seven coats (total thickness 1¼ inches)

○ *Trullisatio* (first coat) which is a first rough coat
   3 – coarse sharp washed sand
   1 – slaked lime putty, 20 mesh
   Goat hair
○ *Arenatum* (second coat) comprising three sand coats
   2 : 1 : 1
   2 – coarse sharp washed sand
   1 – crushed brick
   1 – slaked lime putty, 20 mesh
   2 : 1 : 1
   2 – fine washed sand
   1 – crushed brick
   1 – slaked lime putty, 20 mesh
   1 : 1 : 1
   1 – fine washed sand, 20 mesh
   1 – fine crushed brick, 20 mesh
   1 – slaked lime putty, 20 mesh
○ *Marmoratum* (third coat) made up of three marble coats
   2 : 1
   2 – coarse marble dust, 30 mesh
   1 – slaked lime putty, 40 mesh
   2 : 1
   2 – medium marble dust, 40 mesh
   1 – slaked lime putty, 40 mesh
   2 : 1
   2 – super fine marble dust
   1 – fine slaked lime putty, 40 mesh

Note This final coat lost its plasticity in the demonstration, i.e. it was 'too short' and it has been suggested that it may be improved by adding a small proportion of kaolin or possibly reducing the amount of marble dust (Hill, Holmes and Mather, 1992).

9

Stabilization and other mixes incorporating lime

9.1 Earth stabilization

Traditional uses

Evidence abounds of lime used in conjunction with earth, and its compatibility with soil construction techniques. The setting and stabilizing characteristics of lime, together with its porosity after set, are ideal for the purpose of strengthening earthen structures, as well as improving weather resistance when it is applied as a render and limewash. It is not intended here to detail soil building methods fully, but to identify the principal areas where there are benefits from using lime in conjunction with soil construction.

Research carried out at the Faculty of Architecture, Bahia University, Brazil, into the adobe (mud brick) construction of a nineteenth century house on Ilha das Vacas showed that the adobes were stabilized with lime. The adobe bricks contained lime prepared on site from sea shells.

In addition to the tradition of stabilizing adobe, historical research at Bahia University indicates that lime was frequently used as a stabilizer for *pisé de terre* (rammed earth): a method of construction brought to the colony in the sixteenth century by the Portuguese.

Lime–soil reactions

The Centre for Research and Development in Bahia held a symposium on soil–lime uses, and in 1990 the results were reported at the Sixth International Conference on the Conservation of Earthen Architecture. Specialists at the symposium divided the phenomena of stabilization into two groups, as follows.

○ *Fast reactions*   Absorption of $Ca(OH)_2$ molecules
                     Cation exchange
                     Ion crowding
○ *Slow reactions*   Siliceous cementation
                     Aluminous cementation
                     Ferrous cementation
                     Carbonation

Soils consist of a mixture of coarse material, which is usually quartz sand, fine sand and silt particles, and very fine particles which are clay minerals. Whereas the more sandy soils can be stabilized with cement, the more clayey, plastic or 'stickier' soils are best treated by the addition of lime.

The more common clay structures are composed of crystal wafers of minute thickness, between 0.001μm and 2μm, varying with clay type. The wafers are composed of alternating layers of silica and alumina bonded by ions, cations, and water molecules.

Lime will react with the clay minerals – mainly kaolinite, montmorillonite and illite – in two ways. The first and more immediate reaction is for the calcium in the lime to substitute for the exchangeable alkali elements such as sodium and potassium that exist, together with water molecules, between the thin sheets of the alumino-silicate crystal structure of the clay minerals. Ion exchange can take place between Al, Si, Fe, Mg, Mn, etc. depending on which of the many clay types is stabilized. The clay particles no longer remain in their original dispersed state, but flocculate to form coarser agglomerates of clay. The soil therefore becomes less plastic, will absorb less moisture and it compacts more readily to give an increased compressive strength.

With time, another and most important reaction occurs in which the calcium combines chemically with the silica and alumina in the clay mineral. This follows dissolution of the clay minerals and their recombination to form complex aluminium and calcium silicates. It is a low grade of pozzolanic reaction, for which moisture must be present, and which can be accelerated by a higher temperature. The product is a binding material, comprising insoluble calcium silicate and silica gel. This binding material is also the main mineral component produced when water is added to Portland cement. In addition, and in conjunction with the above reactions, carbonation occurs. The lime reacts with carbon dioxide from the air to form carbonated cements.

There is an optimum quantity of lime for each soil. Generally it ranges between 3 and 10%, tending to be at the middle of this scale for soils containing an optimum clay fraction. The clay fraction of the soil can be determined by sedimentation analysis as shown in Section 11.4. The variation in soils is so great, however, that testing trial samples using various proportions of lime in the mix will probably be the quickest and simplest way of determining the optimum proportion of lime for stabilization.

In general terms, for practical purposes, it may be assumed that most soils need a reactive clay content of over 10% for full stabilization. Temperature is important in the early development of mechanical strength.

The longer that moist curing conditions are maintained for stabilized soil the greater the strength. A minimum of 14, and preferably 28, days is recommended for the initial cure. The longer both hot and moist conditions are maintained the stronger the final results are likely to be.

Field tests are described in the handbook *Building With Earth* by John Norton (1997), who recommends that the amount of lime to be used is established by producing blocks using a consistent compaction method and water content, and testing them as described in the handbook's chapter on performance testing.

9.2 Daub construction

A common method of construction in many parts of the world involves placing mud over a framework of light twigs or laths. In England up to the late eighteenth century this was the usual technique to fill panels of buildings framed with sturdy timbers, often buildings of high architectural quality. But more often the method is now used for low-cost building with no heavy framing. The network of light timbers is called wattling and a common term for this construction is 'wattle and daub'.

A daub in this context is clay-rich soil which has been made into a smooth pug by working it with water, often with various additives, to make it easy to squeeze into place around or between the sticks. The term daub is also used for a thick render material often made from similar ingredients. The most common additives are cow dung for weather resistance and extra plasticity, lime for durability and chopped straw or hair as tensile reinforcement. Straw and chalk can also increase porosity, which helps the pug to dry.

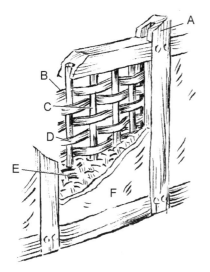

A Upright framing (stud or post)
B Wattle (interwoven mesh reinforcement)
C Staves or stakes: riven oak or ash, sometimes beech branches debarked. Tapered at top in head piece or slid into trenched groove; staves at bottom into auger-bored holes or trenched groove in sill piece
D Cross-slats or laths of riven oak or hazel or large hazel twigs with bark left on, interwoven between staves
E Daub; infilling with 'cats', i.e. slightly damp balls of clay mixed with a small proportion of cow dung, chopped straw, flax or hair. These are pressed in and through the wattle for form one mass to harden before drying out. When daub has hardened, the surface is slightly wetted before receiving the plaster rendering
F Rendering: lime, sand and varying proportions of cow dung mixed with chopped straw or hair. Panels are then finished flush with framing or slightly recessed. The surface is sometimes combed into patterns before receiving coats of limewash (repeated over the years)

Typical wattle and daub infill panel (after K. Reid)

In Gabon, daub is pressed between vertical posts and a horizontal framework of rods. This framing method is common in many parts of Africa. The daub is then pierced through from one side to the other so that when render is applied on both sides the piercing makes it possible for one render to bond to the other.

There is a very wide variety of mixes which have been used for this work. A mix used in 1985 by the Research and Technical Advisory Service at the Weald and Downland Museum in Sussex, England, includes no lime at all:

A   Frame to support staves
B   Upright staves of cleft oak
C   Sticks woven between staves
D   Pug of clay and straw mix
E   Lime plaster and/or limewash
     finish applied to pug surface in
     several layers up to ¼" thick

Sixteenth-century example of lime plaster on wattle and daub, partition in roof space, Plas Mawr, Conway, 1997

12 parts soil (with 10% clay content): 1 part dung: 1½ parts straw

At the same museum another mix used to match old work in the reconstruction of an old building was:

1 part earth (approximately 15% clay content): 2 parts slaked lime: 1 or 2 parts sand: 3 parts chalk granules (pea sized): 1 part chopped straw

The lime in the mix would be considerably more expensive than the soil, but it would be particularly beneficial in clay-rich soils, increasing the strength – and hence the durability – and reducing shrinkage and subsequent moisture movements which might lead to cracking.

Reid (1989) gives the following three examples of daub mixes:

8 parts stiff sandy clay soil: 1 part lime: 1 part cow dung: 1 part straw

4 parts sandy clay soil: 1 part cow dung: 1 part lime plus chopped hair

3 parts reused old daub: 1 part lime putty with 1lb hair per 3 cubic feet.

9.3 *Pisé de terre* or rammed earth

An earth wall may be built up in layers of rammed earth. Each layer is compacted by pounding the earth between rising shutters or formwork. Provided the finished surface is well keyed (see Section 6.3), this will be suitable for taking a protective coating of lime-sand render. Limewash alone may be adequate depending on the quality of finish achieved on striking the shutters.

It is not advisable to render an earth wall before:

○ Sufficient drying out has taken place to ensure there will be little or no further shrinkage. This may take as long as nine months for thick rammed earth. A guide is that the centre of the wall should not contain more than 5% water by weight. Dry weather conditions clearly assist the process.
○ All settlement has taken place. This means that all remaining construction which would add weight to the structure has been completed, particularly anything involving additional loading such as floors and roof.

An alternative to rendering is 'plating' with stabilized earth. During the course of building up the rammed earth wall, stabilized soil is mixed and set aside. The stabilized soil is then placed against the sides of the shuttering as it is filled, with the unstabilized soil in the centre. Both types of soil are then rammed together providing a hard stabilized soil surface to the wall without the cost of stabilizing the whole mass.

Lime may be used as a stabilizer for the full thickness of *pisé de terre* or rammed earth structures. This was common practice by the Portuguese in the sixteenth century.

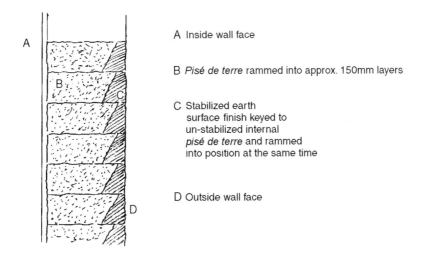

A Inside wall face

B *Pisé de terre* rammed into approx. 150mm layers

C Stabilized earth
  surface finish keyed to
  un-stabilized internal
  pisé de terre and rammed
  into position at the same time

D Outside wall face

Section through plated pisé de terre *wall*

Full details of rammed earth construction, including methods of earth preparation, are given in other publications listed in the Bibliography.

9.4   Lime-stabilized earth bricks and blocks

This section draws on information given in *Building with Earth* by John Norton (1986) with emphasis and amendments in respect of the use of lime for stabilization. Further information can be found in the Overseas Building Note by R.F. Carroll (1992).

Preparation and testing of materials
The traditional methods of block-making use wooden moulds. Blocks have either been slop-moulded or mixed as dry as possible and compacted, and then sun-dried. Naturally the drier and more compact the initial mix, the less drying shrinkage will occur.

Recent developments have made use of hand-operated mechanical presses, hydraulic and motorized presses, and vibration techniques. The majority of machines have been developed for compacted soil, cement-stabilized soil, or sandcrete (sand and cement) blocks. There is considerable potential for the further development of mechanical presses for lime-stabilized soil blocks.

Unlike cement, which works with the coarse particles of a soil, lime works with the clay minerals. The lime reacts with some of the clay minerals and water to produce a cementing effect, increasing the soil's strength and reducing susceptibility to water. Lime therefore works most effectively

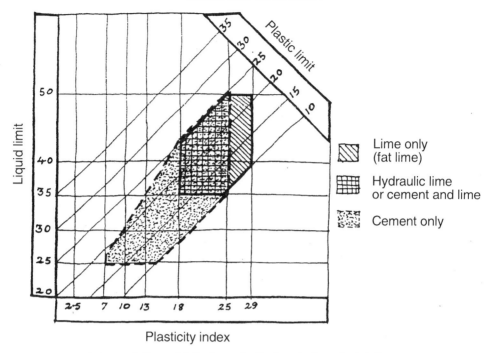

Interpretation of Atterberg limits for choice of stabilizers

as a stabilizer with a high clay content soil, which is not normally suitable for stabilization with cement, nor easily compacted.

The reaction of lime with the clay minerals is slow. This could make it difficult to use as a stabilizer on its own. However, one of the beneficial effects of lime on a soil is to lower its plastic and liquid limit (see the illustration above), by reducing the amount of water the soil can absorb. This has two results: the soil is easier to compact; and cement can be used more efficiently than is normally the case with a high clay content soil. This latter result means that it could be useful to use a small amount of cement to give quick stability, supplemented by the slower strengthening reaction of lime.

Either quicklime or hydrated lime can be used for stabilization. Quicklime has a drying-out effect, which can be most useful with soils that have a high clay content, but it is important to ensure that there are no unslaked lumps in the mixture before it is used.

The amount of lime may be established by producing blocks with consistent compaction and water content, and testing them (see Chapter 11). Select the lowest proportion of lime which will give acceptable results. Some tests have indicated that there is an optimum lime proportion for soil beyond which compressive strength decreases. The proportion of lime is likely to be between 3 and 10% by dry weight, and this will increase as the clay content increases.

158

Mix lime with soil in the same way as preparing coarse stuff for render, with a water content at or just above the optimum. When compacting high clay soils, mix the lime in and allow the soil to stand for a day or two, during which the lime will react with the clay, helping to break it down, and making it easier to compact. Lime-stabilized bricks and blocks should be kept damp for at least two weeks after compacting, and longer if possible.

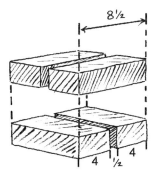

Brick and block unit proportions

Hand-moulded bricks and blocks

The shape and size of the block is first chosen in relation to the type of building, suitability for its location, or standard sizes used locally. Moulds may be constructed from wood or metal. They should have constant dimensions in order to ensure an even wall thickness and good bonding. Rectangular blocks are best made in a proportion of twice their width plus one mortar joint (say 15mm) being equal to their length. Depth should be 20 to 30% of the length and no less than 50mm.

Brick and block unit proportions   The example above is based on approximate equivalents of 1 unit = 1 in = 25mm. Note that the length of the unit is designed to take into account the mortar joint width. For best results it is therefore advisable to set out and lay mortar joints (perpends) consistently to the design width.

Soils suitable for making lime-stabilized blocks should be selected using the soil stabilization tests described in Section 11.5. Topsoil (containing organic matter) should not be included, and grains larger than 10mm should be removed by sieving. Particle size distribution of materials in the mix should be within the range:

Sand	(2.00mm to 0.06mm)	40% to 75%
Lime	(below 0.60mm)	3% to 10%
Silt	(0.06mm to 0.002mm)	10% to 30%
Clay	(less than 0.002mm)	15% to 30%

Earth, water, and sometimes straw, is prepared by mixing all ingredients together. They must be thoroughly mixed and any lumps broken down. The mix is left for a minimum of 24 hours to soak.

After the material has matured it is again mixed thoroughly and the moisture content checked. Lime stabilizer is then added to the quantity of material to be used immediately. The final mixture is then taken to the moulding site, and the moulds filled and compacted by hand.

Productivity depends on the size of the brick or block and skill of the moulders. Once experience has been gained and skills developed, a brick-maker should be able to produce 1500 small bricks or more a day.

Lime-stabilized bricks should be kept out of the sun and moist for as long as possible; this should be a minimum of 14 and preferably not less than 28 days. After one or two days, when the bricks are dry enough, they are lifted out of the moulds and stood on edge on the ground or on pallets.

Sound bricks can be loosely stacked on top of one another after one or two weeks. They should be arranged in a way that will allow air to pass between them and given about three weeks to dry in a tropical climate. There will be a significant increase in drying time required for colder and wetter weather. Bricks should never be used before they have evenly dried through. This may be checked by breaking a brick in half and noting the moisture inside.

The material from any broken or defective bricks may be broken up and reused. The same proportion of lime should be added again to the mix before remoulding.

Lime-stabilized compressed blocks

Manually operated or motorized presses are normally used for compaction. A similar but much drier mix to that used for hand-moulded bricks is necessary. Unlike the hand-moulding technique described previously, immediately the compaction process has been completed the block is removed from the press and set up to cure.

Depending on the size of block and the number of the workforce, manually-operated presses enable an operator to produce between 300 and 1000 blocks per day, and motorized presses have quoted daily production rates in excess of 2000.

Mixing The material used for stabilized compressed blocks should be dryer, and with a slightly higher sand content than for moulded blocks. John Norton (1986) recommends the following particle size distribution:

Sand/fine gravel	45–75%
Silt	15–30%
Clay	10–25%
Lime	3–10%

If dry hydrate is being used as the stabilizer, it should first be mixed well into the material in a dry state. Water should then be added carefully by sprinkling, *not pouring*, on to the mix. No part should be saturated, and all material should become lightly moistened. The optimum water content is between 7 and 16%. A simple way of checking this is with the drop test (see Section 11.5). Lime and soil types vary in their reactivity and setting properties. Some may be improved by giving between one and three days for the reaction to commence after mixing in the lime and before compaction.

Curing   Following compaction, the compressed blocks must be given time to cure in a similar way to moulded blocks, keeping them in the shade and moistening with a light sprinkling daily for at least the first week. The longer they are given to cure, without fully drying out, the longer the pozzolanic reaction has to take place, and the stronger the blocks are likely to be. A 28-day curing period is the preferred minimum.

Output   Compressed block output, using a manual press, is generally given as between 350 and 500 a day. This rate of production depends on an efficient operating team of seven to nine people working an eight hour day. The principal operations need to be carried out simultaneously to keep production flowing. These are: excavating, sieving and mixing the soil; filling and working the press; demoulding; transferring to the curing area; stacking; and keeping the blocks moist.

Block dimensions   The depth, width and length of blocks vary from one press to another, although approximate dimensions of 290×140mm ($11\frac{1}{2}$" $\times 5\frac{1}{2}$") are common. A number of machines can be ordered with different mould sizes, and a few with interchangeable patterns. Tiles and different block shapes can also be made by the insertion of wooden blocks or templates to reduce the volume and change the profile.

Physical properties   A table setting out the physical properties of compressed lime-stabilized soil blocks including compressive strength, drying shrinkage and water absorption is given in Appendix 11. The table also gives comparative information on these properties for bricks and blocks of other materials. Appendix 8 describes various soil types and their suitability for stabilization with lime.

Mortar for stabilized soil blocks   Wall building should follow the basic principles employed for masonry, with attention paid to bonding. Good

Demonstration of limewashed and rendered clay lump (soil block) wall with blocks bedded in lime and clay mortar (Photograph: Stafford Holmes at: Society for the Protection of Ancient Buildings technical day)

quality stabilized compressed blocks can be used like concrete blocks. Lime-stabilized blocks can be laid with a lime : soil mortar in the same ratio as that used for making the blocks, or alternatively with soil : cement : lime in a ratio of 9 : 1 : 2 or soil : cement in a ratio of 8 : 1. Lime improves the plasticity of the mortar, and reduces the likelihood of it cracking, because it dries more slowly. Blocks should be dampened before laying. Mortar joints should be a consistant thickness, kept to the minimum. A good quality block will enable tight joints less than 10mm thick.

A slightly higher sand content in the mortar may help to reduce shrinkage. The adhesion of lime-sand mortar and lime-mud mortar will vary, dependent upon mix proportions. The principles of using lime mortars should be applied, as described in Chapter 5.

Renders Unstabilized block walls will need rendering. In theory, stabilized blocks should not require rendering if well made, but in practice most stabilized walls are covered with a thin coating applied at a fairly liquid consistency. Previous chapters, and Sections 9.5 and 9.6, detail rendering and painting techniques for earth walls.

9.5   Lime and cow dung render and pargeting

It is not unusual for mixes to contain a proportion of cow dung. Cow dung, in a slurried form introduced into the mix, acts as an additional binder and improves plasticity. When used in conjunction with lime there is an additional stabilizing affect and a noticeable improvement to weather resistance.

The effect of dung, especially cow dung (or slurry) on lime is described in Ashurst & Ashurst (1988b). This states that the significant constituent of the dung is a mucus which reacts with lime to form a gel. The gel both stabilizes the clay mineral wafers and supports the lime and sand until the lime carbonation process has been completed and the final strength obtained.

Traditional uses
Pearson (1992) records recent research confirming that lime putty and cow dung mixed in equal proportions have been used for render to soil-based walls in mainland Britain in the past.

Decorative pargeting, which may also incorporate cow dung, is described in Section 8.3.

Traditional mixes
A traditional daub render finish is: 4 parts lime putty to 1½ clean sharp sand to 1 slurried cow dung, all reinforced with 150mm (6") chopped straw. It is essential that the whole mix is thoroughly beaten and rammed as dry as possible before application. A deeply scratched cross key should be applied when the render coat has hardened to a rubber-like consistency. The finishing coat should be 4 lime putty to 1 sharp sand to 1 slurried cow dung. The sand, as for all renders, must be clean and sharp.

Fire resistance
The excellent binding, adhesive, and fire resistant properties of the mixture of lime and cow dung were known and used in England up to the latter half of the twentieth century for parging chimney flues. This was mixed in the same proportions as those given above, sometimes with the omission of sand.

Plane pargeting
Mixtures for decorative pargeting and wattle and daub are described elsewhere in this book. Plane pargeting has been used extensively on soil structures in many countries for centuries. Batty Langley confirms the mix used at the time of his book, *London Prices*, 1738. This was 1 part dung incorporated into 4 parts of lime by beating it well. Innocent (1916) stated that the English plasterers were following an old and widespread tradition in the knowledge that cow dung has excellent setting properties. He confirmed that it was currently in use in parts of North Derbyshire as a

material for parging flues and chimneys. It has been used for this purpose in England recently, at least up to the 1960s for new buildings.

9.6 Renders and slurries for soil structures

Renders

Lime-soil renders can be used on earth walls. These renders are stabilized with lime or cement in proportions of lime : earth between 1 : 5 and 1 : 10, and may be improved if one part of lightly burned brick dust is added to give a pozzolanic reaction with the lime. Soil-based renders have a better adhesion to soil structures than sand-based renders.

Well burnt quicklime granules or quicklime dust fresh from the kiln will stabilize clay-rich soils. The addition of quicklime improves the weather resistance and durability of clays. Dry hydrate and putty may also be used although the lime-soil reaction tends to be slower and less pronounced than with quicklime. Quicklime is highly reactive, however, and health and safety precautions need to be taken as for preparing limewash from quicklime described in Section 4.2 on page 50.

Good rendering depends much on preparing the wall properly so that the render will adhere. Renders which are 'strong' are particularly prone to separation from the wall they are protecting; this is often the case with cement-based renders. When lamination occurs, water penetrating through cracks into the gap between the render and the wall can do great damage. For example, one of the most popular techniques of rendering with cement has been to fix chicken wire to the earth wall, and to use this as a key for a cement-sand render, so that little attention is paid to adhesion with the wall or roof being rendered. The principal danger in using this system, particularly in areas of prolonged rainfall, is that structural damage by water can occur without being visible on the outer surface.

There are various ways of preparing a good key for render, including the chicken wire mentioned above. Chicken wire (or similar) should be fixed at regular intervals to the wall, with spikes or pegs. Alternatively, spikes and nails can be used alone to provide a key, placed in a dense but irregular pattern, and hammered well into the wall. Another method is to face the wall with broken pottery, tiles etc., which project out from the surface, and are either put in at the time of building, or pushed into the mortar whilst it is still damp. A similar effect is achieved by placing fibres in the wall while it is being built so that they project beyond the surface. When working with bricks or blocks, the joints should be raked out to a depth of 15mm or more. The rougher the surface the better the key, and this can be achieved by making grooves or holes in the surface. Further details concerning background preparations are given in Section 6.3.

Surfaces should be brushed down in all cases to remove loose matter and dust, and then dampened before the render is applied. Renders adhere better if applied with force; thrown on with a trowel or in balls. Renders smoothed and pressed on firmly by hand adhere well to rough surfaces, and this is often the traditional way of working. Inevitably the renders will shrink, and cracks may be removed by repeated dampening and scouring, and to some extent by filling with additional mortar. Lime stabilization reduces shrinkage, and other techniques involve adding sand or chalk particles, though they will reduce the durability of the render. It is important to bring the soil to its optimum plasticity with the right water content and to allow enough time for the water to penetrate the clay.

Clough Williams-Ellis *et al.* (1947) describe an earth-lime render mix used in Natal, South Africa. This mix utilizes the red lateritic earth, abundant in Africa and South America, in the ratio of earth to sand to hydraulic lime of 6 : 2 : 1. It is described as being applied as a thin coat after damping the wall. After drying, and having cracked to some degree, it is rubbed all over with a pad of sacking covered with the same plaster mix, but with additional water added to give it a consistency of thin cream. The lime-soil render after drying is then ready for taking a paint or limewash finish.

A lime-soil render recommended by John Norton (1986), who advises that a sandy soil be used, is suitable for stabilized earth walls. The lime to soil mix proportions range between 1 : 5 and 1 : 10. These may be improved either by using a hydraulic lime, or adding a pozzolan in equal proportions to a fat (Class A) lime.

Analysis of existing render to a nineteenth century garden wall in Hampshire, UK, which had stood the test of time for at least 100 years (Pearson, 1992) gave the result by volume:

Lime	7%
Hair and vegetable matter	9%
Crushed chalk	32%
Sand	52%

Slurries incorporating lime

John Norton (1986) has recommended a water, lime, cement slurry, mixed in a ratio of 6 : 1 : 1 and brushed on to the wall like paint, as a weathering coat for an earth wall. Adding clean fine sand helps to give a gritty texture which improves resistance to water. Slurries can last from five to ten years. Alternatively, the cement may be omitted and a natural or artificial hydraulic lime can be used instead. This comprises hydraulic limewash with the addition of fine sand, which will give similar results, although it is slower to set after application. This slurry, with lime only as the binder, has the advantage that it should be more permeable than a slurry incorporating cement.

Lime and pozzolan with sand or soil render

The best known of these renders uses powdered burnt clay with lime, and is known in India as 'surkhi'. Other pozzolans include flyash, burnt rice husks, and volcanic ash. The ratio of pozzolan to lime depends upon the reactivity of the pozzolan and the strength and speed of set required. High pozzolan dosages (say 1 lime : 4 pozzolan) work faster, but 1 : 2 is common as is 1 : 3 with a less reactive pozzolan. A suitable render is 1 lime to 2 pozzolan and 9 sand or soil for use on a stabilized soil construction, or a weaker mix, with less pozzolan, on unstabilized soil.

Gypsum-lime and gypsum-lime-sand render

External renders in very dry climates with a lime to gypsum to sand ratio of 1 : 5 : 4 and small amounts of water can be used, with a final coat leaving out the sand. Internal renders can be prepared without the lime, but lime improves water resistance. Generally, it is not recommended to use gypsum externally if lime is available, as most gypsums are soluble in water.

Traditional internal plasters for earth structures

Earth buildings intended for human habitation are often plastered internally. The lime-sand plasters described in Chapter 6 will be satisfactory and should give the best results, provided it is possible to obtain well-graded clean sand. Earth walls, however, are suitable for receiving a combination of mud or lateritic soil and lime as plaster. Good background for these earth-based plasters is just as important as for lime-sand plaster, and the key should be given as much attention and prepared as described in Section 6.3.

Traditional mud plasters vary greatly, but there are a number of common principles. Generally the first coat is thick, up to 20mm. It may or may not incorporate lime, but when it is rich in clay there is considerable benefit in adding about 10 to 20% of lime. This assists stabilizing and hardening of the first coat. Lime stabilization of lateritic soil for the first coat has been common practice in Zanzibar and other parts of East Africa. Pearson (1992) confirms that render coats of clay and lime have been traditionally used on earth buildings in England.

The first coat, of clay-rich earth and lime, will develop shrinkage cracks which will be more severe in soils with a high clay content if not compensated by a greater proportion of lime in the mix. The second coat, which is frequently also the finishing coat, is applied after the first coat has dried, or shortly before it is completely dry. The finishing coat may be a thin coat of lime putty, or clay and lime, or sand and lime. Whichever mix is chosen, best results will be determined by trials with lime and the local soil. It is important to carry out the preparation and application of lime-soil plasters and renders in accordance with the principles set out in Chapter 6 if a reasonably durable finish is to be achieved. A daub render mix recommended by EARTHA for an initial trial is 1 clay : 2 sharp sand : 1 lime putty.

9.7 Roof finishes

In the tropics there are advantages to be gained in making use of flat roofs for terraces and the creation of cool outdoor spaces. Several of the finishes described for floors in Chapter 10, particularly those with tiles or mosaic, are therefore appropriate for roofs, provided careful attention is given to detail. The roof structure must be adequate to take both the live load of people using it and the dead weight of the surface finish. Arrangements for water run-off and a water disposal system capable of controlling rapid water build up is essential. Good falls, with a minimum gradient of 1 in 40, across the roof to deep gutters, also with good falls to water chutes or gullies, are basic essentials for protection of the building fabric below.

If it is not intended to use the roof as a terrace, less durable and lower-cost finishes may be considered, although these are more likely to require careful maintenance at a greater frequency. The flat roofs of the ancient mud city of Sana'a in North Yemen were traditionally finished with a coating of Ramad. This is a mixture of lime and wood ash carefully pre-pared and thoroughly beaten (Rogers, 1986). Interestingly, the description of it is very similar to the wood ash and lime mix detailed in Appendix 2 on pozzolans. This was used for ash mortar in England in the eighteenth century as described in correspondence between Lord Macclesfield and John Smeaton during the course of the latter's research into water-resistant mortars for the Eddystone Lighthouse.

Roofs that will not be used as terraces, or which will take only occasional light foot traffic for maintenance may be finished with other hydraulic lime mixes, particularly stucco and chunam (Chapter 7) provided they are very carefully prepared and laid.

Common factors in the preparation of these water-resistant finishes is careful selection of fresh well-burnt quicklime and raw materials, the care-ful preparation of lime putty and a thorough mixing and beating of all ingredients to achieve good workability with low water content. Madras chunam and Rajasthan aryash have been used this way for centuries, as may be seen on roofs and domes in India to this day.

In addition to the above finishes, an application of limewash (with addi-tives to improve water-shedding properties) will give increased protection, all as detailed in Chapter 4.

9.8   Tar and lime coating

The base of the wall is the most vulnerable part, being exposed to frequent contact with surface water, abrasion and impact. Although it is preferable to build a mud wall off a stone base, or to provide a stone plinth or underpin course to protect this area, it is not always possible to do so.

If the soil wall has been taken down to the ground, a deep skirting of pitch or tar applied hot to the face of the render will give added protection against splashes and abrasion. Where rising damp is a problem, the tar may also be used to form a horizontal damp-proof course. Tar is a natural bitumen distilled from coal, wood, or peat. It may be applied either neat, or blended with a sharp sand, in two or three coats, and finished with a sand blinding. After the sand-blinded surface has dried, this may be lime-washed.

Bitumen, normally supplied in the form of bitumen paint, may be used as an alternative to tar. Both tar and bitumen have the advantage over other waterproofing materials that they are moderately permeable to water vapour.

An alternative technique for application of this finish is to allow a first coat of tar to dry. A second coat of tar is applied, and whilst still wet, a slurry of lime and fine, sharp sand is mixed into it. This slurry, to the consistency of thick cream, is rubbed into the wet tar with a grass brush. The surface is left rough whilst the tar is allowed to bleed through. It is then limewashed at least twice at approximately three-monthly intervals (Wright, 1991).

This technique is more suitable for cooler climates. If the render is exposed for too long to direct sunlight in warm climates there is the possibility that the tar will be heated to a temperature at which it will melt. Alternative means of waterproofing and strengthening plinths are therefore recommended for the tropics.

9.9   Calcium silicate bricks and components

Calcium silicate bricks and components are made with a mixture of lime and natural sand or crushed rock. The incentive to manufacture calcium silicate bricks is found in both the wide availability of raw materials and in the low cost of production. Use has grown progressively since they were first made commercially in Germany at the end of the nineteenth century.

Manufacture is by mechanical or hydraulic presses which compact the moist mixture of sand and lime into the required shape. After forming, these are hardened by curing in high-pressure steam autoclaves. The reaction of lime with the silica during autoclave treatment produces hydrated calcium silicates, which are the principal cementing agents. Calcium silicate bricks are produced in most industrialized countries in the world. Total annual world production is rated in thousands of millions of bricks per year.

The proportion of lime used in manufacture ranges between 5 and 9% of quicklime, or 8–12% of hydrated lime. The quality of quicklime used must be such that it hydrates evenly and completely during the mixing process which precedes pressing of the bricks. If hydrated lime is used it must be already completely hydrated. These requirements are essential because of the expansion which occurs during the hydration of lime. If hydration occurs in the autoclave, the resulting expansion will lower the strength of the bricks, and can be sufficiently large to cause them to crack or even burst.

The possibility of incomplete hydration of the lime may be due to either the limestone composition, or the way in which it has been burnt. If the lime has been burnt at too high a temperature, or for too long, it becomes over-burnt and hydrates less readily. The presence of iron compounds and magnesia increase the risk of over-burning, making such limes unsuitable for this use. It is therefore essential to be sure of quality control during burning, as well as analysing samples before selecting a suitable lime for brick manufacture.

Criteria that have been established for accepting lime for the manufacture of calcium silicate bricks are:

○ *Available lime content* This is the amount of calcium oxide present, as this is the only part that is reactive and will form the calcium silicate bond. Good quality quicklime should contain 90–95% available CaO, although lower contents are sometimes acceptable. It is recognized that a commercial hydrated lime of good quality will have 68–72% of available lime. A hydrated lime with less than 60% available CaO would not normally be acceptable.

○ *Magnesia content* Magnesia is detrimental in lime for this use, since it is liable to hydrate and give expansion in the autoclave. In the UK limits of 5% in quicklime and 4% in hydrated lime are accepted, but below 3% is preferred. In countries where there is less choice and higher magnesia content is necessary, control of the conditions of burning and hydrating lime for this use become more critical.

○ *Fineness of grinding quicklime* In the UK it is considered sufficient to grind quicklime to pass a standard 1.18mm sieve for the drum hydration process. This is a maximum size, and more finely ground lime is usually preferred. The German DIN standard 1060 requires a quicklime to be ground to pass a 0.63mm sieve for the reactor process.

It may be economic to use waste products from mining or industry to replace some or all of the sand for this type of brick. For example, in South Africa and the CIS, bricks are made with waste from mining residues. Pulverized fuel ash has also been used from coal-fired power stations that use powdered coal as fuel, and this residue has been used as part replacement of the sand. The process can also be applied using some types of slag as aggregate.

The only type of press until the 1950s was the mechanically operated rotary table press. This is still widely used, and has been developed to be fitted with automatic loading and stacking equipment.

A second type of mechanically-operated press, which has a single mould block, presses several bricks in one operation. It has a slightly higher output than the rotary table press. Advances in technology have lead to the introduction of large multi-mould boxes with hydraulic presses of high output. These have tended to replace the mechanically operated types and have been widely adopted in industrialized countries (Bessey, 1974; Everett, 1994).

Automated production methods, together with the economy of increasing the autoclave size, favours a high-capital industrialized system. It is difficult to develop the process on a small scale. This is unfortunate as the raw materials, sand, lime and water are low-cost and generally readily available.

In addition to the production of bricks, calcium silicate may be used for numerous other building components such as external pavers, floor tiles, copings and sills. These can be of very high quality with a satisfactory durability of over fifty years. Like lime-stabilized soil blocks, there is considerable potential for the development of appropriate machinery for the small-scale production of calcium silicate bricks and building components (see Appendix 4 for British Standards; also BRE Digest 157, 1974).

10

Substructure: floors, roads and lime concrete

10.1 Floors and paving

One of the earliest lime concrete floors discovered is dated about 5600 BC. This was one of a number found adjacent to the river Danube at Lepenski Vir in Yugoslavia.

The floor is made of red lime, sand and gravel laid to a depth of 250mm (10") and compacted to form a floor. The lime appears to have been brought from almost two hundred miles upstream (Stanley, 1986).

It is believed that the art of making concrete spread from Egypt and the eastern Mediterranean to Greece by 1000 BC. The Romans developed lime concrete for structures that have not been surpassed, examples of which date from 300 BC.

External cobble paving

Cobbles are hard stones which have been rounded by water action and are often freely available. These can make an excellent hard paving if carefully selected and laid. This is similar to, but less intricate than, pebble work in Pompeii described later in this chapter in the section on floor surfaces.

Correct preparation of the base is essential. Normally it is best to prepare a well-compacted 75mm deep hardcore sub-base. If the subsoil is clay, this may be stabilized and the hardcore omitted. To stabilize a clay subsoil: remove topsoil; sprinkle hydrated lime, or for best results quicklime, over the clay; mix to a depth of 75mm; and dampen. Proportions should be approximately 90% clay soil to 10% lime. The proportion of lime may be reduced to as little as 3% depending on the type of clay.

Whatever sub-base is used, the materials should be well compacted, preferably with a roller or by ramming. Lay a 25mm bed of hydraulic lime and sand (mix $1:2$, or $1:1\frac{1}{2}$) on top of the sub-base. The exact depth to be determined by size of cobbles to be laid. If eminently hydraulic lime is not available additional durability can be achieved by the addition of a pozzolan to the mix. Cobbles may also be laid on sand, aggregate and clay beds without the addition of lime to stabilize the base course and formation. Lime stabilization of the ground below the cobbles improves durability.

Allow approximately 3mm at the narrowest point of joints between cobbles, and ensure careful coursing and bedding. Carefully fill and compact joints with hydraulic lime : coarse sand or pozzolan mix in proportions $1:2$ or $1:1\frac{1}{2}$. Finish joints slightly recessed and avoid feather edges.

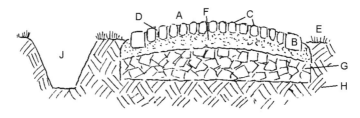

Cobble paving

A: Cambered surface; B: Larger kerb stones; C: Cobbles set as close as possible, allowing 3 to 6mm
width for pointing in 1 : 1 or 1 : 1½ hydraulic lime : sand mortar up to 50mm deep; D: Hydraulic lime
pointing; E: Topsoil ground level; F: Hydraulic lime mortar bed and haunching; G: Lime stabilized soil, or
hardcore or lime concrete; H: Formation base of compacted sub-soil; J: Culvert.

It is advisable to construct stone, brick or timber kerbs at the perimeter
to contain the paved area. This will help to increase durability and prevent
fracturing at the edges. The incorporation of drainage channels also helps
to increase durability.

The figure above is typical of cobble paving constructions which utilize
small stones or cobbles from a wide variety of sources. Some hard material of
this nature is likely to be locally available. Most durable local stone or brick
can be used for hard-wearing paving and flooring in this way.

External paving should always be laid to fall away from the building.
Water may then be directed to drainage channels, gullies and soakaways.
Falls need to be arranged to keep surface water clear of entrances and the
building's perimeter. A simple and effective method of achieving water
run-off from paths and roads is to provide a good camber to shed water
from the centre to culverts either side.

Solid floors

Vitruvius, the Roman architect and engineer, writing in the first century BC
has been quoted previously. He describes two methods of constructing
solid floors using lime as the binder, and these have a potential use even
today. A wide variety of finishes is possible with lime-concrete flooring.
Vitruvius describes concrete floor construction in connection with polished
finishes (Adam, 1994).

Polished finishes would be produced by making use of materials that
could be ground or rubbed down, and oiled or polished to give a smooth
surface. The finishing material would be in the form of chippings of, for
example, marble or soft burnt brick. These would be either mixed into, or
sprinkled on, a hydraulic lime surface screed. Alternatively, these materials
may be treated more selectively for colour, shape and size. This makes
possible an immense range of floor designs and patterns from plain floors
with coloured chippings or terrazzo, to the most elaborate mosaic or mar-
quetry, with different types of stones selected for their colour, and cut
to shape.

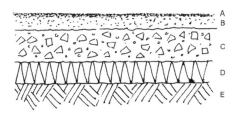

A Opus signinum with polished
  crustae on surface
B Nucleus – 100mm of 3 pulverized
  tile to 1 lime
C Rudus – 225mm lime concrete of
  broken stone to lime at 3 : 1
D Statumen – 225 to 150mm
  compacted hardcore of broken
  stone
E Soil sub-base levelled and
  compacted

Lime concrete floor

The specification Vitruvius gives for lime-concrete flooring to take these polished finishes is:

○ Test the soil sub-base to ensure all areas are solid, and level off.
○ On this firm sub-base lay broken stone, well bedded down. If some filling is necessary to level the sub-base, it is important to ensure the broken stone is well rammed down. The term for the layer of broken stone was '*statumen*', which is the equivalent of today's 'hardcore', for which clean brick rubble is a good alternative to stone.
○ The following layer, the *rudus*, is a thick lime concrete slab composed of small broken stones mixed with lime in the proportion of 3 : 1. Vitruvius recommends that this is beaten down into a solid mass and not less than 225mm (9") thick.
○ The next layer, the *nucleus*, to receive the finish is pounded clay tile mixed with lime in the proportions of 3 : 1. This should be laid not less than 100mm (4") thick. Presumably the importance of the pounded tile in this mix is its pozzolanic qualities which may also be achieved by using other crushed clay products such as soft burnt brick or pottery.
○ The *nucleus*, or equivalent of today's 'screed', is carefully levelled to receive the finish. The most common, and economical, of these was *opus signinum*. This was made with pieces of broken terracotta, brick, or fragments of marble termed *crustae* (probably sieved to sizes ranging between 3 and 10mm (⅛" to ⅜"). These might be scattered at random on the surface of the *nucleus* before it had fully set, or mixed with it. Clearly great care was needed to ensure the set had thoroughly taken place before rubbing down and polishing (Adam, 1994).
○ Vitruvius (tr Morgan, 1960) states that finishes applied to the screed (*nucleus*), after being carefully levelled and set, could also be cut slips, lozenges, triangles, squares and hexagons. This is a reference to the best quality work for principal rooms, and a better quality alternative to the *opus signinum*. Considerable emphasis is placed on careful jointing of all these units on the same plain with one another. Rubbing down was not considered properly finished until all edges were level.

After the rubbing down and the smoothing and polishing process had been completed, powdered marble was sifted on top followed by a

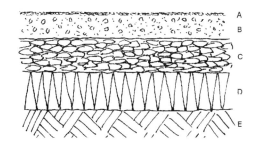

A Ground and polished surface
B 150mm deep gravel lime and ash mix
C Minimum 150mm deep trodden down charcoal
D 150 to 225mm stone or brick hardcore laid to falls and well compacted
E Sub-base formation rammed down to inclined levels to assist drainage

Insulated lime concrete floor

coating of lime and sand. This is presumably the equivalent of today's grouting of tile surfaces. The fine marble dust and lime would fill the joints between the tile or mosaic pieces, and after an initial set be brushed off, although this is not stated.

In the same chapter, Vitruvius gives a specification for an insulated and absorbent floor, describing it as the Greek method of making floors for use in winter dining rooms. The construction of this is carried out as follows:

○ Excavate the ground to about 600mm (2 feet) below finished floor level. Ram down the sub-base to a formation, with inclined levels to assist drainage at its base.
○ Fill and ram down broken stone or brick hardcore, also to falls.
○ Fill in with *charcoal*, and lightly compact by treading down. Level to an approximate minimum depth of 150mm (6").
○ Spread on a mortar mix of gravel, lime and ashes to a depth of 150mm (6"). Carefully level the surface and allow to set.
○ Finish off by smoothing down (polishing) with whetstone (a grit-stone or grinding-stone).

Damp-resistant floors

Numerous materials are used for constructing solid ground floor slabs by compaction. If lime is the binder this must be either naturally or artificially hydraulic to resist damp and wet conditions.

A popular method of solid floor construction in Gloucestershire in the nineteenth century was given the name of 'grip floor'. This was composed of lime and ashes laid moist to a thickness of 100mm to 125mm (4" or 5") on a compacted sub-base and rammed down hard with a heavy timber tamper until a hard and smooth surface was obtained. The principal means of compaction and hardening ground floor slabs was by ramming, scouring and/or polishing, as gypsum could not be added due to its inability to resist moisture. Construction methods that may be used as a precaution against rising damp in the ground floor slab are:

○ Keeping the floor surface well above ground level.

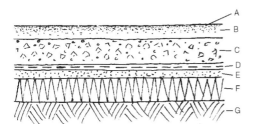

A Surface finish
B 100mm hydraulic lime screed
C 225mm lime concrete
D Damp-proof membrane
E Sand blinding
F Minimum 150mm compacted hardcore
G Compacted formation

Damp-resistant lime concrete floor

○ Forming a drainage trench around the building to intercept groundwater.
○ The provision of a well-compacted hardcore sub-base of broken stone, brick or other inert rubble material which is free draining.
○ A blinding over this hardcore of sand, loam, ash or other fine material to receive a damp-proof membrane.
○ The laying of a continuous damp-proof membrane of any material that will prevent the penetration of damp. This could be in sheet form such as thick polythene sheet, or of bitumen or tar-based materials, oils or resins, or even layers of clay, if the former are not available.
○ On top of the damp-proof membrane construction of the floor, slab, screed and finish was laid, compacted and polished. These could be prepared in one of the ways described above, preferably with either a natural or artificial hydraulic lime.

Suspended floors and 'lime-ash'

Two of the most common methods of constructing suspended floors, i.e. upper floors, are with gypsum and 'lime-ash' laid on timber joists in colder climates, or with coral laid on boriti poles in warmer climates. Both methods take advantage of lightweight aggregates combined with the binder to give a light, low-cost floor slab with an integral finish. Because the floor construction is lightweight, the floor slab may be supported by timber joists of minimum section. This allows greater spans to be achieved, providing larger rooms. The lighter weight of material enables smaller structural timber sections to be used, which are more readily available, thus reducing cost. Further advantages of this construction are that it is vermin proof and fire resistant.

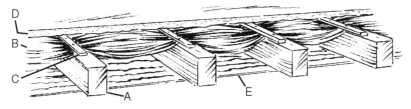

Lime ash (or plaster) floor
A: Timber floor joist; B: Reed or straw; C: Lath nailed through to joist; D: Lime ash or plaster floor; E: Lath and plaster ceiling

Although the first of these methods is called 'lime-ash', gypsum was often used as a quick-setting binding agent for lightweight aggregates such as soft burnt broken brick or tile, and the partially burnt residue from kilns and furnaces. Particularly suitable would be sintered coke, coal and charcoal. The proportion of lime in the mix was variable. If gypsum was not available the set would be slow, and to help overcome this the hydraulic lime content would be increased.

Plaster concrete for upper floors was laid on reeds nailed down to the top of floor joists with timber lath. Straw might be laid over the reed to prevent the plaster percolating through. The plaster concrete was floated fair to about 80mm (3") in thickness, and then after initial curing was finished the following day. To increase hardness and give the best finish some were rubbed down, polished, and coated with linseed oil. There are also records of the addition of egg white or bullocks' blood to improve the quality of finish. When the mix was gauged with gypsum, wood strips would be fixed around the walls prior to laying. These would then be drawn out when the plaster began to set, to allow for its expansion. Further information on materials and mixes for floor finishes is given in the next section.

The lightness of this construction enabled floor joists to be reduced to 90mm (3½") by 65mm (2½") wide fixed at about 350mm (14") centres, and supported by beams (Millar, 1897). These floors were clearly not intended to take heavy loads. Deflection, with inevitable cracking, is likely to occur if heavy items such as furniture are positioned towards the centre of the room, unless floor joists of a larger section are used.

Another method of forming a lightweight upper floor is with coral ragstone on boriti poles. This method has been used extensively in east Africa. Boriti (mangrove) poles are placed between 150mm (6") and 300mm (12") apart, with ends supported on either structural walls or larger floor joists. Pieces of coral ragstone, lightweight due to the large proportion of voids within the coral, are carefully positioned to span between the poles. The underside is lime plastered, leaving the poles exposed whilst the upper

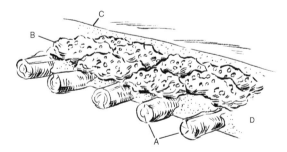

Cut-away of coral ragstone suspended floor
A: Boriti poles; B: Coral ragstone; C: Lime-stabilized laterite screed; D:
Lime plaster ceiling

surface is rendered with a lime-stabilized laterite screed finished with a polished granolithic (or terrazzo) lime surface.

Floor surfaces and finishes

Floors designed to take heavy wear have traditionally been finished with hard materials. One of the least expensive and hardwearing can be produced by carefully setting small pebbles in a hydraulic lime screed. Excellent examples of this work survive from the classical period in Greece. The pavement of via di Porta Marina, (*circa* 300 BC) in Pompeii is finished in pebble-work which still exists, and indicates the quality and durability that can be achieved with this low-cost material.

Small pebbles may also be arranged in geometric patterns, ranging from the simplest to the most complex. The method may include splitting the pebbles to achieve a flatter surface. This technique can be developed further by cutting pebbles and other hard material. Soapstone, marble, and even broken pottery provide the possibility of not only geometric patterns but also elaborate designs in colour. The technique has close similarities to depeter for the decoration of walls, described in Section 8.6. At the highest levels of design and craftsmanship, magnificent murals and floor patterns have been produced in mosaic. These finishes are extremely durable, as demonstrated by the many ancient Greek and Roman mosaic floors existing today.

Recent examples of floors finished with hard-wearing surfaces composed of small units are widespread. In Zanzibar, nineteenth and early twentieth century buildings have floor finishes made of small pieces of broken glazed pottery set out in colourful geometric designs. Villa Saraceno, Italy, completed in the middle of the sixteenth century, has a lime floor incorporating small pieces of broken brick in the surface, polished down to give a smooth finish.

The inclusion of small chippings and pieces of harder material in the screed is common, particularly in Italy where marble is abundant. Chippings or small pieces of the softer marbles are ideal. It is also possible to use this technique for making pre-cast tiles. Industrialized production of terrazzo today relies on the quick set and hardness of Portland Cement. The technique, however, was well known before this, and relied on lime or gypsum as the principal binder. It is important to ensure a thorough set before polishing, and the disadvantage of lime as the only binder, even using the most hydraulic type which would be preferred for floors, is the length of time before final set. In order to speed this process, it became common practice to gauge the mix with gypsum where there was no danger of dampness from the ground.

An inexpensive floor finish makes use of ash and clinker, often from the bottom of the lime kiln. Examples of this are widely recorded from the seventeenth century onwards. Composition was extremely varied, as the general principle was to make use of relatively fine, hard and inert waste material in order to reduce weight without loss of strength. The most economic source of ash and clinker would be waste material from local industry.

It is therefore not surprising to find reference to foundry ashes, gun dust and anvil dust from the forge, which were added to improve surface durability.

Nicholson (c.1850) recommends for a finishing screed a mix of lime and coal ashes in the ratio of 2 : 1, well sifted with a small quantity of loam clay. This is well mixed and tempered with water. It is allowed to stand in a similar way to coarse stuff, for a week to ten days, and then tempered again and allowed to stand for three or four days. This process is repeated with continual tempering until it becomes 'smooth, yielding, tough and gluey'. After the floor base is levelled, the floor is laid with this material about 75mm (3") thick and smoothed with a trowel. It is recommended this is carried out in the hottest weather for best results.

Nicholson also recommends that to make the best floor finish, ragstone lime (possibly hydraulic lime), should be used and the mix well-tempered with white of eggs. It is used as a finishing screed to about 12mm (½") thick and allowed to dry thoroughly. It is then polished and rubbed up with a little oil which will give a fine gloss. Several references state that it is important to apply the finishing screed whilst the 'under flooring' is not too dry, in order that the two layers will be incorporated together (Neve, 1726; Salzman, 1952; Innocent, 1916; Smith, 1834).

Surface hardeners
Techniques for increasing the hardness of lime-based floor finishes given by Millar (1897) include:

○ Brushing the surface with copperas (ferrous sulphate).
○ The application of either alum, zinc or copper sulphate in solution are all recommended, also a drying oil like linseed oil or tung oil.
○ The addition of soapstone or talc to the mix.
○ Two coats of black solution made with 1lb of white shellac, ½lb of powered pumice stone, ¼lb lamp black, dissolved in 1 gallon of pure alcohol.

Other methods of hardening surfaces include incorporating carborundum or granite dust, or other finely divided hard materials such as iron filings, into the surface. These will harden but not reduce dusting, which is best achieved by oiling or waxing.

10.2   Roads

Lime stabilization
The use of lime for stabilizing clay has a long history, dating back more than 5000 years. Much of the detailed practical knowledge of this technique, used extensively in China and India, has either been confined locally to various regions within vast continents or lost over time. It was not until

Lime stabilization of M25 motorway, sub-grade, London, c. 1985

the middle of the twentieth century that soil-lime mixes were evaluated, and the techniques of soil mechanics developed in the USA and the UK to a level suitable for the construction of modern road bases.

Lime stabilization of sub-grades in the UK is carried out in accordance with the Department of Transport's (now the Highways Agency) Specification for Highway Works (1986) reissued in 1998 and last amended in May 2001. Quicklime is usually preferred to dry hydrate in the UK due to the generally wet ground conditions.

The following examples are typical of lime stabilization procedures. Although the machinery described is not always appropriate for low-cost applications, the principles and basic techniques may be applied at any scale. An indication of the reliability of this method is that it is used widely for roads, motorways, airports and car parks in Africa, Australia, America and Europe (Buxton Lime Industries, 1990).

Use of quicklime on waterlogged ground

On building sites or earth roads in the tropics during seasonal rains, work is often hampered and may be suspended altogether for long periods when wet weather makes the ground incapable of bearing traffic. Here lime can provide a simple and proven remedy if the soil contains a certain amount of clay.

Use is made of the reaction between lime and clay. Mixing lime with a wet clayey soil causes an immediate reduction in plasticity. The effect is permanent, and will in time be enhanced by additional slow hardening. Where the initial amount of moisture present is very great, quicklime may be used with advantage in place of hydrated lime to absorb some of the

179

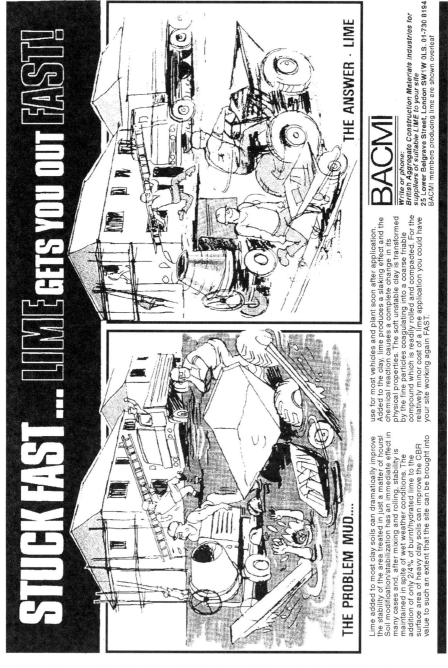

*Advertisement for the lime stablization of clay soils for building sites
(reproduced with permission of BACMI)*

water. This also raises the temperature, which assists drying and helps to speed up the chemical reaction process.

For any reaction to take place there must be a significant proportion of clay present in the soil. The soil may in fact be a clay, loam, or clay gravel, and the greatest strengths are normally attained with the latter, which is know also as 'hoggin' or 'wall-ballast'. The reaction takes place in two stages. The first, which occurs immediately after lime is mixed with the soil, consists of an ion exchange, which results in flocculation of the very fine particles of clay. The effective increase in particle size caused by flocculation brings about a substantial increase in the plastic limit, and the clay behaves as if it were much drier.

The second stage consists of a slow chemical reaction between the lime and the clay minerals, which hardens the soil by the formation of hydrated calcium silicates and aluminates, similar to those formed in the setting of Portland cement. Under cool weather conditions this hardening only becomes really significant after some weeks, but increases with age. The reaction is quicker in warmer climates (Buxton Lime Industries, 1990).

The amount of quicklime required varies from 2 to 6% by weight of the soil. If hydrated lime is used, up to 10% may be necessary. It is best to remove any top soil, which contains appreciable amounts of organic matter, and apply stabilization to the underlying inert layer, usually to a depth of about 150mm (6").

The usual method of application is *mix in place*, where the soil is first scarified and pulverized to the depth required. Hydrated lime or quicklime is spread over it either from a vehicle or by placing bags of lime at regular intervals and raking out the contents. The lime is mixed with the soil either by a rotary tiller or by hand, followed by hoeing and raking over. This is wetted by a water spray, and compacted preferably by rolling.

In the *plant mix* method, the soil and lime are mixed in a mixing machine, spread on the ground and compacted.

Road formation

The method by which clay-rich soils are stabilized by lime has been outlined above and in the previous chapter. Civil engineering contractors make use of this process for road construction. The description given below is based on methods that have been used for the formation (sub-surface base) of roads in Northamptonshire, and parts of the M25 London Orbital Motorway completed in the 1980s. Clay sub-grades have been regularly stabilized with lime for the construction of roads in North America and Europe, where it was accepted as normal practice well before current levels of use in the UK.

Stabilized soil samples are tested prior to proceeding with construction. Tests have shown that after seven days the Californian Bearing Ratio

Lime stabilization of road base
A: 15mm (½") quicklime 'carpet'; B: Clay-rich subsoil; C: Rota teeth
370mm (15") deep; D: Mixed material before rolling

(CBR), which is similar to compressive strength, can rise from 2% to over 30% with the addition of 3% lime.

Clay treated *in situ* to a depth of 350mm (14") in two or more layers forms a capping complying with the Highways Agency standards for road pavement design.

In the Northamptonshire example the top soil was removed and quicklime was spread as a two-metre-wide carpet, 15mm (½") thick. The mixing operation, the next stage, was carried out by a pulverizing machine designed for stabilizing operations. The cutting depth of the rota teeth was 370mm (15").

The formation was then trimmed, lightly rolled to seal the surface and left for a minimum of two days to allow the lime to commence its reaction. After this a second mixing operation was carried out. The formation was then retrimmed and compacted with six to eight passes of a vibrating roller. After seven days the 30% CBR value was achieved (Fulalove, 1982).

10.3   Lime concrete

Many of the most important historic buildings regularly visited and in use today owe their presence and continued stability to lime concrete foundations. Examples in the UK include the Houses of Parliament, Westminster Bridge, Lincoln Crown Court and the British Museum. There are many other examples of the successful use and durability of lime concrete, the most durable being the magnificent engineering achievements of the Romans. Domes, vaults, bridges, viaducts, cisterns and dams using lime concrete have lasted in the order of 2000 years. A number of these continue in use and can be seen throughout Europe and North Africa.

Lime concrete has a long and well-documented history, like most building materials that use lime as a binder. In an agricultural treatise in about 160 BC, Cato wrote a detailed description of the construction of a lime kiln and the burning of lime. He also wrote about lime concrete.

Walls

Lime concrete technology appears to have developed rapidly before and during Cato's lifetime in conjunction with a technique of mixing lime mortar with broken stone or brick rubble to be used for infilling walls (Adam, 1994). It was common practice to build walls of two facing skins and infill with a mixture of lime mortar (coarse stuff) and small broken stones to form a rubble core known as *opus caementicium*. Often the rubble would contain broken tiles, bricks and debris from stone cutting.

Some walls of lime concrete still stand today, examples of which can be seen at Pompeii. Evidence suggests that natural hydraulic limes were seldom used in southern Europe, but artificial hydraulic lime was common. Vitruvius gives a specification for mortars in regular use, selected for different building requirements. These range from a ratio of $1:2$ for lime : pozzolan for maritime works which suffer continually damp or wet conditions, to a $1:3$ lime : sand ratio for parts of buildings receiving less severe weathering. Other mixes included $1:2$ ratio for lime : river sand and $1:2:1$ ratio for lime : river sand : broken and crushed clay tile.

Superstructure

It was realized that by designing a lime-concrete mix incorporating varying degrees of pozzolan, the speed and depth of set, the workability, and variations in the strength–weight ratio could be controlled. This understanding lead to the design of the most remarkable lime-concrete structures. The Pantheon has been mentioned in the introductory chapter. Although it is probably the largest, it is only one of many lime-concrete structures of the period employing the same principle. Arches, vaults and domes were designed as structural forms, in conjunction with specific lime-concrete mixes. Materials, often of volcanic origin, such as pumice and tufa, as well as amphorae (hollow clay pots) buried in the masonry were selected for lightness at the higher levels.

The Pantheon has a total of six zones of differing lime-concrete materials. The lightest mix for the capping at the top of the dome is a lime concrete using tufa and aerated lava as the aggregate. The zone below is of alternating tufa rubble and brick. The next zone, incorporating the springing of the dome, is of lime concrete using only brick fragments. The upper vertical section of the wall has a mixture of tufa and bricks. The lower section of wall is tufa and travertine rubble. The foundations are lime concrete with travertine rubble to a thickness of 4.5m (14').

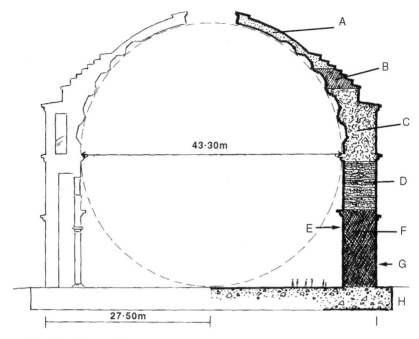

The Pantheon, Rome, 124ad: lime concrete fill between facings (Adam, 1994)
A: Aerated lava and tufa rubble (1.2m thick); B: Brick and tufa rubble; C: Broken brick fill; D: Opus caementicium with mixed tufa and bricks; E: Internal marble lining; F: Travertine rubble and tufa core; G: External brick facing; H: Opus caementicium with travertine rubble only

In addition to the magnificent civic buildings of Rome, the civil engineering structures also incorporate lime concrete. Many of the massive aqueducts, bridges, and reservoirs, although faced in stone or brick, owe much of their strength and stability to a lime-concrete core.

Marine works

Much of the science developed by the Romans for successful lime-concrete structures was lost until the eighteenth century. The growth of civil engineering programmes in Europe for the construction of bridges, harbours and canals gave rise to an immense demand for hydraulic building limes. Extensive research was carried out into natural and artificial hydraulic limes to meet this demand. By the beginning of the nineteenth century, lime concrete was once again being used prodigiously. The type of use was mainly restricted to the sub-structure of large buildings, bridges, canals, harbours and walls. It did not reach the technical level achieved in many of the outstanding engineering feats of the Romans.

The climate and geology of Italy favours the use of artificial hydraulic limes for civil engineering. The abundance of readily-available volcanic material, for example, is significant. The climate becomes progressively colder further north in Europe and there is less natural pozzolan. Both temperature and the reactive quality of pozzolan have marked effects on the speed of set and final strength of the mix. It is not surprising, therefore, that in the nineteenth century, at the time of the industrial revolution, there was extensive research into artificial and natural hydraulic limes.

In massive lime-concrete engineering structures, it is not possible to rely solely on carbonation to provide a set. The research, development and use of locally available natural and artificial hydraulic limes by incorporating pozzolans increased at an accelerating pace about this time. Leaders in the field were J. Smeaton (1724–92) and L.J. Vicat (1786–1861).

Following extensive research, Smeaton (1793) concluded that the most satisfactory mortar for use in construction of the Eddystone Lighthouse was a mix of one part of Blue Lias hydraulic lime from Aberthaw with one part of Italian Pozzolana.

Pozzolans researched and used by Smeaton for other marine projects included Dutch Tarras, Italian Pozzolana, and English Minion, a name given to burnt and crushed ironstone. One way of obtaining this was by using cleaned, powdered and sifted smith's forge scales. He recorded twenty compositions for 'Water Mortar' or hydraulic lime mortar, the principal mixes for which are given below. Variations of these include higher

Table 10.1: Hydraulic mortar mixes recommended by J. Smeaton (1793)

	Hydraulic lime powder	Pozzolana	Sand
Eddystone mortar	1	1	–
Stone mortar	2	1	1
Face mortar	2	1	3
Backing mortar	2	¼	3
	Hydraulic lime powder	Minion	Sand
Face mortar	2	2	1
Mortar for Calder Canal	2	1	2
Backing mortar	2	½	3
	Common lime	Tarras	Sand
Tarras mortar (face mortar)	2	1	0–3 depending on strength required
Tarras backing mortar	2	½	3
	Common lime	Minion	Sand
Face mortar	1	1	1
Backing mortar	2	½	3

proportions of sand for less demanding situations or where the pozzolan and sand available are of excellent quality.

Sand was graded; for example, the sand for the Calder Canal lock was one part coarse sand to one part fine sand. Pozzolana for the Eddystone Lighthouse was from Civita Veccia, Italy.

Smeaton stressed the importance of mixing all the ingredients well in a dry state first, and then with the addition of a minimum quantity of water, beating all very thoroughly to form a paste of even consistency. The Eddystone mortar joint surfaces were coated over with plaster of Paris for initial protection against immediate washing by the sea.

10.4   Hydraulic mortar and concrete specifications

The way in which lime concrete was used before the general acceptance of Portland cement can be best illustrated by some typical nineteenth century specifications collected and published at the time (Rivington, 1899; Macey, 1904; Donaldson, 1860).

Nineteenth century lime concrete specifications in Europe

Foundations at Wellington College A specification for lime-concrete foundations in the UK for the external walls of the towers of Wellington College, near Sandhurst, Berkshire used one part ground stone lime to six parts gravel, first well mixed dry, then wetted and shot from a height of at least 6 feet.

Foundations for house in Grosvenor Square, London   Foundations for a house in Grosvenor Square were specified to be composed of one part fresh burnt ground Dorking stone lime to six parts clean washed Thames ballast. The ballast was sifted coarse and mixed in small quantities with the quicklime. While the mix was hot (still slaking) it was shot into the foundation trenches from a height not less than six feet.

Burnell (1867) strongly recommended that concrete should *not* be placed by shooting in from a great height. Rather that it should be barrowed in for filling the excavation in layers of between 220mm (9") and 300mm (12") depth and firmly rammed down. Depth of lime concrete foundations recommended are between 300mm and 1200mm (1' and 4') depending on ground conditions and weight of superstructure.

Thames ballast was a natural blend of sand and gravel aggregate. This approximated to a mix of sand and small stones in the proportion of 2 : 4 or 2 : 5; the largest of the small stones being the size of a 'hen's egg'. Some of this would be a gravel of intermediate size. In a more precise specification given by Gwilt (1894), the proportion of sand to stone is recommended as 1 : 2. The average of a range of concrete mixes and one corroborated in text books of the

186

period is a ratio of 1 : 2 : 5 hydraulic lime : sand : gravel. In the UK it was often specified that the lime should be mixed in as quicklime fresh from the kiln before adding water. In France the lime was generally mixed in as a putty.

Bridge of Souillac on the Dordogne by L.J. Vicat   Mortar was prepared as a putty in paste form first and then mixed with the aggregate for foundation concrete. The mixture was as follows:

26 parts of hydraulic lime in paste
39 parts of granitic sand
66 parts of gravel

Set out as a simple ratio proportion this closely equates to a ratio of 2 : 3 : 5 of lime : sand : gravel.

Westminster Bridge, London   Foundations for the new (nineteenth century) Westminster Bridge across the Thames between Westminster and Lambeth were specified by the engineer Thomas Page (Donaldson, 1860).

○ '*Lime*: to be best Blue Lias lime, thoroughly burned, and quite free from core, and used hot from the kiln, where practicable.'
○ '*Mortar*: composed of Blue Lias lime in one part with three parts of clean, sharp river sand, free from all vegetable substance and screened. The lime properly slaked and thoroughly mixed with the sand with no more water than necessary to bring it to a proper consistency.' Page emphasizes that on no account is any to be used that has become partially set, nor any water to be added to the mortar after it is once mixed. He also states that the mortar shall not be mixed in a pug mill but shall in all cases be beaten up to the proper consistency, 'as practised in former ·times' (i.e. pounded and turned by hand).
○ '*Concrete for piers*: below high water mark shall be composed of four parts clean gravel and one part well-burnt Blue Lias lime, properly slaked under sand, and well mixed with the gravel. No more water to be used than is sufficient to render the concrete solid.'
○ '*Concrete for filling in abutments, backs of approach walls and spandrels of arches*: composed of five parts clean river gravel and one part lime. The concrete shot, as soon as mixed, into place in all cases from a height of not less than 12', and rammed with broad heavy pinners. No concrete to be mixed or thrown into place during frosty or very wet weather. Heavy stone or iron slag to be used with the concrete as directed by the Engineer.' The concrete was faced in stone or brick, and the piers and abutments were supported on bearing piles of English elm.

Railway bridge at Newcastle, England   Robert Stevenson, for a bridge on the Newcastle and Berwick Railway at Newcastle in 1847, specified

Lyme Regis (Blue Lias) mortar for base piers to a height of 6' above high water, and pointed in Roman Cement. The rest of the work above this level was with mortar from the Fulwell lime kilns at a ratio of 3 : 1, all ground in a pug mill.

Quay wall at Newcastle, England Extension of the quay wall at Newcastle-upon-Tyne, specification by John Dobson, architect.

○ '*Mortar*: For the front ashlar to be of the best Dorset lime from Lyme Regis (Blue Lias), to be burnt at Newcastle, and when slaked to be mixed with one part of clear sharp sand, from the mouth of the Derwent, to one part of lime, to be kept dry until wanted. Then to be added 1 part of iron dust or slag and one part of clear 'scars' which must be previously ground under edge stones, and the whole passed through a screen to separate it from coarse particles.' ['Scars' were probably waste in the form of clinker or slag from the iron foundry.] The work was carried out behind the protection of a coffer dam and principally in stone. A puddled clay wall was built behind the quay wall three feet thick to make the structure impervious to water.

Viaduct at Bawtry, England Bawtry viaduct for the Great Northern Railway, specification by the engineer, W.M. Brydone, 1856. Concrete to be composed of the best, strong, hydraulic lime, mixed with clean gravel in the proportion of one lime to six gravel. Mortar in the piers and abutments to be composed of three sand to two hydraulic lime, and in the arches of one sand to one hydraulic lime. The whole of the mortar for the entire building to be perfectly ground between stones in a pug-mill.

Rapid setting concrete for maritime works George R. Burnell, writing in 1867, quotes a specification by Treussart which is as follows:

'30 parts of hydraulic lime, very energetic, measured in bulk and before being slaked
30 parts of trass from Andernach
30 parts of sand
20 parts of gravel
40 parts of broken stone, a hard limestone'

A similar concrete, recommended by Burnell for the same purpose, but using Italian pozzolan is given as:

33 parts of energetic hydraulic lime, measured before slaking
45 parts of pozzolan
22 parts of sand
60 parts of broken stone and gravel

Burnell recommends that the first of these concretes should be used immediately it is made whilst the second should be mixed and left to lay in the open for about 12 hours before it is put in place.

Further recommendations for placing lime concrete are that it should be spread in layers from 250mm to 300mm (10" to 12") in thickness, and well rammed, until the mortar begins to flush up at the top. Strength increases steadily during the first six or seven months and Burnell recommends that the lime concrete should be left undisturbed for that length of time if possible.

Artificial hydraulic lime for canals and harbours

Vicat records the use of artificial hydraulic lime in the concrete prepared for the canals of Saint Martin and Saint Maur in France at the beginning of the nineteenth century. This was also used for the harbour at Toulon and for bridge foundations. It was composed of hydraulic lime and rubble, in which the lime is slaked before it is mixed with the aggregate. The artificial hydraulic lime used was prepared in one of two ways. Vicat considers the best is made by mixing slaked fat lime (Class A) with a proportion of clay, one dry clay to four lime. This mixture was prepared as a paste, then dried and burnt a second time. He termed this 'artificial lime twice kilned'.

The second method was to take a soft limestone such as chalk or tufa which had been crushed to fine dust and made into a paste with water. This was mixed, usually in the proportions of 1 dry clay to 7 parts of crushed limestone (chalk). The optimum quantity of clay varied with locality and Vicat considered the finest and softer clays were the best.

At a factory in Meudon near Paris, chalk and clay was mixed in a horse-driven mill with harrows and rakes. Four measures of chalk to one of clay were added successively, together with water, for about an hour and a half. This would produce about 1.5 cubic metres of thin paste. It was then drained into a series of pans at lower levels where the paste would settle out, after which the clear water was drained off. (Vicat, Articles 44–55, 1837).

After the excess water had been removed, the firmer paste would be moulded into small prisms which were set out to dry on shelves. Following initial drying they became hard enough to burn in a lime kiln. This artificial hydraulic lime mortar, mixed with sand, gravel and stone aggregate was used for the canals of Saint Martin and Saint Maur, locks, and for the foundation of one of the piers over the Dordogne at Souillac.

10.5   Lime concrete canal lining in India

The Indian Standard IS:7873 (1975) Code of Practice for lime concrete lining for canals was reprinted in June 1990. The crushing strength requirement for the lime-concrete mix given in this standard is 5 N/mm^2 at 28 days, following moist curing.

The standard stipulates a mix of $1:1\frac{1}{2}:3$, kankar lime : kankar grit or sand : kankar aggregate, stone aggregate or brick ballast. Kankar aggregate, stone aggregate or brick ballast is to be sufficiently large for not more than 5% to pass a 20mm mesh sieve. Kankar lime is defined under IS:7873 as comprising:

Calcium oxide (CaO) and magnesium oxide (MgO) = 50% minimum in total

Magnesium oxide (MgO) = 6% maximum

Silica (SiO_2), alumina (Al_2O_3) and ferrous oxide (Fe_2O_3) = 20% minimum in total

Carbon dioxide (CO_2) = 5% maximum

Free moisture content = 2% maximum

Fineness – residue on a 300 micron sieve = 5% maximum

Time for initial set 2 hours minimum

Time for final set 48 hours maximum

Minimum compressive strength 1.0 N/mm² at 14 days and
1.75 N/mm² at 28 days

Kankar lime is another term for hydraulic lime prepared from limestone containing active clays.

Kankar Grit is defined (IS:7873) as a fine pozzolanic aggregate which may be clean, ground cinder screened through an 8 mesh to 1" sieve (2mm apertures), (IS:320). Presumably other pozzolanic materials locally available, ground to the same fineness, such as broken brick or clay tile may also be used.

The thickness of the canal lining is given as 100mm-150mm for normal canal flow rates.

Transport of lime putty and mixed material during hot or cold weather must be in deep containers. This reduces the rate of water loss by evaporation during hot weather, and the smaller surface area tends to reduce heat loss and the risk of freezing during cold weather.

Compaction when laying is to be continuous as the material is spread. All compaction has to be completed within 12 hours of laying. The lining is finished by trowelling up the compacted lime concrete with wood and steel floats.

After trowelling the surface must be kept damp continuously for at least 14 days by fine spraying or covering with damp sand, straw or hessian, which must be kept continuously moist for this period.

10.6 Water mortars for making lime concretes

Lime mortars designed to resist permanently wet conditions and often required to set under water were named 'water mortars' by Smeaton (1793). Both Smeaton and Vicat (1837) stress the importance of taking into account the variations that occur in all the natural materials used. Each material – clay, sand, aggregate, limestone and pozzolan – will vary depending on locality.

The common factor in all hydraulic mixes is the need to provide a strong binder that will set rapidly and remain sound in wet conditions. This is achieved by promoting a reaction between lime and active clays by burning and mixing in optimum proportions. Limestone may contain any amount of this 'active clay' material ranging from nil to 50% or more (see Appendix 1). The best mix will result in chemical compounds similar to, but less complex than, those of Portland cement.

Clay and pozzolans contain varying proportions of silica, alumina and ferrous oxides. In order to achieve the strongest set approximately 35% of this, as a proportion of the total mix, needs to combine fully with the lime. It is likely that some proportion of the clay or pozzolan will not be reactive, particularly the larger and poorly burnt material. This may be part of the reason for Smeaton's (1793) choice of 50% pozzolan to 50% lime for Eddystone (as opposed to 35% pozzolan) in the mix.

The essentials to achieve a good hydraulic lime mortar or concrete are therefore:

○ Well-selected raw materials of even consistency.
○ Well-burnt material. Both clay and lime should be burnt at a low even temperature of approximately 900°C.
○ An optimum proportion of active clay or pozzolan in the mix. This will vary upwards from, 1 active clay to 3 lime, to 1 : 1 or more, depending on local materials, the strength required, and the efficiency of mixing.
○ A thorough mixing of the pozzolan or burnt clay with the lime. This may be achieved by pounding the pozzolanic material to a fine powder and mixing in a dry state first, or by building up a slurry with wet material, drying out and re-firing. Generally particle size is best kept below 0.3mm. Current research (Teutonico *et al.*, 1994) suggests that it is predominantly the material below 75μm (0.075mm) which is likely to be reactive.
○ A minimum addition of water to the mortar mix.
○ Thorough mixing with the sand and/or aggregate before placing.
○ Thoroughly compacting all material in layers as the work proceeds.
○ Protection after completion of the work, particularly under water where the material may wash out. It should be remembered that the initial set may take two or three days or more. Noticeable hardening will usually continue for well over two years before final strength is achieved. If it is allowed to harden out of water it must be kept moist as described for the curing of mortar and pointing for walls in Chapter 5 and in canal linings in IS 7873, 1975 (see Appendix 4).
○ Normal curing requirements as for external render.

Whilst lime concrete is satisfactory when used in bulk for foundations and walls it must not be considered as a direct substitute for Portland cement concrete. Portland cement concrete has both tensile and compressive strengths far in excess of lime concrete. Portland cement is suitable for engineered reinforced structures with large spans. *The science of using lime concrete in a similar way to Portland cement concrete for structural frames has not been developed.* There is, however, considerable potential for further research and development of lime concrete for its application as an appropriate building technology.

11

Limestone recognition, testing and standards

11.1 Field investigation

Methods of investigating limestone areas as potential sources of local building limes are described here; once recognized, they may be investigated further with field tests and matched to their appropriate uses.

Limestone is often a firm rock that forms features on the landscape such as hills, a scarp or cliffs. The more recent formations such as chalk, although sufficiently dense to endure as weathered outcrops, are much softer and less durable. At the same time most limestones are slightly soluble in water, which gives rise to the formation of caves, open crevices and pot-holes in the ground. Soil and plant cover is often thin and the soil, though lying on alkaline rocks, may be slightly acidic due to being well drained.

An appropriately experienced geologist will be able to give general information about limestones in a particular area and advise on availability. Some readers may, however, wish to make their own observations and carry out preliminary investigations. It is helpful to know how limestones are formed as this assists in understanding the way different building limes may be used.

Wingate (1985) details some of the initial steps to be taken when prospecting for limestone. Data concerning the location and preparation of raw materials for building-lime manufacture is given in detail in Chapter 3 of that book. Recommendations include making reference to the Geological Survey, usually found in a department of a government ministry, and to geological survey maps.

There are various locations where geological observations may be made without difficulty. These include areas of natural exposure such as cliff faces, river banks, particularly those cut away by water erosion, wave-cut coastal areas and exposed rock outcrops on hillsides and on stream and river beds.

Artificial exposures can also be a useful source of information. A great deal may be learnt from observing banks at roadsides where they have been worn down by traffic. Artificial exposures include small excavations such as where ditches, foundation trenches and wells have been dug, or on a larger scale, railway cuttings, road cuttings and canals. Geological observations may be made of the sub-soil and rock strata below normal ground level at these and similar locations.

11.2   Geological origin of rocks

Recognition of the various limestone types can best be discussed in relation to their origin. The geology of the differing limestone types is therefore described here in some detail.

Sedimentary rocks

Sedimentary rock originated as sediments, usually derived from the weathering and disintegration either of previously existing rocks or of debris from marine life. This fine-grained material was produced by water or wind erosion, and it was carried, largely by rivers, to be deposited in lake and ocean depressions, or spread over the surface of the sea bed. Limestone consists mainly, or entirely, of material produced by plants or animals, or from calcitic material precipitated from water by bacterial or chemical action.

The skeletons and shells of marine animals are mainly, if not entirely, calcium carbonate. When the animals die, their shells and bones fall to the sea bed and mix with accumulating inorganic sediment. The inorganic sediment is produced by weathering and disintegration of material, usually from land formations. The eroded material is washed away and discharged into seas or lakes. The further the inorganic material is from its origin, the

Quarry face of oolitic limestone showing the strata of the sediment laid down, Daglingworth quarry, Cirencester, UK, 1996

greater the proportion of calcareous material. In many cases calcareous material can make up virtually the entire deposit, which produces a pure limestone used in many manufacturing processes including the production of 'pure' Class A building lime.

The sediments that make up limestone can accumulate simultaneously with those of clay, silt and sand. Some of these impurities are the origin of the 'active clay' component of hydraulic limes and natural cements. One of the most favourable conditions for a build up of sediment is near the coast of seas and lakes, often in shallow water, and where there is little or no wave action on the coastline. The silts and sands effectively 'dilute' the lime and give rise to the lean Class B limes.

Igneous rocks
The word 'igneous' is derived from the Latin word for fire. Igneous rocks were once molten material which emerged by volcanic action from below the earth's crust. Igneous limestone is rare, but an example may be found near Tororo, Uganda.

Metamorphic rock
Derived from the Greek meaning 'change of form', this is rock that has undergone a transformation, usually as a result of extremes of heat and pressure. Originally these were sedimentary or igneous rocks, subsequently completely altered in texture and mineral composition by extremes of heat, pressure and chemical change. Examples are marble, schist and slate. Marble is formed by heat and pressure acting on limestone. Pure limestone is recrystallized into tightly interlocking calcite crystals. Impure limestones tend to result in lime silicate minerals with more colourful variations, and are suitable for cutting and polishing for decorative finishes. Marble was, and is still, regularly used for floor and wall finishes. Marble (often in the form of quarry waste) can be burnt to produce building limes. Where it is abundant, such as in Italy, it has been used extensively to produce lime for mortars and renders.

11.3   Limestone recognition
Fossiliferous limestone
Many limestones contain fossils of plants and animals or their remains, such as shells, laid down during the sedimentary process. These fossiliferous limestones occur in many parts of the world and are not difficult to identify. Coral deposits, for example, are quarried inland for lime burning in East Africa, and in a number of other countries today. Young coral is a very new material in geological terms, although it also occurs as easily recognizable fossils in older rock formations which can date back as far as 400 million years. Other fossiliferous limestones include identifiable plant and animal remains such as the fossils or imprints of oyster and other mollusc shells, crinoids, bryozoa and brachiopods.

Fossiliferous limestone (Natural History Museum, London)

An oolitic limestone (Natural History Museum, London)

Oolitic limestone

Some limestones are composed of a finer sediment of much smaller fossils and a matrix of calcitic cement. The structure of oolitic limestone consists of grains which may vary in size from the diameter of a pea to smaller than a pin's head. Stones composed of the largest grains are called pisolite, or pea-stone. The growth of the oolite grain was often a combination of chemical and mechanical processes. After the calcium carbonate is deposited, there may be some picking up of foreign matter as the grains move about. On the West Indian coral reefs it was observed and first recorded by de la Beche (1853), that at the centre of the grains there are fragments of shells, corals and foraminifere. Very fine layers of calcium carbonate are

196

deposited on these grains and with the build up of each layer they become more spherical.

The result is a fine-grained, evenly-textured stone resembling fish roe in appearance. Due to the evenly distributed high calcium carbonate content, it is usually light in colour unless stained with pigmentation from adjacent material. The more compact beds of oolitic stone can be accurately sawn to ashlar blocks or roughly dressed. It can also be split on its bedding plane. It is therefore used extensively for building construction in many forms. The calcium carbonate content is mostly between 75 and 96%, so it is also suitable for burning to produce building lime as a binder.

Chalk

Geological evidence suggests chalk was laid down in relatively shallow water of not more than 150 fathoms (North, 1930). In many areas, chalk contains minute spheroidal bodies less then 100 microns in diameter, too small to discern with the naked eye. These may be similar to oolitic grains, or they may be the remains of microscopic animals, shells and *coccoliths* (calcareous algae). This process of gradually building up microscopic calcitic animal remains is common in seas and lakes where the conditions are favourable. An example where this is taking place at present is in the sea off the Bahamas. The further from land that the chalk deposits are laid down, the less they are mixed with silt brought down by rivers and carried into the sea. As the land-derived sediment becomes less, the proportion of calcium carbonate increases, until virtually nothing else but the calcareous material accumulates. The exceptionally fine grain, soft texture and whiteness of the pure calcium carbonate of chalk are distinctive characteristics. This white chalk will produce highly reactive quicklime when burnt, a pure, Class A non-hydraulic lime putty, and an excellent material for internal plastering. On the other hand, the grey chalk from the muddier deposits will produce a lime with hydraulic properties.

Magnesian limestone

Most aquatic organisms, in addition to contributing calcium carbonate ($CaCO_3$) for the limestone, also contain magnesium carbonate ($MgCO_3$) to varying degrees. Analysis of the skeletal remains of calcareous sponges, starfish and crustaceans show that they contain up to 14% or more magnesium carbonate. Those of calcareous algae range between nil to over 25% magnesium carbonate (Twenhofel, c. 1900). The calcareous sediment is therefore likely to contain greater proportions of magnesium carbonate where there has been a concentration of this type of sea creature. In addition, the magnesium carbonate tends to pass into solution in water. The percolation of magnesium carbonate-bearing water through accumulating sediment can result in greater chemical concentrations as the magnesium and calcium carbonates unite forming the double carbonate, dolomite ($CaCO_3.MgCO_3$). In the Pacific Ocean, the coral of the atoll of Funafuti has a small percentage of magnesium carbonate at the surface. This increases continuously with depth to 300 metres (1000 ft), where the rock is almost entirely dolomite (Sollas, quoted in North, 1930).

Many limestones therefore contain magnesia in varying proportions. Opinions differ as to the amount that constitutes a magnesian limestone, but more than 20% is generally accepted, and it would not normally be considered as such below 15%.

The double carbonate of calcium and magnesium as a mineral, dolomite, contains 45.65% magnesium and 54.35% calcium (North, 1930). Strictly speaking therefore, there is a distinction between magnesian limestone which may contain variable quantities of magnesium carbonate $MgCO_3$, and dolomite which is a mineral composed of the double carbonate $CaCO_3.MgCO_3$. Truly dolomitic lime should logically therefore contain a significant proportion of this double carbonate.

Magnesian lime may contain magnesium carbonate and calcium carbonate separately, and not necessarily the mineral dolomite. These terms are used loosely and, to simplify definitions, usually only the proportion of magnesium carbonate is taken into account.

The American standard ANSI/ASTM C51–71:1976 gives the following limestone definitions:

High-calcium limestone – containing from 0 to 5% $MgCO_3$.
Magnesian limestone –   containing from 5 to 35% $MgCO_3$.
Dolomitic limestone –   containing from 35 to 46% $MgCO_3$.

Limestone suitable for hydraulic lime

Limestone suitable for producing hydraulic lime contains finely disseminated argillaceous material with potential pozzolanic properties, more simply described as 'active clay'. Chemically this is silica and alumina, probably also with ferrous oxide and other compounds. Clays incorporated in the stone are composed of minute inorganic particles, individually too small to see with the naked eye. The same compounds may also occur in larger particle sizes such as sands and silts which will not be reactive.

A typical rock form that will produce hydraulic lime is Blue Lias of the Lower Lias formation. This is a bluish grey colour, thinly bedded, on average 50mm to 250mm (2" to 10") in depth, sometimes separated by thin beds of shale. It is a combination of calcareous and argillaceous deposits, each bed containing varying proportions of silica and alumina. In some areas the original deposits may be of calcareous mud derived from land made up of carboniferous limestone. Some Lias beds contain a large proportion of fossils, including oyster shells and ammonites.

In a number of the Lias beds, very fine deposits of sediment laid down in alternating layers of calcium carbonate and clay can be clearly seen.

Section through Blue Lias limestone

A typical section of newly broken Blue Lias rock is shown 50% of actual size above. Methods of testing to determine the clay content of argillaceous limestones are given in Section 11.4. As most limestone is of sedimentary origin, providing the possibility that 'active clay' may be deposited at the same time as the calcareous material, certain carboniferous and meta-morphic limestones will also produce the full range of hydraulic limes.

Carboniferous limestone

Another term often used to describe this rock is mountain limestone. Its composition includes varieties that contain fossils of closely-packed shells, crinoids and coral, or fragments of these. It is a much older rock than chalk and oolitic limestone and appears to have been subjected to greater pres-sures. The term 'mountain limestone' indicates its nature; being generally dense and hard, and deposited to a great depth, between approximately 30m and 2000m (100 feet and 6000 feet). It can be seen in the form of moun-tainous ridges and imposing cliffs. Its specific gravity is in the order of 2.7.

Metamorphic limestone

During the course of geological time, material deposited on the earth's crust in horizontal layers has been subjected to movement and extreme pressure, throwing these layers into folds. Deeply buried material, and that subjected to volcanic action, has been affected by extreme heat which has changed the mineral composition. The older the formation, the more it is likely to have been affected by movement of the earth's crust, and the longer has been the

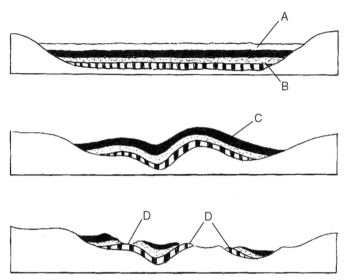

Sections through the earth's crust showing the changes that take place over geological time
A. Sea or lake; B. Sedimentary deposits; C. Movement of the earth's crust causes folds in the sedimentation layers; D. Erosion at the top of the folds exposes the lower strata of older formations.

period of hardening. Metamorphic limestones have been subjected to varying degrees of pressure and heat, which has produced the most dense rock. The hardest rocks are the least affected by erosion and are therefore often found in mountainous regions. The heat, pressure and turmoil to which the material has been subjected often result in rocks of very mixed colour which are so hard that they are very difficult to break.

Metamorphic rock may be of variable mineral composition, with ill-defined strata. It may be composed of a wide variety of mixed mineral

Table 11.1: Increasing weight and density of limestone relative to age

Stone	Geological period	Age (millions of years)	Weight per cubic foot (lbs)	Typical pore space (%)
Chalk	Cretaceous	70–135	100.7	46
Doulting stone	Middle Jurassic	159–180	129.1	14.46
Hopton Wood stone	Carboniferous	270–345	141.4	8.36
Carrara marble	Metamorphic	Over 500	146.2	0.78

Source: North, 1930

colours, or a bed or intrusion of one mineral, or it may be pure limestone which has been converted to marble. The colour variations seen in many polished marbles used for decorative finishes typify its variable appearance. These variations have come about by the formation of different minerals from impurities in the original rock. Pure limestones will be various shades of cream or white. Granular crystalline marbles are the most dense limestone form.

Calcareous nodules (septaria)

This type of nodule is formed in clay under similar conditions in various parts of the world. Fossils or shells in the mud give rise to a calcium carbonate-rich patch of clay which acts as a nucleus. Crystallization of the calcium carbonate produces a hardening of the outer surface. This is followed by further crystallization of the interior, subsequent shrinking and the development of cracks. The general arrangement of these cracks is polygonal (North, 1930, pp. 282–288). Percolating water then deposits calcite in the fissures formed resulting in clearly identifiable patterns of white/yellow calcite against a background of dark brown.

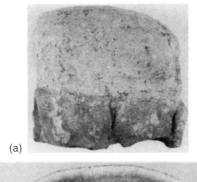

(a)

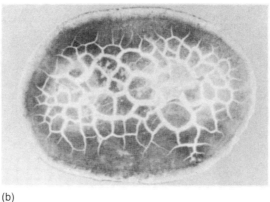

(b)

Septarian nodule 'as found' (above) and polished section through septarian nodule, England (Kirkaldy & Bates, 1988)

James Parker first took out a patent in 1796 to manufacture natural cement by the process of burning and grinding septaria found in layers in the London clay. The natural cement produced was termed Roman cement. It is a hydraulic cement that sets rapidly under water.

'Cement stones' have been discovered and used for producing 'Roman cement' in places as far apart as Illinios, Ohio and Virginia in the USA, Vassy and Theil in France and Calderwood in Scotland (Reid, 1869, p. 28).

Precipitation

The percolation of slightly acid water, and water containing dissolved carbon dioxide, over limestone causes it to dissolve to calcium bicarbonate. Calcareous matter that has been taken into solution is then deposited in crevices and on surfaces over which the water flows or percolates. These deposits are familiar in the form of stalagmites and stalactites inside caves, but also occur as tufa and travertine. Tufa is of even texture, usually light, porous and soft, whilst travertine is hard, compact and will take a polish. White is usually the predominant colour, but these deposits often contain impurities which produce yellows, browns, reds and sometimes green in various shades.

Calcium carbonate can crystallize as either calcite or aragonite, both of which are chemically entirely $CaCO_3$. Calcite crystals are hard, with a specific gravity of 2.72, rhombohedral, and normally appear translucent or transparent, without colour unless stained from adjacent impurities. They tend to form in small cavities, voids and fissures within or adjacent to limestone. Fibrous calcite sometimes occurs in narrow veins in the limestone bedding plane. This is a well known feature which some quarrymen term 'beef'.

These dissolved and redeposited calcium carbonates are seldom used independently for the production of building limes. Their recognition, however, will assist in confirming the existence of the main limestone deposits with which they are associated.

Calcite crystals and dolomite

The presence of calcite crystals in rock can be an indicator that the rock in which it is found is limestone, or that limestone is in close proximity. To test whether a crystal is of calcite, its hardness on the Moh hardness scale (3) can be checked by scratching with other materials of a hardness either side on this scale. A fingernail will not be able to mark it, but it can be scratched by broken glass or a copper coin. Crystals of quartz may look similar, but are much harder and cannot be scratched by glass.

To test chemically for calcite, using dilute hydrochloric acid, calcite (and pure marble) will effervesce vigorously and leave no residue. A 30% solution of aluminium nitrate $(Al\ (NO_3)_3)$ will stain calcite blue but will not stain dolomite. For another test, dolomite and calcite can be treated with dilute hydrochloric acid followed by spraying with Alizarin Red. The calcite will stain pink or red whilst the dolomite will not change colour (Wingate, 1985).

11.4   Field tests for lime

Following an initial investigation, or more detailed geological prospecting (Wingate, 1985), simple field tests can provide a wealth of information. The way in which the lime will perform in buildings can be assessed by some of these tests, which do not require laboratory equipment.

It should be noted that field test results, whilst extremely useful in giving a general indication of the lime type and its performance, cannot give the precise definition required by National Standards. National Standards for building limes set out methods of testing, most of which are performed under laboratory conditions, including control of ambient temperature and humidity. Tests of this nature are outlined in Section 11.6.

Limestone evaluation

In addition to visual identification, limestones may be field tested to assess the proportion of calcium carbonate, and to determine the presence and extent of active clay. The quickest and most straightforward test is chemical by use of hydrochloric or nitric acid, or possibly distilled vinegar. Information may also be gained by constructing a simple test kiln to burn a sample of limestone.

Each bed of limestone is likely to vary in depth and composition. This variation can be seen clearly in the Blue Lias formations mentioned previously, which have bed depths ranging between 50mm and 250mm (2" to 10"). These beds are well-defined, being interspersed with thin bands of shale. Other limestones may have been laid down to a much greater depth, but the composition of each bed is also likely to vary. In addition, these variable beds may either be adjacent to one another or interspersed with the strata of sedimentary rock containing no calcium carbonate at all. It is therefore most important to identify and record precisely the bed from which the test sample has been taken. Accurate evaluation will enable the development of selective and cost-effective quarrying in order to manufacture a product of consistent quality.

Determination of calcium and magnesium oxides

The calcium and magnesium content of limestone can be established in broad terms with a simple field test using dilute hydrochloric acid.

The amount of limestone required for a sample on which a field test is to be carried out need be little more than a few handfuls, enough to half fill a litre (quart) measure. The stone should be carefully selected to ensure that it is representative of the strata to be evaluated. The sample is broken up and crushed to dust. This can be done with a club hammer or similar. The stone should be crushed on a hard, clean surface and the powder sieved off into a small container. The container needs to be of clear glass or plastic; a glass jam jar or tall measuring flask will be adequate. Weigh the container, half fill it with the powdered stone and weigh again.

Slowly add either dilute hydrochloric acid (diluted approximately 1 : 10) or obtain this ready-prepared as a brick cleaner. Gradually add the diluted hydrochloric acid to the powdered limestone, stirring it all the time with a piece of wood or glass rod. Continue to add the acid in small amounts until the effervescence ceases.

Evaporate the solution once the effervescence has stopped, by heating gently until the liquid is reduced to a paste. Then mix the paste with half a litre of water, and filter. This separates the salts and the clay remains as a residue on the filter. Dry and weigh the remains of the sample to determine the amount of residue left, consisting of calcium and magnesium oxide, silica etc., deduct this from the original weight of the sample to determine the amount of carbon dioxide driven off. The greater this loss in weight, equivalent to the content of carbon dioxide, then the purer the limestone. A pure calcite limestone would show a weight loss of 44%.

If hydrochloric acid is unavailable, distilled vinegar may be substituted. Nitric acid can also be used for this test. Take great care with the acid as it will burn the skin if in direct contact.

Field test for clay content

Following the above test, the impurity that remains will contain varying amounts of clay, silt and sand. To determine the proportions, they may be separated by adding water and decanting to allow them to settle out in a flask or jar as described in the sediment test for sand later in this chapter. The greater the percentage of active clay, the more hydraulic will be the lime. Some clays are less active than others in terms of pozzolanic effect, but generally the more clay there is, the more likely it is that the limestone will produce a hydraulic lime. The proportions of active clay required to produce differing classes of lime to varying degrees of hydraulicity are given in Appendix 1. The less the proportion of clay and the greater the amount of silt and sand, the more lean the lime will be. All proportions in this test should be determined by weight (Burnell, 1867; Reid, 1869; Cowper, 1927). This is a field test, which will give only a general indication of the clay content of the stone. In more accurate tests, the quantity of calcium chloride remaining would be calculated, if not removed by titration.

Vicat (1837) did not recommend the above chemical analysis as he considered results too approximate. For the purpose of an initial field trial, however, this test does provide helpful information.

An alternative method of confirming the clay content is to burn the residue in a similar manner to that used in clay tile or brick production. The hardness of the resultant burnt clay, and its proportion in relation to the original sample, should give an indication of the class of hydraulic lime that may be obtained (Smeaton, 1793).

Firing trial field test

Whilst a general indication of the class of building lime that might be obtained from a limestone will be given by chemical analysis, a more detailed evaluation is possible with small-scale firing trials. The amount of stone required for the first stage of evaluation is small, as little as 3kg should suffice. The stones to be tested need to be broken into small lumps about the size of a walnut or small plum, say about 25mm to 50mm (1" to 2") in diameter. These can be burnt in a test kiln, which may be made of local material such as stone, brick or rammed earth. Advice on building a test kiln, as well as kilns for small-scale lime production is comprehensively set out by Wingate (1985). For the purpose of small-scale trials, small industries operating locally may be a source of kilns that could be used. Fired pottery, brick and tile works for example, will have kilns that might be suitable. It will be necessary to raise the temperature of the stone sample to a little over 900°C (bright cherry red) and maintain that for about four to five hours in a ventilated kiln to achieve full calcination.

After burning, field tests may be carried out to determine the class of building lime that can be produced from this limestone. Field tests for adequate calcination are given in this chapter in the section headed 'Field tests for quicklime'.

Classification by burning, slaking and hydraulic set

The method of classification was described by Vicat (1837), and the burning and slaking techniques were also described by Cowper (1927), Burnell (1867) and Reid (1869).

STAGE 1 – BURNING AND SLAKING

Firstly, fill a litre (quart) measure with the burnt quicklime lumps prepared by the firing trial method described above. Take care when handling the quicklime, which is caustic, by wearing protective clothing, particularly gloves and goggles.

Empty the measure of small lumps of quicklime into an open container such as a small woven basket, kitchen colander or sieve. Dip the container and contents into a bucket filled with fresh clean water so that the quicklime is fully covered. Hold it in position below the water for six seconds only, lift out the container, allow it to drain and empty the contents on to an inert surface such as metal, pottery or stone for observation. A large mortar (grinding bowl) or small metal bucket would be suitable.

The lime will behave in one of the following ways, which are also set out in summary form in Appendix 1 under the heading 'slaking rate'.

○ *Pure lime (Class A)* The lime hisses, swells rapidly, decrepitates, increases in temperature sufficiently to produce water vapour, and turns to powder almost immediately or within a few minutes.
○ *Lean lime (Class B)* There is no initial activity for up to six minutes, following which there is an energetic reaction by the lime as for pure lime.
○ *Slightly hydraulic lime (Class C1)* The lime is inactive for a longer period than for lean lime, up to quarter of an hour before there is any change. This will tend to be the slow opening up of cracks with little or no falling to powder. A small amount of vapour may be seen, but considerably less and cooler than for Class B.
○ *Moderately hydraulic lime (Class C2)* Similar to slightly hydraulic lime, but the change of state does not commence for at least an hour or more after immersion.
○ *Eminently hydraulic lime (Class C3)* An alteration in the state of the lime is barely noticeable, increase in temperature is slight and cracks formed are very small and in some cases do not appear at all.
○ *Natural cement (Class D)* Natural cements may contain up to twice as much active clay as eminently hydraulic lime and may therefore not slake at all. One conclusive field test that this is calcareous, other than by observation of fossil content, will be by testing with dilute acid as described in the section on chemical analysis.

The classification test may be developed by grinding the burnt stone to powder without the addition of water, then adding a small amount of water to make a paste to the consistency of stiff potter's clay. The paste is transferred to a tall container such as a drinking glass, jam jar, pot, or open-topped can, to about three-quarters of its height. The container should be struck on the underside gently to ensure the paste is uniformly concentrated from the bottom upwards. The container is then filled to the top with clean water. A natural cement will set rapidly under water within a few hours and in some cases in as little as 15 minutes (Rivington, 1899). There will be very little or no expansion of the material.

Natural cements were produced extensively in America and Europe in the 19th century and a substantial amount is still in production today, despite the advent of artificial cements. Parker's Roman cement made from burnt and ground septaria, would sometimes set in less than one hour and regularly under two. Other natural cements take the same order of time to set, some a little longer but mostly in less than a day.

STAGE 2 – HYDRAULIC SET
Lime of Classes A, B and C may be tested for setting time in a similar way to natural cement, with a small variation in preparation of the paste as

more energetic slaking occurs. After the initial slaking a small amount of water is poured down the inside face of the container, not directly on to the lime. The lime is stirred with a spatula at the same time and a pestle may be used to work it up to a paste the consistency of very stiff potter's clay. Care is taken to add only sufficient water and not to drown it.

The lime paste is left for a minimum of three hours, or until it has fully cooled, whichever is the longer. It is then worked over again with the pestle and brought to a final consistency similar to that of clay ready for making pottery.

The procedure of filling a tall glass or other container with the paste and immersing it in water is the same as described above for natural cement.

In order to judge when the paste has set, the simplest test is to press a finger into it at arm's length. It is considered set when no depression or alteration to its form occurs until it breaks.

A more controlled setting time field test, useful for the comparative testing of several limes, may be carried out with a simple piece of equipment. This consists of a knitting needle, bone or metal rod with a sharpened point of one millimetre (0.04 of an inch) square at one end. At the other end is fastened a standard weight of 0.3kg (say 10oz). Gently lower the point on to the lime at intervals, carefully noting the time from immersion of the sample. The lime is taken as set (initial set) when it bears the point of the needle without forming a depression in the surface.

Both the length of time before set, and the expansion, are further indicators of the class of lime produced. It must be noted, however, that these are field test results only. It will be necessary to obtain verification by laboratory analysis to substantiate a formal classification.

Classification of limes by setting time and expansion
Since the mid eighteenth century the following classification by setting time and expansion rate has been broadly accepted:

- *Pure lime (Class A)* Consistency of putty remains unchanged and will never set under water. Volume is at least doubled by slaking.
- *Lean lime (Class B)* Consistency is similar to pure lime but there is also likely to be a residue which usually sinks to the bottom and can become quite firm after a few weeks. Expansion is variable, up to double the volume.
- *Slightly hydraulic lime (Class C1)* This will set slowly, the initial set taking up to a month or more. Rivington (1899) suggests between 15 and 20 days. Final set to the consistency of hard soap takes about one year. The increase in volume is similar to that of lean lime.
- *Moderately hydraulic lime (Class C2)* Sets in six to ten days following immersion and hardens progressively up to one year, to consistency of soft stone. Expansion is small (25% or less).

○ *Eminently hydraulic lime (Class C3)* Sets rapidly, usually between two and four days from covering with water; hard and insoluble after one month and fractures under a hammer blow after six. Expansion is normally small, similar to moderately hydraulic limes.

The speed of set and compressive strength of all hydraulic limes and natural cements will be affected by higher burning temperatures (1250 to 1400°C) and fineness of grinding. Hydraulic limes do not have to be ground if fineness is controlled by sieving or air separation. There is likely to be greater consistency and reliability where sieving or air separation is used as a method of quality control, as it removes the possibility of over-burnt and under-burnt material being ground and introduced into the product. On the other hand, there may be economic reasons for the producer to omit this step.

○ *Natural cement (Class D)* This is prepared by burning a lime with high clay content at higher temperatures than fat lime, and grinding the sintered material. It is not slaked. Set is very rapid and will be affected by burning temperature, fineness of grinding and whether sand is added to the mix. Set may be expected to take between 15 minutes and two hours. Very fine grinding, optimum burning temperature and little or no sand (1 : 1 or less) will all increase speed of set.

Field tests for magnesian limes

If carefully burnt, and given sufficient time to hydrate, a magnesian lime can be an excellent material. If not burnt and prepared with care, or disturbed when setting, however, lime with a high magnesium content may not bind at all, and will fall to powder. Calcined magnesia (MgO) does not slake with the addition of water like calcium oxide (quicklime) but combines with water gradually (Rivington, 1899).

The conversion of magnesium carbonate ($MgCO_3$) to magnesia (MgO) begins at 725°C, which is much lower than 900°C for the equivalent conversion of calcium carbonate to quicklime. The consequence of this is that if a magnesian limestone (which contains both magnesium and calcium carbonates) is burned at the higher temperature, the magnesia will be over-burnt. In that form the quicklime will not normally slake fully – if at all. This quicklime is harder and absorbs water at a far slower rate than a high calcium quicklime.

When magnesian limes are burnt at these higher temperatures in commercial production, they are usually hydrated under pressure in an autoclave, but can also sometimes be slaked over a very long period in a lime pit. The alternative is to burn them at the lower temperature so that the calcium carbonate remains unconverted. Identification of magnesian limes is clearly very important, and the following tests may be used:

Using the dilute hydrochloric acid test, magnesian limestone will fizz slowly, while pure dolomite will dissolve only if the acid is heated (Wingate, 1985).

Another test is to crush the stone to powder and place a small quantity in a crucible. Heating this suddenly will make it jump if it is a magnesian limestone, possibly enough to leave the container completely. In comparison, calcite can be safely heated the same way without this effect.

Provided magnesian lime is not overburnt and it is left undisturbed, it is able to harden under water, although this is best achieved by allowing the paste to dry well before immersion. This set is also assisted if a very small (up to 5%) proportion of clay is present (Burnell, 1867). When magnesium carbonate exceeds 30% it enables the lime to set, independently of any active clay content (Rivington, 1899, p. 153). It will make a hard and durable mortar or render when mixed with sand in the proportion of 3 or less sand to 2 lime. It should set within two to three days of immersion if undisturbed (Vicat, 1837).

Dolomites are slightly heavier and harder than limestone without magnesia of a similar texture and porosity. Pure dolomite is white but impurities present, often iron, tend to tint it red, brown or yellow. The process of dolomitization often produces minute rhombohedral crystals which line small internal voids. This process, due to the marginally higher specific gravity of dolomite over calcite, tends to reduce bulk and creates a porous texture. This, combined with the rock's hardness, can give it a similar appearance to sandstone.

Field tests for quicklime

Well-burnt limestone will produce good quicklime when the stone has been fully calcined. Quicklime exposed to the air will immediately start absorbing carbon dioxide as well as moisture. This is termed air slaking, and will eventually convert the lime back into inert calcium carbonate which has no binding properties. Ways in which to ensure that the lime used is at its most reactive and will maintain its binding power and qualities of workability are either to use it fresh from the kiln (i.e. the same day following burning), or to slake it under water, also immediately after burning. Stored under water it cannot absorb carbon dioxide. Fat lime stored this way will therefore remain indefinitely as an excellent putty in the form of calcium hydroxide, and improves with age.

Hydraulic limes are also best slaked fresh from the kiln, but can only be stored as a dry hydrate. They must be stored in waterproof and air-tight containers, usually bags, for similar reasons.

Field tests to ensure that quicklime has been correctly burnt are as follows:

SOLUBILITY IN WATER

Pure lime [CaO or $Ca(OH)_2$] is fully soluble in water if the water is frequently changed. A test specimen of fully converted pure lime should therefore dissolve completely if continuously subjected to washing with clean fresh water. Calcium carbonate, and any insoluble impurities, will remain as a residue. A little sugar previously dissolved in the water will greatly increase its solvent power and increase the speed of the test (Higgins, 1780; Vicat, 1837).

UNDER-BURNT LIMESTONE

This will be heavier than a fully burnt stone of the same size. It will contain a central core which has not calcinated. The core is recognizable by its different colour, texture and density from the surrounding quicklime. Its core would remain as residue in the water solution test described above.

OVER-BURNT LIMESTONE

The method of burning the stone, fuel used, type of limestone and weather conditions will all affect the quality of quicklime produced. Over-burning is most unlikely when wood is used as the fuel, but extremely high temperatures (up to 1400°C) can be reached with coal, coke and even charcoal. All limestones will be adversely affected by temperatures above 1100°C as the various impurities they contain start to melt and fuse. In extreme cases considerable quantities of clinker may be formed. Impurities in the fuel may also combine with the clinker.

The result is that in addition to hard fused surfaces the overburnt stone is also likely to be discoloured with fuel contaminants. The quicklime under these conditions will clearly be far less reactive under water and is likely to leave clinker residue. Generally the higher the temperature and the longer this has been maintained the greater the quantity of clinker produced. Pure lime can become deadburned and will lose its reactivity. Hard burnt particles may take weeks or months to slake. In addition to observing these signs, a further check is to test for reactivity to compare with well-burnt lime.

Field tests to ensure quicklime has been fully calcined and is fresh, without having absorbed carbon dioxide or moisture are:

GAIN IN WEIGHT

The process of burning limestone to convert it to quicklime drives off carbon dioxide, reducing the weight of pure limestone by 44%. In re-absorbing the carbon dioxide as well as moisture from the air, the quicklime gains weight. A sample of the quicklime under test may therefore be carefully weighed for comparison to a sample of fresh quicklime of identical source and volume. The initial control samples must be taken fresh from the kiln immediately following a good burn. A good burn can be judged by the successful conversion of all, or at least 95% of, the stone in the batch. The difference in weight will be that of the moisture and carbon dioxide absorbed. The amount of carbon dioxide alone may be checked by heating a sample at, say, 80°C for half an hour, to drive off the moisture, and re-weighing it. As a guide, specifications for commercial lime in the UK state that the carbon dioxide content should not exceed 5%.

HYDROCHLORIC ACID

Fully slake the quicklime with minimum water and add dilute hydrochloric or nitric acid. If the limestone has been fully burnt, it should dissolve without effervescence (Vicat, 1837).

PHENOLPHTHALEIN

This turns a bright pink when in contact with calcium oxide or quicklime (CaO) but there is no colour change when it is applied to calcium carbonate ($CaCO_3$). If the lump of quicklime under test can be cut in half, a clear change in colour at the edge of the new face will indicate the precise depth to which carbon dioxide has been absorbed.

QUICKLIME REACTIVITY

This is a comparative test based on the amount of heat produced by the chemical reaction of calcium oxide with water. It is more appropriate for the purer limes. A fully calcined, freshly burnt pure limestone will rapidly raise the temperature of water shortly after immersion. This reaction can be measured by timing alone if the water boils, or by the rate of temperature rise.

○ *Time measurement*
Using a small 2 litre (quart) container, half fill it with one litre of water maintained at a set temperature, say 25°C. Fully immerse half the volume, 0.5 litres, of a representative sample of quicklime. All quicklime lumps in the sample need to be the same size, about 25mm diameter. Record the exact time taken for the water to be brought to the boil from the moment of immersion.

Test the quicklime produced at each firing or from different kilns. If the quality of quicklime used in each test is consistent, the time taken to raise the same volume of water from the same temperature to boiling point should also be consistent. If it takes longer or does not boil at all this indicates the quicklime is less reactive, probably containing calcium carbonate due to underburning or having been left exposed to the air for too long. Alternatively, the quicklime may have been prepared from stone taken from a different bed in the quarry that contains a lower proportion of calcium carbonate.

○ *Temperature measurement*
This method is more precise but requires more sophisticated equipment. It is more useful for hydraulic limes where the time to reach boiling point is longer, and for eminently hydraulic limes where the temperature rise may be very small.

Use the same sample volumes, equipment, and process as above, but use a thermometer to record the rate of temperature rise. It is important that the temperature of the water is exactly the same at commencement of each test, when the quicklime is introduced. Take the temperature every 30 seconds for pure limes, but for hydraulic limes these intervals will need to be increased in proportion to the degree of hydraulicity. The slaking rate becomes progressively slower the more lean or hydraulic the lime.

The time and temperature taken at each reading can be recorded, preferably in graph form, and compared to previous readings or related to experience with other limes.

Ground (powdered) quicklime can be tested the same way as lump lime provided it is sieved to ensure that there is a single particle size which is exactly the same for each test.

Temperature changes for the slower slaking limes can be slight and are more difficult to record. To make measurement easier, the container should be well-insulated, or a vacuum flask could be used.

○ *American Standard*
ASTM C110 gives a guide to reactivity of a 100g sample of high-calcium quicklime that will pass a 3.35mm (no. 6) sieve immersed in 400ml of distilled water at 25°C and agitated with a whisk at about 400rpm as set out in Table 11.2.

Table 11.2: Reactivity of high-calcium quicklime

Quicklime reactivity	Temp. rise in centigrade	Maximum time for temp. rise	Time reaction complete
High reactive quicklime	40°C	3 minutes	10 minutes
Medium reactive quicklime	40°C	6 minutes	20 minutes
Low reactive quicklime	40°C	over 6 mins.	over 20 mins.

Field tests for lime putty

SOUNDNESS

A test to ensure lime putty is sound establishes quality generally, and is particularly relevant where the quality of finish is important, such as internal plasterwork. Hard over-burnt lime particles and impurities may slake very slowly, causing pitting and popping in the surface of the finished work months after completion. If they have been ground fine and incorporated into dry hydrate they are difficult to detect. One simple field test is to spread a thin layer of putty, about 2mm (1/12") thick on a sheet of glass or clear plastic and hold it in front of a strong light. If dark spots can be seen, these indicate the probability of over-burnt material and the possibility of defects occurring in the finishes at a later date (Young, 1913).

All putty for mortar and render base coats should pass through a no. 8 mesh sieve, aperture size 2.36mm, and for finishing coats a 20 mesh sieve, aperture size 0.85mm, leaving no residue (ASTM C5–79). If the putty is to be used for work of a high standard such as internal plaster or decorative stucco, it should pass a no. 50 mesh sieve, aperture size 0.3mm or 300 microns. In order to achieve this finer material, the putty should be washed through the sieve in a diluted form and then allowed to settle out as a putty again. The putty should not have to be 'punched' through in a firm state. Alternatively, production of the best putty can be by suspension in water, overflowing through weirs to lower storage vats, the sieve test only being carried out as a random check for quality.

DENSITY

An upper limit of 1.45g/ml is set in BS 890 for lime putty of standard consistency. The putty density can be calculated with any size of container provided it is of sufficiently regular shape to maintain a precise and consistent volume each time the container is filled.

It is filled first with very clean, preferably distilled, water to establish the volume. The weight of water is equivalent to its volume in metric units, i.e. 1 millilitre weighs 1 gram. Deduct the weight of the container from the total weight when it is filled. This determines the weight of water and hence volume inside the container. Fill the container with the putty and ensure all air is expelled by tapping it down until no further putty can be added. Carefully strike off surplus from the top. Continue to tap down, strike off and add putty until there is no increase in mass.

The density is calculated by dividing the maximum mass of the putty in grams by its volume in millilitres.

A typical putty density vessel is shown in BS 890. It is 90mm high and 60mm in diameter, and holds approximately 250 ml.

In a worked example, if the vessel is filled with putty that weighs 375g, the density is:

$$\frac{375 \text{ g}}{250 \text{ ml}} = 1.5 \text{ g/ml (or kg/l)}$$

Clearly the simplest field test method would be to use a container that holds exactly one litre. This would be carefully filled with the putty as described above and weighed. After deducting the weight of the container, the putty weight in kilograms is the same figure as the density. Accepting the British Standard above, the maximum weight for one litre should be 1.45kg. Therefore, in the example above, the putty is slightly too dense for the British Standard, and water should be added to bring it to the correct density.

WATER RETENTION

WATER RETENTION

When lime putty is received from the supplier, the amount of water separating from the putty can be measured to indicate water retentivity of the lime. The putty supplied is first thoroughly mixed for sixty seconds to an even consistency at an average day-time temperature. A 1.5 kg sample is weighed out and left to stand undisturbed in a sealed and covered bucket for exactly one day. The surface water and lime in suspension is then poured off into a measure. The lime in suspension is allowed to settle for half an hour in the measure. The water volume, excluding the settled lime, read off in the volumetric measure should not exceed 25ml. *(BS 890 – 1972 and BS 6463 Part 4-11-1987).*

PLASTERING AND WORKABILITY

One of the many advantages of a good lime putty is its ease of workability. This means that it is both easy to spread off the plasterer's trowel and at the same time has 'suction' qualities that provide good adhesion to the background whilst it remains soft and plastic. A field test for this is known as the Carson Blotter Test. The materials required are: a large piece of blotting paper (or other paper of similar absorbent qualities!); a container the size of a drinking glass; a can or cup; and a spatula, small trowel or large knife. The lime is mixed to a standard consistency (as described in the next section) in the cup and left covered for a few hours, or overnight if made from dry hydrate, to temper. The lime is then spread over the paper like butter. The distance of spread is noted for comparison with other limes, plastering materials or a standard lime of good quality. It requires little experience before differences in plasticity can be reliably assessed for the main work, (Cowper, 1927, pp. 32–33).

STANDARD CONSISTENCY

Prepare equipment similar to that used for field testing the setting time of lime putty. In this case, to make an approximate assessment of whether the putty is close to standard consistency, the needle or plunger should be 12.5mm (½") in diameter. This may be a rod with its lower end closed (a pipe or hollow tube having one end filled solid would be convenient). The bottom of the plunger should be perpendicular and smooth without curvature or shoulders. The total weight of the plunger, including any attachments for support or increasing weight if required, should be exactly 30g (1.06oz) *(ASTM C110)*. The advantage of using a hollow pipe is that it can be filled with a heavy granular material until the precise weight is achieved.

Prepare the putty to be tested by taking a one litre (1 quart) sample and thoroughly mixing it for 30 seconds. Remove the mixing equipment, scrape down any putty adhering to the sides of the bowl and equipment and re-mix for a further 30 seconds. Fill a small, smooth flat-topped container, preferably circular with a diameter about 70mm by 40mm high (3" diameter × 2" high) with the putty, ensuring no air pockets remain, and strike off flush at the surface. Gently lower the plunger vertically on to the putty. The penetration by weight of the plunger only should be between 15mm and 25mm (⅝" to 1") for a putty of standard consistency. These limits could be marked on the plunger.

The test can be improved by using a modified Vicat apparatus to lower the plunger accurately and to record the depth of penetration. This is based on the ASTM method of testing putty prepared from dry hydrate. The principal purpose in the standard is to determine the optimum amount of water that should be added to the dry hydrate to bring it to a putty of standard consistency. It is also useful as a simple field test for fat lime putty.

Many national Standards (such as BS, DIN, ASTM) refer to a 'flow table' for testing putty consistency, and this is described below in Section 11.5.

Field tests for dry hydrate

FINENESS

Sieve testing will give an initial indication of the quality of a dry hydrate. If production, packaging and storage have been in accordance with the recommended standards, the lime should pass simple particle size tests.

National Standards usually require the majority (99%) of all hydrate to pass an 80 mesh (180 micron) sieve. This fineness is advisable for plastering, but not necessary for the majority of other applications for which building limes are required. In terms of fineness only, the hydrate will normally be acceptable if it passes a 20 mesh (0.85mm aperture size) sieve after continuously sifting 100g for five minutes, and leaves no residue. The sieving process should be by shaking without brushing, rubbing or punching the lime through.

CARBON DIOXIDE CONTENT

If dry hydrate is left exposed to the air, it absorbs carbon dioxide and moisture in a similar way to quicklime. The rate of absorption varies with ambient temperature and humidity, making the rate of deterioration difficult to predict. It is important to use the hydrate when it is reasonably fresh from manufacture, at the most within two or three weeks, or to ensure that it is stored dry, in well-sealed air-tight containers. If these precautions are not taken, the dry hydrate will progressively revert to calcium carbonate, eventually losing all binding properties.

Field tests to establish carbon dioxide content are similar to those described for quicklime. Tests with hydrochloric acid and phenolphthalein will be able to give an indication of the lime's condition generally. Heating to drive off moisture and carefully weighing, again as the test described for quicklime, can give a fair indication of the amount of carbon dioxide absorbed.

There are a number of laboratory tests set out in various national standards which give detailed descriptions of chemical analysis methods to determine the precise carbon dioxide content. These are outlined in the following section and listed in Appendix 4.

SOUNDNESS TEST — FAIJA APPARATUS

A test for soundness makes use of the way chemical reactions are accelerated in hot and moist conditions. A small steam cabinet or cooking vessel that can be used in a similar way is required. The lime is prepared as a pat of firm paste, up to a maximum of 100mm (4") in diameter and 10mm (⅜") thick. It is allowed to set in air for 48 hours and then placed on a metal plate ready for insertion on a rack or other support in the upper part of the steam cabinet.

Water at the bottom of the cabinet is heated to just above boiling temperature. The water is maintained at 105°C for a period of no less than four hours (DIN standard 1060, Appendix 4). The test specimen is then examined after having been saturated with steam in the cabinet vessel. If the sample shows no sign of expansion, disintegration, or pitting, the lime is considered sound.

DENSITY

The density of dry hydrate may be determined in a field test, as described previously for lime putty, by using a density vessel. Some national Standards give a range of maximum density figures for each class of building lime. The German Standard DIN 1060:1986 part 1 and the French Standard NF P 15–310 (Appendix 4) give guideline values for maximum bulk density: see Table 11.3.

Table 11.3: Maximum densities of dry hydrate

Class	Dry hydrate of lime	Bulk density (g/ml)	
		German Standard DIN 1060:1986	French Standard NF P 15–310:1969
A	White (pure) lime	0.5	–
C1	Feebly (slightly) hydraulic	0.7	0.65
C2	Moderately hydraulic	0.8	0.60 to 0.75
C3	Eminently hydraulic	1.0	0.9

11.5   Field tests for sands, pozzolans and mortars

Field tests for sand quality

The types of sands and aggregates best suited for mortars, renders, plasters and other mixes have been described previously. Field assessment of sand can be carried out mainly without tools although a few accurately graded sieves are very helpful.

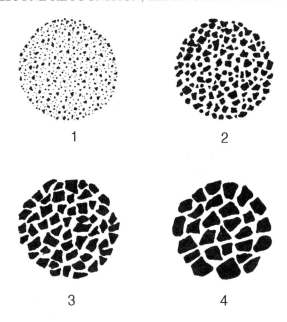

Particle size grading and recognition by eye
1. fine sand – 0.06mm to 0.6mm; 2. medium sand – 0.6mm to 2mm; 3.
coarse sand – 2mm to 4mm; 4. grit – 4mm to 6mm

OBSERVATION
If clean sand is rubbed between moist hands it should leave no stain. The size and sharpness of grains can initially be judged by eye and feel. Recommended particle size grading is set out in the relevant chapters for mortar, render and plaster. These describe the ideal sand as having an optimum mixture of coarse through to fine grains. In some cases, for wide joints or for lime concrete, a proportion of grit is required with a grain size in the order of 3mm to 6mm.

Nearly all sands will be composed of a mixture of different size grains but generally, for the purpose of judging sand by eye, coarse sand may be assumed to be between 4mm and 2mm ($\frac{3}{16}$" to $\frac{3}{32}$") and medium sand between 2mm and 0.65mm ($\frac{3}{32}$" to $\frac{1}{32}$"). There may also be very fine sand or dust from 0.65mm down to 0.06mm (60 microns). Material with a particle size even smaller than this falls into the category of silt or clay, which can be determined by the sedimentation test. Salts in the sand can be detected by taste.

SEDIMENT TEST
This field test is described in connection with sand, but it is also suitable for testing other aggregates, as well as soils, to determine the proportions of clay and silt.

As silt particles (0.06mm to 0.002mm) and the particles of clay (below 0.002mm) cannot be judged with the naked eye, a simple test to determine the proportion of these in the sample makes use of the way sediment settles in still water. Particles tend to settle according to size, with the largest falling quite rapidly followed by the smaller particles, and then the smallest which may be much slower, settling last of all.

A cylindrical flat bottomed container made of clear material such as glass or plastic is used for this test. A jar is adequate, but to help judge proportions a tall and narrow flask or bottle over 150mm (6") high with a volume of about 1 litre (1 quart) or more will assist measurement. The top of the container should be capable of being made water-tight. If this test is to be carried out regularly, a volumetric flask marked with 5mm graduations over the lower 100mm or 200mm to half way up from the bottom would be ideal.

Use a representative sample of the sand and quarter fill the container (250ml). Add clean water until it reaches the top, and a teaspoon (5g) of common salt. Seal the opening and turn it upside down. Shake the container vigorously for one minute. Stand it down on its base on a firm horizontal surface. Leave it for an hour then shake again, repeating the process described above, following which it should remain undisturbed for

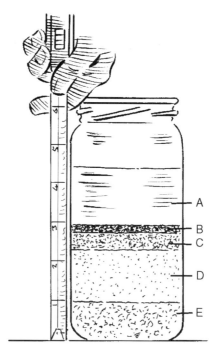

Sediment test equipment
A. water; B. clay; C. silt; D. fine sand; E. coarse sand.

two days. Allow the material to settle. It will do this in layers with the largest particles at the bottom. The sand should settle within about five minutes, the silt eight hours and the clay two days. The boundary between silt and clay can be difficult to see, but can be distinguished by gently drying out the residue. When thoroughly dried the clay layer will cup and fracture (Ashurst and Ashurst, 1988b, p. 97).

The depth of each layer may be read off against the scale, and the percentage of the total calculated. The maximum total for silt and clay that can be tolerated for lime : sand plaster is 6%. Optimum proportions for other mixes are given in the respective chapters.

If it is not possible to obtain clean sand from a local source for the main work, and if it contains salts or excess silt and clay, it should be washed with clean water as described in Chapter 3, and tested again before use.

SAND BULKING

When measuring mortar and plaster mixes by volume and when, at the same time, it is important to keep proportions consistent, it is sometimes advisable to check for bulking. This occurs particularly where the moisture content of the sand is most likely to be variable, i.e. after heavy rainfall or a new delivery. This test is based on the fact that the volume of saturated sand is the same as when it is dry, but when it is damp the same sand has a larger volume.

A container the same as or similar to that used for the sediment test described above, is suitable. Pour a sample of the sand into the container, without packing it down, until it can be levelled off at exactly 100mm.

Empty the sand into another clean vessel. Half-fill the original container with water. Carefully reintroduce half the sand into the original container and prod it through gently to ensure all air is removed. Repeat the process with the remainder of the sand and level it off where it has settled down well below the water line.

Measure the depth of the saturated sand, which will be lower than the damp sand first introduced. The percentage bulking is calculated by using the formula:

$$\% \text{ bulking} = \frac{OR - NW}{NW} \times 100$$

where
$$OR = \text{original depth of sand}$$
$$NW = \text{new depth of sand}$$

Worked example: Assuming the saturated sand drops to 80mm

$$\% \text{ bulking} = \frac{100 - 80}{80} \times 100 = 25\% \text{ bulking}$$

In this example, if the sand is normally used dry, 25% more will be required when in the damp (and bulked) state at the time of the test.

The density of the sand, with or without compaction, can be checked as described above for testing the density of lime putty.

PARTICLE SIZE ANALYSIS

This can be a simple test but it does require accurate sieves. To carry out a detailed check that the sand has the recommended grain size distribution for internal plaster, as shown in the table in Section 6.4 for example, a series of eight sieves would be required. Laboratories carrying out particle size analysis will be equipped with a series of sieves in greater numbers then for manual testing, stacked and operated mechanically.

Field test equipment can be reduced to possibly three sieves of a quite small diameter, say 150mm (6"). Weight can be reduced further by using interchangeable sieve mesh bases for a single frame. The amount of sand passing through a sieve mesh aperture size of 5mm and retained on meshes of 2mm, and 0.6mm apertures will give a good initial indication of the overall particle size distribution, i.e. the relative quantities of coarse, medium and fine sand in the sample.

A sand with an optimum variation of grain size, that will give the very best results, will have a mix that enables all voids between the larger grains to be filled with the smaller ones. This optimum can be determined by using a container similar to that described for the previous tests, using the following method.

Take a representative sample of dry sand and divide it by sieving into coarse, medium and fine grains. Gently transfer all coarse sand into the container without vibration or compaction and record its height. Secondly, introduce the medium grains and shake down. Note the height, and repeat for the finest grains. If the smaller grains fill voids between the larger ones exactly, there will be no increase in the volume and height of the sand when the medium and fine grains are introduced. In practice there is likely to be some increase in volume, but the smaller this is the better the particle size distribution. If the range of grain sizes is far from ideal it can be improved for the best quality work by sieving out the unwanted excess of any particular size.

This test can be taken one stage further to establish the optimum proportion of lime putty for the sand that is to be used. Gently pour water from a volumetric flask into another flask containing a measured amount of dry sand. Stop when water saturation reaches the top of the sand. The volume of water used relative to the original sand volume will equal the optimum proportion of putty for that sand (Vicat, 1837).

Field tests for pozzolan reactivity

In this test the pozzolan reacts with milk of lime. The milk of lime (lime putty thinned to the consistency of milk) is poured into a tall narrow glass or jar until it is one third full. This is followed by an equal measure of pozzolan sample which has been finely ground. For a comparative test it is important that the milk of lime is the same consistency for all pozzolans. The simplest way to achieve this is probably to test each pozzolan at the same time using a series of similar containers and the same milk of lime mix.

Shake the container every 12 hours for a week. Measure the depth and observe the bulk of the sediment shortly after shaking. Compare this with a fresh mixture of the same material or with another pozzolan given the same treatment. After seven days the increase in the volume of the solid matter will indicate the extent of pozzolanic reactivity. This can be measured by its increased height up the jar.

The chemical reaction between the 'active clay' of the pozzolan and the calcium hydroxide will form hydrated calcium alumino-silicates of a colloidal nature. They will therefore flocculate and settle at a far slower rate than the fresh pozzolan (Cowper, 1927).

The speed and strength of set of the pozzolan can be determined by pressure of the finger or a Vicat needle as described for the setting time field test for lime putty earlier in this chapter. A list of pozzolans is given in Appendix 2.

Tests involving crushing 50mm cubes to determine the strength of the mixes can be found in Indian Standards IS 1727, 1344 and 4098. Similar tests are given in American Standards ASTM C593 and 109 (see Appendix 4). Further reading on this subject can be found in Spence and Cook (1982, pp. 144–57) which contains an excellent section on pozzolans.

Field tests for mortars and plasters

CRUSHING STRENGTH

Two important reasons for requiring mortars and plasters to set are the need to impart durability to the building surface and to assist the strength and stability of the structure. Comparative compressive strength requirements for mortars and load-bearing structures are given in Appendix 10. From this it can be seen that the compressive strength of the weakest lime mortar is more than adequate for ordinary loads in one- and two-storey buildings.

Compressive strength is therefore not usually of concern for the load-bearing capacity of domestic buildings. Knowledge of the precise crushing strength, which tends to depend on density, can be of assistance, however, due to its correlation with porosity and to some extent permeability. If the materials and workmanship that have gone into making a mortar or plaster are of the standards recommended here, crushing strengths will be adequate. Crushing strength requirements are set out in detail in most national Standards in connection with hydraulic lime mixes and these are discussed in the following section.

WORKABILITY OF MORTARS AND PLASTERS

The Indian standard IS:1624:1986 (Appendix 4) describes a test for mortar workability that can be carried out on site and in field conditions. The cone mould used in this test measures 100mm (4") diameter at the bottom, 70mm (2¾") diameter at the top and is 50mm (2") high. A representative sample of mortar prepared for the main work is used to fill the cone mould, which is supported on a 1mm-thick galvanized steel plate 120mm (4¾") square.

The plate and filled mould are raised 300mm (12") above a second plate of mild steel 300mm square. The smaller plate is quickly slid out horizontally and the mortar allowed to fall freely on to the plate below. The spread of mortar should average 150mm (6") to 160mm (6¼") for good workability. For an initial assessment without equipment, a similar sized ball of mortar may be dropped on to a flat surface.

RATE OF CARBONATION

Carbonation is extremely important to surface durability. The rate of carbonation is variable as this depends on temperature, moisture content and air movement over the surface, as well as the texture of the surface itself and the reactivity of the lime. A test which gives a very clear indication of the depth of carbonation can be carried out with phenolphthalein indicator solution. This remains colourless at pH 8.4 and below. It turns red (or bright pink) at pH 10.0 and above and will therefore show up clearly on uncarbonated areas whilst the mortar that has carbonated remains colourless.

If phenolphthalein is not available, a similar test can be carried out using a neutral metallic solution containing a dark-coloured oxide which will be precipitated by caustic lime. There is no reaction on carbonated areas but the oxide 'adheres' to the uncarbonated surfaces. J.T. Smith (Vicat, 1837, pp. 36–37) advised that a freshly prepared solution of ferrous sulphate acts in this way, depositing green ferrous oxide. He also describes other solutions that will give similar results, such as chloride and nitrates of mercury which show up as bright yellow, brown or black precipitates. The silver nitrate shows black. The tincture of the *Terminalia chebulica* plant, common in India, shows dark green and slowly turns chocolate.

Vicat records, in a series of tests he carried out, that the average depth of carbonation for a lime sand mix (in a Mediterranean climate) was about half a millimetre in one week, 3.3mm in one month and nearly 11mm in one year. The rate of carbonation is increased the greater the porosity and permeability as well as the rougher the surface texture. Research by structural engineers (Alan Baxter and Associates) in connection with lime mortar for the construction of large expanses of new brick walling in London in 1995 have confirmed this general trend, and the variable nature of the carbonation rate.

SETTING TIME

The initial setting time of mortars and plasters may be tested with the Vicat needle and apparatus or its modification, as described for lime putty and paste earlier in this chapter. Both the initial and final setting times will largely be a function of the class of building lime used, the proportion of aggregate, and ambient conditions (temperature, humidity and air movement). Severe dampness in buildings can prevent carbonation.

If time allows, it is advisable to make up small samples of proposed mixes to test them for rate of carbonation, durability and the effect of weathering, before proceeding with the main work.

FROST RESISTANCE AND DURABILITY

Frost resistance may be tested by placing sample pats, at varying stages of set, in a domestic refrigerator or freezer for varying time periods, say for 12 hour intervals, and noting the effect. A more severe trial of a similar nature is the freeze-thaw test to determine the number of freeze-thaw cycles the sample will withstand without breaking down. Where freezers are not available, the durability can be judged by tests with salt solutions, since the destructive power of salt crystallization is similar to that from ice crystals. The sample in this test is alternately saturated in salt water and dried out in similar time cycles to the freeze-thaw test.

Test for presence of sulphate in background material

It is important that structural walling materials such as bricks and blocks do not contain excessive soluble sulphate if they are to be plastered, as the salts will adversely affect the finished work. Neville Hill has suggested the following test.

Soluble sulphate in a sample of finely crushed brick, for example, can be detected by shaking 60g of the dust with distilled water for about half an hour. It is then allowed to stand until it settles. Some of the clear water is decanted off and added to a solution of barium chloride. Any sulphate present is precipitated as insoluble barium sulphate.

11.6   Field tests for soil stabilization

Drop test to determine approximate water content of stabilized soil

Method Take stabilized soil that has had some water added to it. Squeeze the damp mix into a ball in your hand. Then with arm straight out at shoulder level, drop the ball on to a hard, smooth, clean surface at ground level and observe the result.

○ If the mix stays in one piece it is too dry: add water and try again.
○ If the mix is still in one piece the clay content is too high.
○ If the mix breaks into many pieces, it is too wet: leave it to dry a while and try again.

○ When the dropped ball breaks into only a few pieces it is close to the optimum water content, and suitable for use.

Continue to use the drop test to check the water content of the mix as it is being used (BS 1377 (see Appendix 4); Stulz, 1988; Norton, 1986).

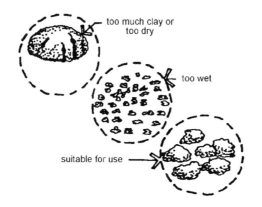

Drop test samples of clay

Clay content test

To gauge clay content the best method is to test the soil's cohesion as follows:

○ Make a roll of soil about the size of a sausage with a diameter of 12mm (½").
○ The soil should not be sticky and should be capable of being shaped so that it makes a continuous thread 3mm in diameter.
○ Place the thread in the palm of the hand. Starting at one end carefully flatten it between index finger and thumb to form a ribbon of between 3 and 6mm (⅛" and ¼") in width and as long as possible.
○ Measure the length obtained before the ribbon breaks.

Long ribbon (250 to 300mm/10" to 12")	High clay content
Short ribbon (50 to 100mm/2" to 4") obtained with difficulty	Low clay content
No ribbon at all	Very low clay content

Compressive strength of stabilized soil blocks

John Norton (1986) suggests that dry compressive strength values for compressed unstabilized mud brick are at least $15kg/cm^2$ ($1.5 N/mm^2$), after one month curing. Compressive strength values for stabilized soils are given as wet strengths, since this is the critical strength condition. These values should be at least half the dry strength value. A suggested minimum for cement-stabilized blocks is 14kg/cm² (1.4 N/mm²) wet compressive strength after one month. Much higher strengths can be achieved and may be necessary. Lime achieves its strength more slowly than cement, and to allow for this the time before testing is doubled.

FIELD TEST FOR COMPRESSIVE STRENGTH

For stabilized earth, the sample should be immersed for 16 hours in cool water and then allowed to drain for 30 minutes before testing.

If using laboratory compression testing equipment, the sample should be cushioned between two plywood sheets 2.4–4.8mm (⅛"–¼") thick, which just overlap the edges of the sample.

When the very large weights required for compression tests on full size blocks are not available, it is common to make small test samples, 50mm in diameter or square, and 50mm high.

Practical equipment for compression testing using a lever system is shown in the illustration below. Cover the sample with plywood or a board 20mm thick (more for larger samples). Place weights on the end of the lever arm, or suspend them from it.

Calculate the compressive load (C) as follows:

$$C = W \times D \div A$$

where

W = weight (this must include the weight of the lever arm calculated from its centre)

D = distance from weight to point of resistance (variable);

A = distance from point of resistance to centre of the sample (300mm).

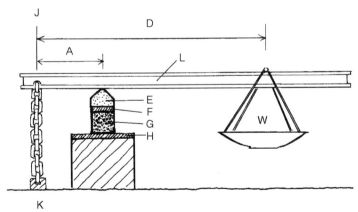

Crushing strength field test
A. Distance from point of resistance; D. distance from weight to point of resistance; W. Weight; E. Pivot point of hard material such as stone or metal; F. Plywood; G. 50mm × 50mm sample; H. Plywood; J. Point of resistance; K. Firm anchor; L. Lever arm

Compressive load is increased by increasing either W, or D, or both, until the sample fails. Divide the compressive load by the surface area of the sample for the compressive strength. Test five samples for an average compressive strength.

A simple quick field test, for wet stabilized bricks, is to try to scratch the brick surface with one's thumbnail. Normally no mark should appear on a brick intended for one or two-storey construction. However, an exception should be made in very dry regions, where a scratch on the surface might not suggest an unacceptable brick.

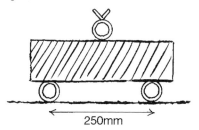

250mm

Standard bending strength test for brick or block

BENDING STRENGTH TEST

There are straightforward tests to establish how much central pressure a brick or block supported at its two ends can take before it breaks. The resulting 'modulus of rupture' value for mud brick should be at least 2kg/cm^2 (0.2 N/mm^2) and preferably between 3 and 3.5kg/cm^2 (0.3–0.35 N/mm^2).

To carry out this test, place a brick or block across the gap between two parallel bars 250mm apart, (less with smaller bricks). With a third bar, apply a load using weights or compression equipment, evenly across the width of the brick at its centre. Record the weight at which the brick breaks. Calculate the modulus with the formula:

$$M = \frac{1.5\ LW}{XY^2}$$

where L = distance between parallel bars
     W= weight applied to brick
     X = width of brick
     Y = depth of brick

Note: in this case L = 250mm.

Test three or more samples for an average.

For a rough appraisal use a large block set up in the same way on two supports, and stand on it to apply pressure (see illustration opposite). With large blocks space the supports 300mm apart to compensate for the foot's extra width. Do not use a person who is very light! (Norton, 1986).

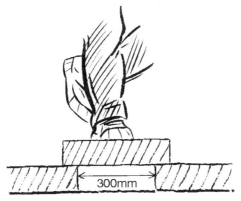

Field bending test for bricks and blocks

11.7 Standard test methods

Most National Standards for lime are written with the intention of providing a guarantee of quality for the production, supply and application of industrial limes, some of which are not building limes. Good standards promote confidence in a reliable product and encourage best practice for its use. Poor standards may discourage the use of a material to the point of elimination, especially if the demands of that standard are too onerous and impractical to apply. National standards are often enforced by law. Poor standards can therefore be extremely harmful to the industry for which they are written.

National Standards presume the availability of precision laboratory equipment and a wide range of chemical reagents. The control of air humidity and temperature within the laboratory is also necessary for most standards. The standards are subject to copyright and are prohibitively expensive for low-income groups. These costs are compounded by the need to cross-reference to other standards, so that several must be purchased to arrive at sufficiently comprehensive information. For example, there may be separate standards for lime, mortar, plaster and external render. There may also be codes of practice for workmanship, sampling and methods of testing, sometimes given as individual standards or sub-sections of the main standard. In addition these standards are regularly amended, expanded and revised.

Whilst this wealth of information is detailed and thorough in the extreme, it is presented in an inappropriate form for developing countries, small-scale industry and low-income groups. There are, however, exceptions to this generalization, particularly where standards have been written with the express intention of being both practical and helpful. Excellent examples of this are given in the Indian Standards IS:1624 and 1635 (see Appendix 4).

A comparative study of the most widely available standards on lime shows that there are several features common to six principal tests. All standards use similar methods for these tests, with minor variations, to establish lime quality. Various properties of lime, directly relating to its performance in terms of workability, binding power, reliability and setting, are the subject of these tests. The requirements for these properties are similar, but not exactly the same, in most standards and are for:

○ Carbon dioxide content
○ Fineness
○ Soundness
○ Putty consistency
○ Setting time of mortar.
○ Crushing strength of mortar.

Field tests previously described deal with ways of checking these properties sufficiently to ensure an adequate quality of lime for most building purposes. The tests in the National Standards are therefore discussed as a guide to the very best quality that can be achieved. Test apparatus normally used to assess lime to this degree of accuracy is also described. A select list of National Standards relevant to the use of lime in building is given in Appendix 4.

Carbon dioxide content

Strict limits for the carbon dioxide (CO_2) content of lime as a product ready for use are set by most National Standards. As this is directly proportional to the amount of calcium (and magnesium) carbonate in the sample, it can be an extremely accurate indicator of lime quality. The CO_2 content should be checked if there is any doubt concerning the length of time between manufacture and use of lime, storage conditions, method of transport and packaging, or excessive core from under-burning.

Acceptable CO_2 content ranges from 3% for lime at the place of manufacture in the American (ASTM) Standard, to 12% for moderately hydraulic lime in the German (DIN) Standard. Some standards stipulate between 5% and 7% for all classes of lime, whilst others differentiate for each. The European ENV Standard (see Appendix 4) gives a maximum CO_2 content of 4% for fat lime, 7% for dolomitic lime and 12% for lean lime.

The test method favoured by most standards is to use hydrochloric acid and to measure the amount of CO_2 released. Laboratory equipment is necessary to measure small granular samples of lime or calcium carbonate between 1g and 10g. An accuracy of 0.1g is required by BS 6463. Each National Standard varies, but the principle is to absorb the carbon dioxide into solution such as barium or potassium hydroxide. The indicators given in BS tests and DIN tests include phenolphthalein, bromophenol blue, and methyl red. The DIN test measures the volume of CO_2 gas in a modified

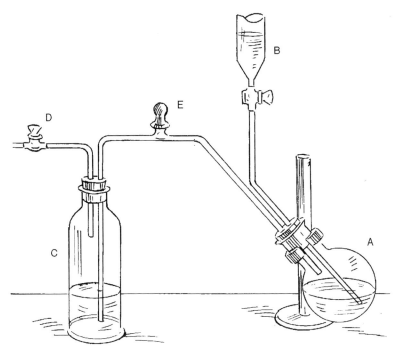

Apparatus for determination of carbon dioxide content (BS 6463)
A. Flask of 10g dry hydrate of lime in solution (100ml); B. Funnel 60ml
dilute hydrochloric acid; C. Bottle of barium hydroxide; D. Tap; E. Safety
valve (rubber teat)

burette, and the BS test measures the difference in volume of acid between two titrations (see figure). Using this equipment, the carbon dioxide liberated from the sample by the addition of hydrochloric acid is absorbed by the barium hydroxide solution. To the resulting precipitate is added phenolphthalein indicator and excess alkalinity is removed using hydrochloric acid. This is followed by a further titration with hydrochloric acid, using bromophenol blue as indicator. The volume of acid used is calculated in terms of the percentage carbon dioxide in the sample.

Fineness
The degree of fineness advisable for both lime putty and dry hydrate has been given in broad terms in the section on field tests. There is considerable variation between different National Standards as to the level of fineness required and the extent to which this is measured. DIN 1060–1986 requires all lime, both putty and dry hydrate, to pass a 2mm mesh. Preferably all should also pass a 630 micron (0.63mm) mesh, but any residue retained on this must be given the soundness test.

229

The Indian standard IS 712–1984 permits up to 5% residue retained on a 300 micron (0.3mm) sieve for dry hydrate, and generally all putty must pass through 850 microns (0.85 mm). BS 890 allows 6% dry hydrate residue on a 90 micron sieve, and for putty 5% on a 1mm mesh followed by 7% on a 250 micron (0.25mm) mesh.

ASTM C5–79 differentiates between the fineness necessary for mortar, render coats, and plaster finishing coats. Putty must pass through 2.36mm for mortar and first render coats and 2.00mm for finishing coats, and be stored for two weeks. Dry hydrate for finishing coats must be capable of being washed through 0.6mm with limited residue on a 0.075mm (75 micron) sieve (ASTM C 141 Specification E11).

The fineness of lime advisable for mortar is less critical than that for plaster, as recognized by ASTM. In practice it has been found that fresh, well-burnt and matured slaked lime putty, all of which passes a 20 mesh (0.85mm aperture size) sieve is likely to be sound. In the case of dry hydrate, however, the test is more demanding, possibly due to the tendency of manufacturers to add back ground material. It is advisable to ensure that dry hydrate will pass 50 mesh (0.3mm). Any material retained on this sieve should be tested further for soundness.

Soundness

If fresh lime is slaked to a dry hydrate and, without grinding, it passes the fineness test leaving no residue, it should be sound. Many manufacturers, however, grind the burnt product. This may include under-burnt or over-burnt material, which can be the cause of unsoundness. This unsoundness may manifest itself due to slow slaking with moisture in the atmosphere, over a long and uncertain period extending to three months or more. As a result, most National Standards employ a steam cabinet or autoclave to speed the slaking and testing procedure. Two methods frequently adopted are the 'pat test' and 'Le Chatelier mould'.

The pat test consists of making up pats of lime putty by mixing dry hydrate gauged with gypsum or cement (to speed set) and placing this in ring moulds, or by making pats shaken down from lumps of lime putty placed between glass plates. The size range depends on the standard. Three 100mm (4") internal diameter and 5mm (¼") deep brass ring moulds are specified in the British Standards. In other standards they range from 100mm to 50mm diameter and smaller. The pats are dried, measured, and placed in a steam cabinet with water at the base of the cabinet, and kept at over 100°C from three to five hours.

The pats or 'cakes' are then examined for expansion, pitting and popping. The lime is considered as having passed the test if the pats are firm and without expansion cracks. ASTM C–141–67 gives a limit, after autoclaving, of 1% expansion in the length of a sample bar (rather than a round pat) gauged with 25% Portland cement.

The German Standard, DIN 1060 (see Appendix 4), describes a simple cold water test for eminently and moderately hydraulic lime, using the pat test principal and without steam treatment. 200g of hydrate is worked into a stiff paste with up to 90g of water. This is divided into two lumps which are sandwiched between two lightly oiled glass plates and gently shaken down until the pats are 10mm thick and up to 70mm in diameter. The pats are allowed to harden in moist air for 24 hours and then detached from the glass. They are placed in water and monitored for four weeks.

If warping or wide cracks at the edges appear on their own, or with a network of cracks over the face of the pat, it is considered unsound and fails the test (see photo). The lime also fails the test if the bottom of the pat warps to a camber of more than 2mm.

  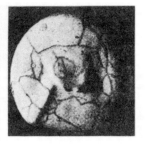

Sample trouble-free   Sample with expansion cracks   Sample with shrinkage cracks
                                                                   (lime trouble-free)

Samples of pats illustrating results from soundness tests
(DIN 1060, reproduced with permission)

A number of National Standards require soundness tests to be carried out with Le Chatelier moulds. These are designed with a squat, split cylinder to contain the lime, to which are attached two 150mm (6") long parallel indicators (see photo overleaf). 30g of the dry hydrate is first mixed dry with 10g of Portland cement and 120g of standard sand. It is then mixed with 20ml of water. The mould is filled and the indicators checked to ensure that they are parallel. The apparatus is allowed to stand for a total of three hours and is then placed in a steam cabinet for a further three hours. Any expansion of the sample causes an amplified change in the distance between the ends of the indicators. BS 890 allows expansion up to a maximum of 10mm between the ends of the indicators before failure. IS 712 table 2 and IS 6932 part 9 give a maximum of 5mm expansion between the ends of the indicators for natural hydraulic lime and 10mm for kankar lime.

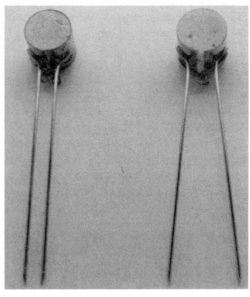

Sound   Unsound

Le Chatelier mould before and after test, showing excessive expansion of unsound lime. The specimen fails the test if the indicators move apart more than 10mm.

Putty consistency

The majority of National Standards examine lime putty in connection with four principal qualities:

○ Fineness
○ Soundness
○ Consistency, which includes density and workability
○ Water retention.

Fineness and soundness of putty are determined in a similar way to dry hydrate described above. The equipment, sieves for fineness and Le Chatelier mould with steam cabinet for soundness, are common to most standards. This apparatus, however, must be manufactured strictly in accordance with each National Standard, which varies from one country to another. Variations in testing methods and equipment are being reduced in Europe at the time of writing (1997 and 2001) by the introduction of a common European standard based on the pre-standard EN 459 parts 1, 2 and 3: 2001 (see Appendix 4).

Parameters for the *consistency* of lime putty are set by stating limits for *density* and *workability*. Density is established with a standard density vessel and test procedure similar to that described for the field test on lime putty, earlier in this chapter. Clearly density and workability are closely related, but most National Standards determine each of these qualities separately.

232

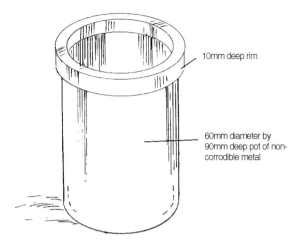

British Standard density vessel (BS 890: 1972)

Workability is tested by an apparatus termed a 'flow table', detailed in many standards including ASTM C230–68T, BS 4551, BS 890, BS 6463 Part 4 – 1987, DIN 1060–1982, and in Central Africa the previous standard RNS No. A15:1963 in what were Rhodesia and Nyasaland and are now Zimbabwe and Zambia and Malawi. There are variations in the dimensions of the flow table from one country to another, but the principle of the test is the same.

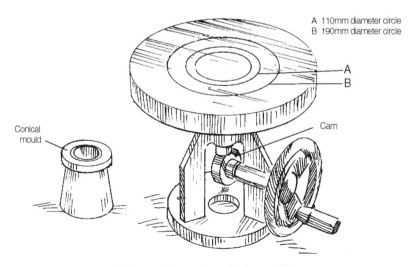

Flow table and conical mould

It is important that the surface on which the putty flows is level and smooth for every test to ensure consistent results. It is therefore usually a requirement that the flow table is made of ground and polished mild steel or, as in the DIN standard, glass.

A conical mould 90mm (3½") high and internal diameter 66.5mm (2⅝") reducing to 38mm (1½") with a hard and smooth internal surface is also required. The mould is placed at the centre of the circular flow table and filled with lime putty. This must be done carefully to ensure there are no trapped air pockets and the top is struck off flush. The mould is carefully lifted vertically leaving a cone of putty to slump slightly at the centre of the table.

The table and support shaft is designed to be of an exact weight, 6.58kg (15lbs), and supported in such a way that it is free to drop vertically 19.1mm (¾"). The table top is marked with concentric circles. The smallest of these is used to locate the cone at the centre of the table, and the larger ones are used to gauge spread or 'flow' of the putty outwards to 110mm (4⅜") and 190mm (7½"). The flow table is raised on a cam and allowed to drop to create a bump at the turn of a handle. At each bump the putty will slump and spread further outwards. On a table of the dimensions described the putty is considered to be of *standard consistence* if it spreads to 110mm after one bump. A tolerance of plus or minus 1mm is allowed, and an average of three overall diameter readings is taken. For the further tests, a putty must be adjusted to achieve this standard consistence.

The putty of standard consistency is considered to be of acceptable *workability* if it reaches a spread of 190mm in *not less than* fourteen further bumps. Temperature and humidity will affect results, and strict parameters for these are given in most standards. As a general guide, however, if testing is carried out at reasonably comfortable room temperature and the weather is not exceptionally dry or humid, conditions are likely to be satisfactory.

Setting time

The apparatus used for establishing the setting time of mortars and plasters specified in current standards is named after its inventor, L.J. Vicat. An adaption of the Vicat apparatus and its use has been described in the section on field tests. Similar tests using the full laboratory apparatus are set out in ASTM C191:1952, and in BS 4550:Part 3:1978 for the testing of cement paste.

The test can be carried out in two stages using the same apparatus but with interchangeable needle and plunger attachments, the plunger to check mortar consistency and the needle to establish setting time.

The Vicat needle is fixed at the end of a moveable rod guided by a steel frame. The total weight of all moving parts is 300g (10.6oz).

A mortar sample is made ready for testing by filling a conical ring mould. The BS dimensions are 70mm (2¾") inside diameter tapering to 60mm (2⅜") and 40mm (1½") high.

It is set on a 100mm (4") square glass plate. The BS test for consistence of cement paste uses a 10mm diameter plunger attachment. The paste is

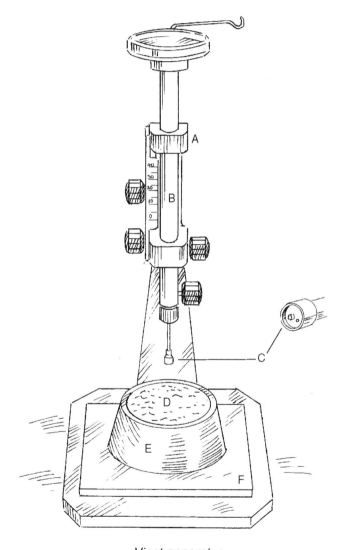

Vicat apparatus
A. Steel frame; B. Moveable rod; C. Setting time needle; D. Mortar sample; E. Ring mould; F. Glass plate

considered of standard consistence when it allows the plunger and move-able rod to settle under its own weight to 5mm (³⁄₁₆") plus or minus 1 mm from the bottom of the mould.

The test for setting time is common to most standards. After filling the ring mould the top of the mortar sample is carefully levelled off. A final setting time needle is attached to the rod. The needle projects 0.5mm below an integral 5mm diameter surrounding ring. The test sample is considered set when the needle is lowered gently on to its surface, the 300g weight is carried fully by the needle and the surface is not marked by the 5mm diameter ring.

Crushing strength

In principle, this is a simple test and may be used as a guide to the classifica-tion of hydraulic limes and cements, as set out in Appendix 1. Tradi-tionally, both tensile and compressive strength tests have been a means of establishing cement quality. Initially, basic testing apparatus using bulk weight or multi lever-arm systems were used, but now testing of crushing strength with hydraulic machines is commonplace. Tensile strength re-mains a quality to be considered, but most national standards have relied increasingly on compressive strength as one of the principal means of evaluation.

The method of measurement is expressed by stating the weight that will be supported by the unit area of one side of a cube of mortar. Imperial measurements, and variations of feet and inches, have been used by most European countries over the last 2000 years. Compressive strength or res-istance is also described as crushing strength, as it has traditionally been assessed by the amount of load per square inch that a cube of mortar will take before being crushed. The load was measured in pounds (lbs) weight

Table 11.4: Minimum crushing strengths for mortars

Classification	French N.F. P15–310:1969 (MPa)	German Din 1060 1986 (MPa)	European ENV 459–1 1994 (MPa)	American ASTM-C141 1972
Slightly hydraulic	–	–	–	
Moderately hydraulic	3	2	2–5	500 psi (3.4 MPa)
Eminently hydraulic	6	5	3.5–10	
Natural cement also described as eminently hydraulic	10	15	5–15	Natural cement mixed at 1 : 1 ratio of cement and sand 1000 psi (6.9 MPa)

and the area in square inches. The crushing strength was expressed in pounds per square inch, abbreviated to lbs/in^2 or psi.

Metrication of measurement has generated a series of new units less comprehensible than a pound per square inch. The generally-accepted unit of measurement for crushing strength at present is Newtons per square millimetre, abbreviated to N/mm^2. The previous French standard was in bars which were approximately equal to kilograms per square centimetre (kg/cm^2). These must be divided by ten to equate to MPa or N/mm^2. Crushing strength equivalents are:

1 bar = 14.72 lb/in^2 ≃ 1 kg/cm^2
1 N/mm^2 = 147.2 lb/in^2 = 1 MPa resistance ≃ 10kg/cm^2

National standards recommend minimum crushing strengths as shown in Table 11.4. These strengths, in N/mm^2, are for mortars mixed in the ratio of 1 lime : 3 sand, and cured for 28 days. Standard sand, proportions of water content, method of preparation and curing are all strictly specified. The cube size is usually 50mm × 50mm (2" × 2").

There will be major differences in crushing strength with varying quantities and quality of sand and aggregate and so a 'standard' sand is often specified. The traditional mixes for natural cements are in the order of one or two sand to one lime, sometimes substituting pozzolan for the sand. The ASTM standard takes this into account to some extent by testing natural cement mixed at a ratio of 1 : 1 with sand, not 1 : 3.

Building limes and natural cements show marked gains in strength over long periods. This gain is substantial for up to two years. Standards usually stipulate testing at 28 days (and less), which fails to take this long-term strength gain into account. This gain is variable, but can be in the order of 40% above the 28 day strength in one year, increasing to 50% after two years for fat limes. It can increase by two or three times the 28 day strength for hydraulic limes.

11.8   National Standards

The principal tests in most National Standards indicate that there is a degree of consensus on the properties to be tested and quality required. There is, however, a marked lack of uniformity between one country and another. This is to be expected when standardization methods attempt to bring uniformity to a natural material with extremely diverse origins and characteristics.

One of the delights of building lime is its diversity. The variations in this material are an asset which has both functional and aesthetic benefits. Limestone varies with geological formation from one region to another. There are good reasons, ecologically and economically, for developing limestone and building lime production on a small scale as a local resource. Each region will benefit most from identifying its own best practice for making optimum use of the limestone types specific to its area. Regional requirements to make best use of local resources are unlikely to be fully compatible with all-embracing national, and even less international, standards.

It is important that standards take account of the diversity of both the materials and the methods of use. It is most important, if quality of work is the objective, for standards to be helpful and informative to the users. Practical advice, possibly in the form of guidance notes, needs to form part of the requirements. Materials and workmanship are interdependent when the objective is to achieve an agreed standard for the end product.

Building limes are able to meet a wide range of requirements for differing conditions and locations in a building, provided appropriate specifications are followed. There is an optimum lime type and mix for each element, exposure, type of weathering, and use that each part of a building will receive. These variations need to be be recognized in standards and codes of practice.

There is immense demand for a low-cost, locally available, and durable binder and building material that is simple to maintain. Building lime is one of these materials, provided the best methods of production and use are understood.

The tendency for standards to give priority to new work is to be expected. Existing buildings, however, are an important asset and their maintenance, repair and improvement tends to be more demanding in scope than for new build.

In addition to the general need to repair existing buildings, the immense value of conservation, ecologically and financially, is increasingly recognized. Historic buildings and towns of national and international importance, therefore, must be cherished and maintained with care. The careful use of lime for conservation is probably the most demanding in terms of materials and skills connected with building limes. The size of that part of the industry that is responsible for historic buildings is significant world-wide. Most important are the skills, experience and knowledge of the craftsmen involved. It is therefore essential that standards for building lime acknowledge this sector.

Existing standards indicate a general acceptance that the quality of certain building lime properties needs to be stipulated, or at least agreed. These standards have been set out in the preceding section. There is, however, variance between standards in deciding precise values, as well as in terminology, and methods of measurement. Some standards appear to be written principally for producers and others for users.

Whilst national or even international standards may be of assistance in broad terms for large-scale producers, their ability to address the specific and varied requirements for regional use is limited. Present standards are inadequate if the best use is to be made of this abundant, but variable, resource. There is a need for regional guidance notes and codes of practice which are helpful and informative to the users of building limes. These need to consider local differences such as climate, available limestone types, aggregates, pozzolans and available skills. Above all, standards must address the needs of users as well as providing practical guidance in response to specific regional demand.

12

Maintenance guidelines

12.1 Introduction

It is not the intention of this book to act as a maintenance manual or repair guide, although the principles for the way in which building limes may be used, described in previous chapters, apply equally to repairs. Information concerning repair methods, particularly for historic buildings, has been thoroughly covered in publications by a number of eminent organizations specializing in this field. The Bibliography includes recommended literature for repairs to buildings of historic importance published by The Society for the Protection of Ancient Buildings (SPAB), Historic Scotland and English Heritage, as well as organizations specializing in the care and repair of earth-based structures.

The importance of caring for buildings by carrying out regular inspections and taking early action to remedy defects, however small, cannot be over-stated. Non-hydraulic lime-based mixes are especially vulnerable to excessive and continuous moisture penetration. Specific maintenance considerations in respect of the care of lime-based materials, principally mortars, renders and plasters, applicable to new buildings, have therefore been selected in this chapter for particular attention.

12.2 Structural movement

Cracking may occur due to the introduction of new load patterns, either by the addition of new furniture or partitions on upper floors, breaking out new door and window openings, an increase in storage areas, or changing the use of spaces in other ways. Cracking caused by subsidence may also occur due to poor load-bearing ground conditions, often created by defective or uncontrolled drainage arrangements.

If movement of the structure is suspected it can be monitored by the installation of devices called 'tell tales' across cracks. Take readings from these, or otherwise record details such as length and width of cracks. Keep a record of areas that are redecorated, or cracks that have been made good, in order that future checks can be made to determine any movement. The information should be recorded on a schedule broken down into ceilings and walls, and if sufficiently extensive, room by room.

Following changes of load, the rate of monitoring should be increased, and in areas of high loading (either dead load or live) monitoring should be carried out on a regular basis. After remedial measures and improvements to the structure have been made, and if records show that there is no further movement, the frequency of monitoring may be reduced.

12.3   Roof maintenance

Keeping roofs clean

Inspection of roofs should be carried out at least yearly to ensure all areas where water flows are clear and free from obstructions. This includes gutters and catchpits.

Only soft brushes, wood or plastic shovels and dustpans should be used for cleaning silt and debris from roofs and gutters. Hard or sharp metal equipment should be avoided to minimize risk of damaging the surface.

When on the roof, whilst carrying out cleaning operations, the opportunity should be taken for a general look at the building fabric at roof level. Any obvious defects in the roof surface should be repaired immediately.

On occasions inspection should be made during heavy rainfall in order to establish how the gutters are flowing. In any areas where build up of water is noted, ponding or inadequate flow should be rectified.

Leaks

Where rainwater penetration and subsequent staining or damage is noted, the source of the leak should be found and the appropriate remedial action should be taken without delay.

12.4   Rainwater goods above ground

General

Ensure all channels taking surface water drainage are kept clear of silt and plant growth. It is surprising how quickly seeds blown by the wind can establish themselves in small amounts of silt. Once established, grass roots and particularly tree roots can give rise to extensive damage.

Keeping rainwater goods clear

Look in inspection covers. Check that rainwater heads are clear and devoid of bird's nests. Check for rainwater staining on walls near downpipes. Where this is observed, determine whether this is from a faulty joint, hole in the pipe or overflowing hopper. Check for vegetation in rainwater goods and clear it away. Check that gullies are clear. Carrying out these inspections during and after heavy rainfall is advisable.

Eaves gutters

Ensure all eaves gutters are clear of debris. This should be done weekly during heavy leaf fall, otherwise every six months. Check falls for flow of water when raining.

Fixings

When clearing gutters and checking rainwater pipes, the condition of gutter brackets and fixings should also be inspected. Some fixings may be made into timber plugs that can work loose. Iron fixings may corrode and damage adjacent render. Where movement or corrosion of fixings has cracked render, this should be noted so that remedial action can be taken before fragments are forced free.

In cold climates, during freezing weather, any blocked rainwater pipe may be split by trapped water turning to ice. Consequently it is essential that regular inspections are made at such times.

12.5   Drainage below ground

Foul drains
A yearly inspection of manholes, inspection chambers and outlets should be augmented by attending to any problems that may be raised during the course of the year. Inspection chambers and manholes should be cleaned and repaired as necessary.

Surface water drains
It is essential that surface water drains are operational and that their associated gullies be kept clear. These may take large quantities of water discharged from roofs and rainwater pipes. If the water is not properly discharged, it will promote decay of walls at low level, internal finishes, and affect the stability of foundations. Particular attention should be paid to the disposal of surface water where discharge positions are close to the building.

Gullies and their associated gratings may clog up with leaves, gravel and rubbish. Such materials should be removed to leave a free passage for surface water disposal.

Inspection after or during heavy rainfall may be particularly informative. Blockages in drains may clear slowly. Consequently, after heavy rainfall, a backlog of water may appear at the gully. In such cases the drain should be rodded to ensure that it is clear and functioning properly.

New or replacement surface water drainage gullies can incorporate silt traps which will collect loose gravel, silt, leaves and debris from path surfaces. These should be checked and emptied at least quarterly, and after heavy leaf fall, which will substantially reduce the risk of drain blockages and the need for rodding.

12.6   Sanitary fittings

Check that all lavatories, cisterns, urinals, wash basins, showers, baths, sinks and the like are functioning properly, securely fixed and not broken. Overflows, dripping taps and leaks should be repaired immediately. Ensure all waste traps are clear.

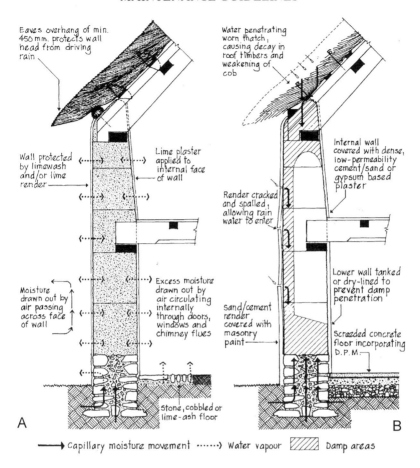

Eaves overhang of min. 450mm. protects wall head from driving rain

Water penetrating worn thatch, causing decay in roof timbers and weakening of cob

Wall protected by limewash and/or lime render

Lime plaster applied to internal face of wall

Internal wall covered with dense, low-permeability cement/sand or gypsum based plaster

Render cracked and spalled, allowing rain water to enter

Moisture drawn out by air passing across face of wall

Excess moisture drawn out by air circulating internally through doors, windows and chimney flues

Sand/cement render covered with masonry paint

Lower wall tanked or dry-lined to prevent damp penetration

Screeded concrete floor incorporating D.P.M.

Stone, cobbled or lime-ash floor

A

B

⟶ Capillary moisture movement   ┈┈⟩ Water vapour   ▨ Damp areas

The causes and effects of dampness in cob walls
A. Wall of unaltered cob building showing how a state of moisture/air
equilibrium is achieved; B. Neglect combined with inappropriate repair/
maintenance can upset the balance and lead to rapid deterioration.
(Source: Devon Earth Building Association; Keefe, et al. 1993)

12.7   Wall finishes

Carrying out a regular inspection of the wall finishes is most important, in order to identify problems and to carry out remedial measures as soon as possible. It helps to be aware of locations where damage may be caused by water leaks, impact, inappropriate cleaning, or abrasion. Where problems are observed, the cause of damage should be identified in order to establish what action is appropriate. Damage and wear of decorative finishes, if left unattended, may result in the loss of building fabric, and detracts from appearance.

Masonry

The walls in general should receive a regular visual inspection. Inspect for signs of water penetration, rising damp, efflorescence, or other signs of distress (say) every three years. The inspection should make note of various defects, cracks, erosion, insect attack, vegetation and the like. The cause of the defect should be determined and rectified. In many cases distress may be due to inadequate water disposal, which should be remedied at source. Minor defects should receive prompt attention to prevent their development into more substantial problems. Such action would include removal of plant growth, particularly roots, cleaning and treating the pockets with a solution of sodium chlorate or other weed killer, and repointing.

Pointing   Repointing should be undertaken only where mortar has weathered to leave open or deeply recessed joints vulnerable to water penetration, or where the mortar is very soft or loose. Sound areas of mortar should be left undisturbed. Mortar joints are an essential part of the building fabric.

Mortar mixes   Different mixes are selected and applied, depending on the location. Factors affecting the mix include: for what purpose it is to be used (bedding, pointing, high-level masonry), the degree of exposure to the elements, strength of masonry units, and what gives a suitable colour and texture match. Mortars vary widely from one area to another due to the difference in local materials. It is most important that repair mortars are compatible with adjoining work. Over-strong mortars cause severe damage to the fabric. A poor match of colour and texture is visually disturbing and undesirable. In damp situations, weak mortars will not survive. Selection of the sands, aggregates and binder is critical. When carrying out mortar repairs these aspects need to be considered in conjunction with the recommendations given in Chapter 5.

Decorative finishes   Finishes such as limewash need to be inspected to establish whether they have weathered to a degree where their protective nature is no longer adequate, or whether they are sufficiently worn to require attention on the grounds of improving appearance. Where a decorative finish has broken down, it should be established whether or not its defective state is having a detrimental effect on the material it covers. The material below should be inspected to determine whether any repairs need to be undertaken before redecoration covers up the defect. Where the condition of the decorative finish is solely of visual concern, subsequent action will usually be by personal preference.

Cleaning plaster   A method of cleaning plaster recommended by Millar (1897, p. 566) is to coat it with a thin paste of starch which should be peeled off when partly dry.

Stubborn stains caused by deposits of soot, smoke or carbon that remain after cleaning and washing off may be removed by washing over several times with strong soda water. Ordinary household soda is satisfactory for this. It is important to rinse off well with clean water and a sponge after the application. The surface when dry, and after rubbing down with a fine sand paper or glass paper, should be satisfactory for repainting (Jennings & Rothery, c.1935).

Limewash   Where walls have a limewash finish they should not be washed down unless it is the intention to remove the paint. Where there are signs of deterioration (small flakes, efflorescing salts etc.) investigation should be carried out to determine the source of the problem. Making good of limewash decorations must be executed with the same material. Application of other paint types is not appropriate as they will be liable to peeling and flaking. In cases where stains are exceptionally stubborn, careful experimentation with chlorine or laundry bleach and liquid dish detergent may prove worthwhile. Care must be taken, however, not to soak or saturate the surface and to sponge off well, in order to keep moisture to the minimum throughout the cleaning process. Mould growth should be cleaned off with fungicide. Following these cleaning methods, which will tend to remove the paint, the area will need to be limewashed again.

Distempers   Distempers may be of two main types, soft distempers and oil-bound distempers. The former will wash off if wiped with a damp cloth. Consequently such cleaning techniques are *not* recommended. Oil-bound distemper is strengthened by casein and a small amount of linseed oil. This produces a paint which is wipeable but not strongly washable. It is advisable to allow new plasterwork and render six weeks to carbonate before painting.

Emulsion paints   Modern porous water-based alkali-resistant emulsion paints are usually of a form that is washable. Water-thinned, textured or coarse mineral aggregate-filled emulsion coatings are also usually washable. It is, however, most inadvisable to apply them over limewashes , other lime-based finishes or distempers. If used, they should be applied direct to the lime plaster or render surface when fully dried and carbonated. A minimum period for new plaster to be left to carbonate before painting is six weeks in a dry, well-ventilated environment. A minimum of three months is advisable for the best quality work if the carbonation tests described in Chapter 11 cannot be applied.

12.8   Ceilings and decorative plasterwork

A general inspection should be carried out about every 5 years to check for signs of movement, deflection, mechanical damage or loss of key. Any signs of staining from water ingress should be noted, and if necessary, opening up should be carried out to ensure that the plasterwork is secure.

Lime plaster maintenance

The basis for most plasterwork will be lime and sand. To this may be added hair and gypsum. The finer decorative plaster may have a higher gypsum content. These materials will normally remain sound indefinitely if undisturbed.

Defects, usually in older buildings, tend to be due to the result of failure of the structure to which the plaster is applied, rather than the plaster itself breaking down. Wood lathing and supporting timbers may have suffered from attack by wood-boring beetle, termites, or fungal growth. Failure of ferrous fixing may manifest itself by sagging in the ceiling, or by long continuous cracks occurring on the underside of the main supporting beams. Where ceiling joists have shrunk over the years they may have introduced stresses in the plaster, which consequently cracks.

Discolouration of the plaster or severe flaking of the surface may be a sign of dampness from leaking pipes, roofs or water ingress through external masonry. Such defects should be investigated immediately. Floor and roof timbers may sag progressively over time, causing some fracturing in the plasterwork.

Movement may also be promoted by excessive floor loading (dead or live) from above. In more serious cases beam ends buried in masonry walls may have decayed. Fine cracks in an irregular line across a ceiling are not necessarily dangerous, but if they are noted to have widened, or if one edge appears lower than another, then it is advisable to investigate the cause and remedy the defect. The materials used for repair should be selected to match the existing material in its various qualities. Replacement of any defective plaster and/or backing should be carried out by a plasterer with knowledge and understanding of the original materials and methods used.

Patch repairs

Loose material should be cut out, a key formed, and new matching material applied.

The first decision to make is how much plaster round the patch to take down. Plaster which appears to be weak should not necessarily be taken down. Very often thin laths will have a certain amount of spring or give and this may be accentuated if the area to be repaired is some distance from the main supports. It is unnecessary to remove adjacent plaster that is well-keyed. Avoid making the joint to the old work over a joist or stud supporting the lath, as the plaster will not have a good key through the laths at this position.

Patch repair; laying on first coat of lime plaster to existing lath background, Warwick Castle, 1995

All loose plaster in the patch should be removed, and the laths, and spaces between the laths, cleaned. Trim the edges of the old plaster well back from the front face to form a dovetail or undercut in the old work. This will act as an additional key for the new plaster.

Defective laths should be replaced with new before trimming the edges of the patch, and any loose laths renailed.

Moisture will be absorbed from new material by the old plaster at the edges unless treated. Trimmed edges of the existing plaster should therefore be painted or coated sufficiently to reduce excessive suction. Otherwise, new plaster patches will be apt to crumble at the join and fall out if too much moisture is absorbed by the old plaster.

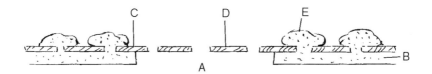

Trimming back edges of plaster on lath to form a dovetail
A. Area to be repaired; B. Old plaster; C. Old lath; D. New lath;
E. Existing plaster key

Coating edge of existing plaster before filling out

Laths are dampened in the normal way before filling out the patch with the first coat. It is important to keep the mix as dry as possible to reduce shrinkage, unless it can be gauged with gypsum. A notched rule is used to rule off the coarse stuff (first coat) about 3mm (⅛") back from the existing face.

The new material is scratched when partially set, undercutting the scratching to give a good key for filling out the patch with the second coat.

248

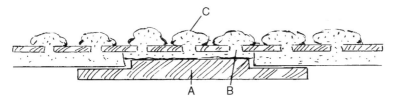

First coat ruled off 3mm from original face using a notched rule.
A. Notched rule; B. First coat of new plaster; C. New plaster key

The second coat is again given a scratched key, all as described previously for plain plastering in Chapter 6.

The finishing coat is best in lime putty gauged strongly with gypsum to the consistency of thick cream. If gypsum is not available, the putty should be knocked up very thoroughly as dry as possible, to minimize shrinkage. The material is laid on tight with the laying trowel and levelled off. Very fine (silver) sand may be added to the mix in the proportions of 1 : 1 or 1 : 2 and the fine stuff for the finishing coat prepared, applied, and finished, all as described for plain plaster in Chapter 6.

This method of carrying out patch repairs to ceilings is also suitable for wall plaster (Verrall, c.1930).

12.9   Metalwork

Signs and brackets
Check the security of sign and bracket fixings yearly. Include inspection of adjacent render for fractures caused by corroding iron. Review the condition of decorations, making a note of any areas of corrosion that need to be arrested.

Miscellaneous iron work
Inspect ironwork embedded in masonry for signs of damage from corroding metal (e.g. iron hooks etc.). Remove all ferrous fixings if possible and replace with non-ferrous. Make good defective render with new.

12.10   Floors

Floor finishes should receive regular checks to monitor wear and ensure that they do not present any hazards. Worn, chipped or delaminated areas should receive prompt attention to prevent accelerating deterioration. Areas of heavy use should receive more frequent monitoring. These include kitchens, bathrooms and principal circulation areas.

Stone paving
Brush down with a soft brush. Repoint joints in a similar way to repointing walls with hydraulic lime and possibly with the addition of a pozzolan. Take additional care to compact the mortar well. Protect for as long a time

as practical, preferably 28 days or more before use. In some cases a lime mortar including tallow or oil will be appropriate.

Marble and stone chippings (terrazzo)

Carefully dust down with a soft mop or cloth to remove dust and dirt. Use soap, or dishwashing liquid, not powdered or abrasive detergents, as a cleaning agent. Do not over-wet, and dry thoroughly. Finish off by renewing oil or wax surface protection.

Tiles

Tiled floors should be brushed down to remove grit and dirt that may grind into the surface. Quarry tiles may be periodically wiped down with an oily rag using boiled linseed oil. Repoint if required as for stone paving above.

12.11   Roads and paths

The wearing course of roads and paths should be inspected to determine if fractures and pot-holes are appearing due to heavy wear. Maintenance of the wearing course is essential in order to prevent damage to lower structural layers which would be more costly to repair. In addition, severe defects may present a safety hazard.

Paths

Inspect condition of paths for loose stones, fractures and unevenness. Clear vegetation every six months.

Surface water drainage

Check culverts and surface water drains are clear and flowing. Clean as necessary. Inspect monthly and after heavy rainfall.

12.12   Vegetation

General

Cut back creepers to prevent blocking of gutters, growth into ventilators, roof voids, and around windows etc. every six months.

Vegetation may provide a number of problems with regard to maintaining building fabric. Creepers must be cut back to avoid growth blocking gutters and pushing out under slates, tiles etc. The sucker pads on various climbers will damage paintwork and should be regularly trimmed away from painted surfaces.

Plant growth in rainwater hoppers or weathered joints and masonry can cause extreme damage. Blocked rainwater goods will discharge water where it may penetrate the fabric of the building, damaging internal finishes, and promoting fungal decay. Plant growth in open mortar joints may cause movement (e.g. copings to parapet walls) or more substantial failure (e.g. pier movement to river bridges).

Where plants are removed, repointing should be carried out to prevent water ingress. The use of biocide may be beneficial in relatively inaccessible areas to reduce frequency of attention. These are manufactured to various toxic levels. They should only be used sparingly, taking care to avoid affecting adjacent areas, especially water adjacent to marine works.

Marine works
The constant presence of water encourages rapid plant growth on embankment walls. Cutting back vegetation on banks, river bridges, harbours and quays, and treating the area against further growth is an essential maintenance operation that should be carried out on a regular basis to prevent decay. During this operation, any masonry units that have been dislodged by root growth should be re-set. If roots are allowed to develop unchecked they will eventually destroy the structure.

12.13 Summary

Preventive maintenance
The above guidelines are suggested methods of preventive maintenance applicable to all buildings whatever their age. It is equally important to care for new buildings on a regular basis, if maintenance costs are to be kept to the minimum, and the existing building stock is to be retained.

Regular monitoring to deal with problems before they develop will reduce, or even eliminate, the need for major repairs at a later date, and is cost effective. It is surprising how soon a structure, however well built, can be adversely affected by apparently minor external influences such as shrinkage and expansion, due to temperature and moisture changes, vibration, new load patterns, plant growth, and blocked drainage.

References and bibliography

Adam, J-P., *Roman Building Materials and Techniques*. (A. Mathews, Translator), B.T. Batsford Ltd., London, 1994.

Adams, J.G. and Elliott, C.A., *Rambles among our Industries: Lime and cement*. Blackie & Son Limited, London and Glasgow, c.1925.

Agevi, E., Ruskulis, O. and Schilderman, T., *Lime and Alternative Binders in East Africa*. Intermediate Technology Publications, London, 1995.

Architectural Press *Specification No. 30*, 1928.

Ashall, G., Butlin, R., Martin, W. and Teutonico, J.M., 'Development of lime mortar formulations for use in historic buildings'. Report on the Smeaton project in *Proceedings of the Seventh International Conference on Durability of Building Materials and Components*, Stockholm, Sweden, May 1996; edited C. Sjöström, London, E & F.N. Spon, 1996.

Ashurst J. and Ashurst N., *Practical Building Conservation, Volume 3: Mortars, Plasters and Renders*. English Heritage Technical Handbook, Gower Technical Press, Aldershot, 1988a.

Ashurst J. and Ashurst N., *Practical Building Conservation, Volume 2: Terracotta, brick and earth*. English Heritage Technical Handbook, Gower Technical Press, Aldershot, 1988b.

Ashurst, J., *Mortars, Plasters and Renders in Conservation*. Ecclesiastical Architects' and Surveyors' Association (EASA), London, 1983 (2nd edition in press).

Ashurst, J., *External Renders*. Ancient Monuments Technical Note 6, DoE, London, 1977.

Ashurst, J., *Earth Floors and Lime Concrete*. Ancient Monuments Technical Note 12, Department of the Environment, London, 1981.

Ashurst, J., *Lime Ash Floors*. Ancient Monuments Technical Note 13, DoE, London, 1977.

Ashurst, J., 'The cleaning and treatment of limestone by the lime method, part I' in Monumentum, Volume 27, Number 3, Butterworths for ICOMOS, September 1984.

B.R.E., Digest 157: *Calcium Silicate (sandlime, flintlime) Brickwork*. HMSO, Watford, 1974, new edition, 1992.

B.R.E., Digest 362: *Building Mortar*. HMSO, Watford, 1991.

B.R.E., Digest 410: *Cementitious Renders for External Walls*. CRC Ltd., London, 1995.

B.R.E., Digest 410 (formerly Digest 196): *External Rendered Finishes*. HMSO, Watford, 1976.

BACMI, *Quicklime – Use on Waterlogged Construction Sites*. Data Sheet, Lime 1, British Aggregate Construction Materials Industries, London, (c.1970).

Bandyopadhyay, S., Kulkarni, S.G. and Rajagopalan B., 'An Alternative Cement for Mass Houses'. *Lime* Vol. 2. Khadi and Village Industries Commission, Bombay, 1975.

Bankart, G.P., *The Art of the Plasterer*. B.T. Batsford, London, 1908.

Baradan, B., 'Lime stabilized fly ash' in N., Hill, S. Holmes and D. Mather, *Lime and Other Alternative Cements*, Intermediate Technology Publications, London, 1993.

Batty Langley, *Builders Compleat Assistant*, 1738.

de la Beche, *Geological Observer*, 1853.

Bessey, G.E., *Sand–Lime Bricks*. Department of Scientific and Industrial Research, Special Report no. 21, HMSO, London, 1934.

Bessey, G.E., *Calcium Silicate Bricks*. Overseas Building Notes no. 154, Building Research Station, Garston, 1974.

Bessey, G. *Production and Use of Lime in Developing Countries*. Overseas Building Notes no. 161. Building Research Station, Garston, 1975.

Bouwens, D., *East Anglian Earth Construction Information Sheet No. 1, practical repair and maintenance*, EARTHA, West Harling, 1996.

Bowyer, J.T., *Small Works Supervision*. The Architectural Press Ltd., London, 1975.

Boynton, R.S., *Chemistry and Technology of Lime and Limestone*. New York. 2nd edition 1980.

BQSF, *Lime in Building*. The British Quarrying and Slag Federation Limited, Croydon, 1974.

Building Research Establishment, *Decay and Conservation of Stone Masonry*. Digest 177, 1976 revised 1990.

Building Limes Forum, *Lime News*. Journal Volumes 1–4, Edinburgh, 1992–96.

Burn, R.S., *The New Guide to Masonry, Bricklaying and Plastering*. John G. Murdoch, London, c.1880.

Burnell, G.R., *Rudimentary Treatise on Limes, Cements, Mortars, Concretes, Mastics, Plastering etc*. Sixth edition, Virtue & Co., London, 1867.

Buxton Lime Industries, *Limebase Manual* (previously: *Lime Stabilisation Manual*). Tunstead Quarry, Wormhill, Buxton, Derbyshire SK17 8TG, 1990.

Carpenter, R., *Pargetting*. SPAB News, Vol. 4 No. 2 pp.19–21, London, 1983.

Carroll, R.F., *Bricks and Blocks for Low-Cost Housing*. BRE Overseas Building Note No. 197, BRE, Garston, 1992.

Cathedral Works Organisation, *French Natural Hydraulic Lime 'XHN'* Technical Sales leaflet, 1992.

Caxton House Editorial, *Specification with which is incorporated the Municipal Engineers' Specification for Architects, Surveyors and Engineers when Specifying*. No. 11, London, 1908–9, and No. 30, 1928, The Architectural Press, London.

Coburn, A., Dudley, E. and Spence, R., *Gypsum Plaster its Manufacture and Use*. Intermediate Technology Publications, London, 1989.

Coldstream, N., *Medieval Craftsmen, Masons and Sculptors*. British Museum Press, London, 1991.

Constantinides, I., *Power Flowers*. Report on casting cornice moulds in lime mixes for the Mansion House at Stowe, SPAB News, Vol. 13 No. 1, London 1992.

Corkhill, T., *Brickwork Concrete and Masonry*. Vol. VIII, Sir Isaac Pitman & Sons Ltd., London, Bath, Melbourne, Toronto, New York, 1931.

Cowper, A.D., *Lime and Lime Mortars*. Department of Scientific and Industrial Research, Building Research Special Report No. 9., HMSO, London, 1927.

Davey, N., *A History of Building Materials*. Phoenix House, London, 1961.

Department of the Environment, *Sands and Plasters, Mortars and Renderings*. Advisory Leaflet 15, HMSO, Birmingham, 1975.

Department of Transport, *Specification for Highway Works*, 1986.

Dethier, J. *et al. Des Architectures de Terres*, Centre Georges Pompidou, Paris, 1982.

Dibdin, W.J., *The Composition and Strength of Mortars*. The Royal Institute of British Architects, London, 1911.

Donaldson, T.L., *Handbook of Specifications or Practical Guide to the Architect, Engineer, Surveyor and Builder* Part II Atchley & Co., London, 1860.

EARTHA see Bouwens.

Eckel, E.C., *Cements, Limes and Plaster*. John Wiley & Sons, New York, 1922.

Everett, A., *Materials*. Mitchell's Building Construction, B.T. Batsford Ltd., London 1970, revised 5th edition by Barritt, C.M.H., 1994.

Fiddler, J., 'A good rendering', *Traditional Homes*, March 1992.

Fulalove, S., 'Lime Mix Stabilises Subgrade'. *New Civil Engineer*, London, 23 September 1982.

GRET (Groupe de Recherche et d'Échanges Technologiques), *La Chaux*. République Française, Ministère de la Coopération et du Développement, Paris, 1981.

Gibbons, P., Scottish Lime Centre Trust, *Preparation and Use of Lime Mortars*. Historic Scotland Technical Advice Note No. 1, Historic Scotland, Edinburgh, 1995.

Grundy, R.F.B., *Builder's Materials*. Longmans Green & Co., London, 1930.

Gwilt, J., *An Encyclopaedia of Architecture*. Revised by Wyatt Papworth, J.B., Longmans Green & Co., London and New York, 1894.

Hartley, P., *Introduction to the Repair of Lime-Ash and Plaster Floors*. SPAB Information sheet 12, The Society for the Protection of Ancient Buildings, London, 1996.

Hawksmoor, N., James, J. and Gibbs, J., *The Builder's Dictionary: or Gentleman and Architect's Companion*. Association for Preservation Technology, Washington, 1981. Facsimile of 1734 London edition.

Hepworth Refractories Ltd, *Data sheets*. Head Office: Swanwick Court, Alfreton, Derbyshire, DE55 7AP.

Higgins, B., *Experiments and observations made with the view of improving the art of composing and applying calcareous cements and of preparing quick-lime*. T. Cadell, London, 1780.

Hill, N., Holmes, S. and Mather, D., *Lime and Other Alternative Cements*. Intermediate Technology Publications, London, 1992.

Holmes, S., *Advice on the Use of Lime in Traditional Building, Zanzibar.* Report to ITDG, Rodney Melville & Partners, Leamington Spa, 1989.

Holmes, S. and Wingate, M., 'Zanzibar – old buildings, old and new skills'. *Appropriate Technology*, Vol. 19 No. 3, London, 1992.

Holmes, S. and Wingate, M., *Report and Advice given to the STCDA for Emergency Repairs, Traditional Lime Technology and Small Scale Lime Production* on behalf of ITDG for the Ministry of the Environment of Finland, Rodney Melville & Partners, Leamington Spa, 1992.

Holmström, I., *Suitable materials for use in repair of historic structures.* Conference on structural conservation of historic buildings B–19/9/1977 Rome.

Houben, H. and Guillaud, H., *Earth Construction a Comprehensive Guide.* Intermediate Technology Publications, London, 1994.

Hudson, K., *Building Materials.* Longman, London, c.1970.

Hughes, P., *The Need for Old Buildings to 'Breathe'.* SPAB Information sheet 4, The Society for the Protection of Ancient Buildings, London, 1986.

Induni, B. and Induni, L., *Using Lime.* Induni, Taunton, 1990.

Induni, B., *Lime and Magic.* A.S.C.H.B. Transactions, Volume 14, Association for the Conservation of Historic Buildings, London, 1989.

Innocent, C.F., *The Development of English Building Construction.* University Press, Cambridge, 1916.

Intermediate Technology Development Group, *Lime: An introduction.* Low-cost cements information sheet, ITDG, Rugby, 1993.

ITDG, *Hydraulic Lime.* Low-cost cements information sheet, Intermediate Technology Development Group Ltd., Rugby, 1993.

Jaggard, W.R. and Drury, F.E., *Architectural Building Construction.* Vol. two, second edition, The University Press, Cambridge, 1946.

Jennings, A.S. and Rothery, G.C. *The Modern Painter and Decorator*, Caxton Publishing Company, London, c.1935.

Jensen, M. and Trampedach, K., *Materials and Proportions for Mixtures Used in External and Internal Restoration Work on Church Masonry.* Nationalmuseet Bevaringsafdelingden, Lyngby, 1991.

Johnston, D., *A Guide to Traditional Mortar.* Masons Mortar, Edinburgh, 1994.

Keefe, L., Bedford, P., Induni, B. and Induni, L., *Appropriate Plasters, Renders and Finishes for Cob and Random Stone Walls in Devon.* Devon Earth Building Association, Exeter, 1993.

Kemp, W., *The Practical Plasterer.* Fourth edition, Crosby Lockwood & Son, London, 1912.

Kirkcaldy, J.F. and Bates, D.E.B., *Field Geology, Minerals and Rocks.* New Orchard Editions Ltd., Poole, 1988.

Lea, F.M., *The Chemistry of Cement and Concrete.* Edward Arnold & Co., London, 1935.

Limestone Federation, *The Uses of Lime in Building.* The British Lime Manufacturers, London, 1963.

Lynch, G., *Brickwork History, Technology and Practice.* Vol. 1., Donhead Publishing Ltd., 1994.

Macey, F.W., *Specifications in Detail*. Second edition, Crosby Lockwood & Son, London, 1904.

Meek, T., *Case Studies of Traditional Lime Harling: Discussion Document*. Historic Scotland, Edinburgh, 1996.

Millar, W., *Plastering Plain and Decorative*. B.T. Batsford, London, 1897.

Mitchell C.F., *Building Construction, First Stage*. Eighth edition, B.T. Batsford, London, 1911.

Moxon, J., *Mechanick Exercises or the Doctrine of Handy-Works*. Dan. Midwinter and Tho. Leigh, London, 1703.

Neve, R., *The City and Country Purchaser and Builder's Dictionary: or the Compleat Builder's Guide*. David & Charles (Publishers) Ltd., Newton Abbot, 1969, facsimile of 1726 edition.

Nicholson, P., *Dictionary of Architecture*. The London Printing and Publishing Company, London and New York, c.1850.

Nicholson, P., *The New Practical Builder and Workmans Companion*. Thomas Kelly, London, 1823.

North, F.J., *Limestones: Their Origins, Distribution and Uses*. Thomas Murby & Co., London and New York, 1930.

Norton, J., *Building with Earth*. Intermediate Technology Publications, London, 1986. (New edition published 1997.)

Oliver, P., *Shelter, Sign and Symbol*. Barrie & Jenkins Ltd., London, 1975.

Orton, J.R., *Lime and Other Alternative Cements*, Appendix 16, Intermediate Technology Publications, London, 1992.

Pearson, G.T., *Conservation of Clay and Chalk Buildings*. Donhead Publishing, London, 1992.

Politis, E. 'Decorated houses of Pyrghi, Chios', in *Shelter, Sign and Symbol*, Barrie & Jenkins Ltd., London, 1975.

Potter, T., *Concrete: its uses in building*. B.T. Batsford, London, 1908.

Price, C.A. and Ross K.D., The Cleaning and Treatment of Limestone by the Lime Method, Part II. *Monumentum*, Volume 27, Number 4, Butterworths for ICOMOS, December 1984.

Redgrave, G.R. and Spackman C., *Calcareous Cements: Their Nature, Manufacture and Uses*. Second edition, Charles Griffin & Company Limited, London, 1905.

Reid, H., *A Practical Treatise on Concrete and how to make it*. E. & F.N. Spon, London, 1869.

Reid, K., *Panel infillings to timber-framed buildings*. SPAB Technical pamphlet no. 11, London and Margate, 1989.

Renton, K.H. and Lee, H.N., Lime Mortars and Plasters in Building. *Building Technology and Management*, April, May, 1989.

Rivington, N., *Series of Notes on Building Construction* Part III Materials, Fourth edition, Longmans Green & Co., London, New York and Bombay, 1899.

Rogers, H., 'Sana'a in the Twentieth Century' in *The Architect*, RIBA Journal, January, 1986.

Salzman, L.F., *Building in England down to 1540*. Clarendon Press, Oxford, 1952.

Sawyer, J.T., *Plastering*. Edward Arnold (Publishers) Ltd., London, c.1950.

Schofield, Jane, *Lime in Building: A practical guide*. Second edition, Black Dog Press, Crediton, 1995.

Schofield, J., *Basic Limewash*. SPAB Information sheet 1, The Society for the Protection of Ancient Buildings, London, 1985, reprinted 1994.

Schreckenbach, H., *Wall Finishes for Earthen Walls – Based on Studies in Ghana*. BASIN News, Issue No. 1, St. Gallen, 1991.

Simpson & Brown Architects, HS Technical Advice Note No. 2: *Conservation of Plasterwork*. Historic Scotland, Edinburgh, 1994.

Singer, C., Holmyard, E.J., Hall, A.R. and Williams, T.I., *A History of Technology*. Vol II, Oxford University Press, New York and London, 1956 reprinted 1967 and Vol. IV, 1958.

Siravo, F. and Pulver, A., *Planning Lamu, Conservation of an East African Sea Port*. National Museums of Kenya, Nairobi, 1986.

Smeaton, A.C., *The Builder's Pocket Manual Containing the Elements of Building, Surveying and Architecture*. M. Taylor, London and New York, 1837.

Smeaton, J., *A Narrative of Building and a description of the Construction of the Edystone Lighthouse with Stone*. Second edition, G. Nicol, London, 1793.

Smith, G., *Essay on the Construction of Cottages for the Highland Society of Scotland*, Blackie & Son, Edinburgh, 1834.

Smith, R.G., *Alternatives to OPC*. BRE Overseas Building Note no. 198, BRE, Garston, 1993.

Spence, R.J.S., Lime and surkhi manufacture in India in *Lime and Alternative Cements*, Intermediate Technology Publications, London, 1975.

Spence, R.J.S. and Cook D.J., *Building Materials in Developing Countries*. John Wiley & Sons, Chichester, New York, Toronto, Brisbane, Singapore, 1982.

Stagg, W.D. and Pegg, B.F., *Plastering, a Craftsman's Encyclopedia*, 2nd edn., BSP Professional Books, Oxford, London, Edinburgh, Boston, Melbourne, 1984.

Stanley, C.C., *Highlights in the History of Concrete*. Cement and Concrete Association, Slough, 1979, amended 1986.

Stenning, D.F., Richards, P.M. and Carpenter, R.R., *Pargetting, Traditional Building Materials in Essex*. No. 1, Essex County Council, Chelmsford, 1982.

Stulz, R., *Appropriate Building Materials*. SKAT and Intermediate Technology Publications Ltd., St. Gallen and London, 1981; revised with Mukerji, K., 1988.

Stewart, J., Glover, R., Holmes, S., Proudfoot, T. and Seeley, N., Traditional Lime-Mortar Formulations at the National Trust. *Transactions*, Vol. 19 Association for Studies in the Conservation of Historic Buildings pp.21–38, 1994.

Swann, S., 'The History and use of Roman Cement'. *Lime News*, Edinburgh, 1997.

Teutonico, J.M., (ed.) *The English Heritage Directory of Building Limes*. Donhead, Shaftesbury, 1997.

Teutonico, J.M., McCaig, I., Burns, C. and Ashurst, J., *The Smeaton Project: Factors affecting the properties of lime-based mortars*. Eurolime Newsletter No. 2, pp.71–77, 1994.

Thomas, W., 'The Execution of Flint and Rubble Walling'. *The Builder*, pp.605–6, September 24th, 1853.

Torraca, G., *Porous Building Materials*. Third edition, ICCROM, Rome, 1988.

Townsend, A., *Rough-Cast for Historic Buildings*. SPAB Information Sheet 11, The Society for the Protection of Ancient Buildings, London, 1989.

Twenhofel, W.H., Treatise on Sedimentation, c.1900.

UNCHS (Habitat), *Earth Construction Technology*. Vols.1–4, United Nations Centre for Human Settlements, Nairobi, 1986.

UNCHS (Habitat), Earth Construction Technology, Technical Notes, no. 11, Part 1, *The Basic Parameters of Soil as a Construction Material*. UNCHS, Nairobi, 1987.

Verrall, W., R.C.P. *Plastering*, Sir Isaac Pitman & Sons Ltd., 1931.

Verrall, W., *The Modern Plasterer*. Vols. 1 and 2, Caxton Publishing Company Limited, London, c.1930.

Vicat, L.J., *A Practical and Scientific Treatise on Calcareous Mortars and Cements, Artificial and Natural*, J.T. Smith, (Translator) London, 1837.

Vitruvius, M.P., *The Ten Books on Architecture*. M.H. Morgan, (Translator), Dover Publications Inc., New York, 1960 (first published by the Harvard University Press 1914).

Williams, G.B.A., *Pointing Stone and Brick Walling*. SPAB Technical Pamphlet 5, The Society for the Protection of Ancient Buildings, London, 1986.

Williams-Ellis, C., Eastwick-Field, J. and Eastwick-Field, E., *Building in Cob, Pisé and Stabilized Earth*. Country Life Limited, London, revised and enlarged edition 1947.

Winden, J.van, *Rural Building*. Vols. 1 & 2, Stichting Kongregatie F.I.C., Maastricht, 1982 second impression 1986.

Wingate, M., *Small-Scale Lime-Burning*. Intermediate Technology Publications, London, 1985.

Wingate, M., *An Introduction to Building Limes*. SPAB Information Sheet 9, The Society for the Protection of Ancient Buildings, London, c.1990.

Wood, M., *The English Mediaeval House*. Bracken Books, London, 1983.

Wright, A., *Craft Techniques for Traditional Buildings*. B.T. Batsford Ltd., London, 1991.

Young, R., 'Cement Scorned, Report on External Lime Rendering to No. 33 Gloucester Street, Cirencester'. *SPAB News*, Vol. 12 No. 1, London, 1991.

Young, S.E., 'Pitting of plaster'. *American Ceramic Society Transactions*, Vol. 15, p. 659, 1913.

Zacharopoulou, G.P., *A Review of Recent Research on Lime Based Mortars for Conservation*. Thesis submitted for the Degree of Master of Arts in Conservation Studies, Institute of Advanced Architectural Studies, University of York, 1993.

Glossary

Accelerator: an ingredient added to a mortar or plastering mix to hasten the set.

Active clay: any clay which will produce an active pozzolan by firing at a suitable temperature. These are likely to be fine and soft clays, but the mineralogy is significant.

Active hydraulic binder: a hydraulic binder which acts without the addition of an activator such as lime. In effect this includes hydraulic cements and hydraulic limes, but excludes pozzolans.

Adobe: a method of earth construction in which the clay soil is first made into blocks which are allowed to dry out before they are used in the masonry.

Aggregate: the hard filler materials, such as sand and stones, in mortars, plasters, renders and concretes.

Agricultural lime: any lime used for soil conditioning, but usually a term to describe ground-up chalk or limestone which is calcium carbonate. In building terms, this is not called lime.

Air limes: limes which set through carbonation rather than through chemical reaction with water.

Air slaked lime: the mixture of calcium (and possibly magnesium) carbonate, hydroxide and oxide which results when a quicklime slakes naturally in moist air. For most purposes this is a debased material.

Air-entraining agents: materials which cause air to be included in a mortar mix. This air may either be as bubbles in the matrix or air-filled pores.

Aluminates: compounds of aluminium and oxygen.

Aragonite: the mineral form of calcium carbonate with an orthorhombal crystal structure.

Arènes: a class of sands described by Vicat and having irregular and unequal grains and a clay content of between 25% and 75%. A mortar prepared with a fat lime and arène can harden underwater and has been used for repairs to hydraulic engineering work in the Dordogne region of France.

Argillaceous: containing clay substances, normally used in the context of rocks or marls.

Armature: a rod or framework of iron or other material built into a surface, usually a wall or ceiling, for the purpose of strengthening or providing additional support to build up plaster or render to form features in relief, usually decorative.

Artificial pozzolan: a man-made material which will react with lime and water to give a hydraulic set. For example, reactive brick dust.

As dug (sand): sand exactly as it is dug from the quarry, without any sieving or washing.

Ashlar: squared and regular masonry.

Autogenous healing: the self-healing of fine cracks in a mortar or render from the binder already in that mortar. Free lime is transported by moisture into the cracks.

Background: the masonry, lathing or other surface on to which the plaster or render coats are built up.

Backing coat: the first of two or more coats in a plaster system.

Bagged lime: usually dry hydrate of lime. Calcium (and perhaps magnesium) hydroxide in a dry powder form and sold in sacks. Bagged lime may also refer to bagged quicklime in small lump or granular form (ground lime) but this definition is less common.

Banker: a raised board on which plaster is stored beside the plasterer for immediate use.

Battens: light timbers fixed (in this context) to carry the plastering laths.

Bead: a small round moulding.

Bevel: a slope made by the cutting of an angle.

Binder: the material which forms the matrix between aggregate particles in a mortar, plaster, render or lime concrete. It is a paste when first prepared, but must then harden to hold the aggregate in a coherent state. Examples include, lime, clay, gypsum and cement.

Blue Lias lime: a hydraulic lime prepared from some of the limestones in the Lias formation which runs across England and the south of Wales. This was used extensively for engineering and external work in the nineteenth century.

Bond: 1. the overlapping of stones, bricks or other masonry units in a wall or other structure, 2. the adhesion between two surfaces, for example a render and its backing.

Bordeaux mixture: A mixture of copper sulphate, lime and water used on plants as a fungicide.

Brandering: to brander a ceiling is to fix battens at right angles to the joists before fixing the laths. Fillets or grounds may be fixed to flat surfaces to support and raise laths in order to allow a plaster key to be formed. The whole process is called brandering.

Breatheability: the extent to which a building material is able to allow moisture to move to the surface and evaporate harmlessly.

Building lime: lime of a suitable nature and in an appropriate state for building uses. For example, hydrated dolomitic lime should be fully hydrated. The composition and classes of building lime are given in Appendix 1. All classes of lime may contain varying proportions of magnesia or dolomite.

Calcareous (material): material containing chalk or other forms of calcium carbonate or lime.

Calcination: in this context the conversion of carbonate to lime, but the word has a much wider meaning including the conversion of metals into their oxides by strong heating.

Calcite: the mineral form of calcium carbonate having a rhombohedral structure. This is the form which gives strength to a well-carbonated lime mortar. It occurs naturally as Iceland Spar and has a unique double refraction of light which may be the reason for the exceptional appearance of limewashed surfaces.

Calcium: Ca, a soft white metallic element.

Calcium carbonate: $CaCO_3$, the material from which lime is prepared. Natural forms are limestones, chalks, shells and corals. It is also formed as an industrial by-product, as in acetylene manufacture. Mortars, renders and plasters containing calcium hydroxide take up carbon dioxide from the air to form calcium carbonate, which develops the set.

Calcium hydroxide: $Ca(OH)_2$, the chemical name for slaked lime or hydrated lime; also lime putty and milk of lime.

Calcium oxide: CaO, commonly called quicklime.

Cantilever: a projecting bracket.

Carbonation, carbonated: carbonation is the process of forming carbonates, and in this context the formation of calcium carbonate from calcium hydroxide when a lime develops its set. A lime mortar is said to have carbonated when the binder has reacted with carbon dioxide from the air and developed strength beyond that which is achieved simply by drying out.

Carbonic acid: H_2CO_3, the very weak acid which is formed when carbon dioxide gas dissolves in water. The salts of this acid are the carbonates and the bicarbonates.

Casein: a protein in milk with many industrial applications including glue making. It can form an adhesive with lime.

Cement: in this context a quick-setting binder for making mortars and concretes. By far the most widespread cement is the Portland Cement formed by grinding a clinker which has been prepared at high kiln temperatures from a mixture of clay and limestone. There are, however, other forms of cement including 'natural cements' formed from naturally occurring nodules of calcareous clay (such as Septaria). A distinction between these and other hydraulic limes is that cements must be ground to a fine powder before they can slake.

Cementation index: a formula for assessing the likely early setting properties of hydraulic limes by their chemical composition. For example, from

Boynton (1980), C.I. = $(2.8 \times S + 1.1 \times A + 0.7 \times F) / (C + 1.4 \times M)$ where S = % reactive silica, A = % alumina, F = % ferrous oxide, C = % calcium oxide and M = % magnesia in the sample. The Index ratings for each class of lime are given in Table 2.1.

Chalk: a common form of calcium carbonate with a very fine structure. A limestone, cretaceous in age, usually very porous and fine-grained ranging from white to pale grey in colour.

Chalk lime: lime calcined from chalk. This may be Class A, Class B or Class C1 depending on the impurities in the bed from which the chalk was taken.

Chamfer: a bevel.

Chunam: a fine stucco based on very pure or shell-lime, fine aggregate and extensive polishing used for the highest quality finishes, often to external walls and roofs, widely used in India. Also referred to as Arayash and Sudha.

Class A lime: Air limes. Non-hydraulic limes. Rich or fat limes. Pure limes. 'White' limes (though the colour is not a safe guide).

Class B lime: see 'Lean lime'.

Class C lime: naturally occurring hydraulic lime. Lime containing an appreciable amount of active clay which can enable it to set by combination with water.

Clay: the smallest particles produced by the weathering of rocks, each particle is less than two microns across. Chemically, clay particles are hydrated alumino-silicates, and physically they are usually in the form of thin plates which stack together.

Clinker (cement clinker): a hard solid material formed by the fusion of other materials (limestone and clay for a cement clinker) at high temperatures.

Coarse stuff: a mixture of lime putty and aggregate which is stored to mature for use as a plaster, render (1st and 2nd coats), or mortar.

Cob: one of the forms of construction of earth walls. Soil plasticized with water is mixed with straw and placed on the wall top with a fork. It is trampled into place and any excess is pared off with a cutting tool.

Colour fastness: the ability of a pigment to retain its colour even against the actions of lime and of strong light.

Composite mortar, compo: a building mortar with cement as its binder and lime to give it workable qualities. The aggregate would normally be sand.

Concrete: a structural building material which can be cast in a fluid state but will set to a firm solid. It consists of sands and stones with water and a binder such as cement or hydraulic lime. This differs from mortar in containing much larger aggregate sizes.

Conservation (conserved): In the care of old buildings, a primary concern is to protect the individual elements such as the bricks and stones, but in the wider context of the whole building and location. The work to conserve the stones of a façade may involve changing an unsuitable pointing mortar to allow the individual stones and the building as a whole to survive for longer.

Corbel: a projection jutting out from the face of a wall, usually to support the weight of a structure or ornament above.

Core (of a wall): in some forms of masonry construction the walls are built with carefully set facing units on the two faces, and the space between these is filled with a rubble concrete which is known as the core.

Core (in quicklime): often a lump of quicklime will contain a core of calcium carbonate which has not converted to calcium oxide due to under-burning in the kiln. In modern methods of preparation this may be re-moved, but in old work it can often be seen as part of the aggregate in a mortar.

Cornice: 1. a series of mouldings crowning a wall or on façades of buildings, 2. the top part of an entablature.

Counter laths: spacing laths running behind and at right angles to the main laths which carry the plaster. This may be to even up the surface, or to allow a space for the nibs to form a key when the plaster is pressed through.

Cross screeds: the secondary screeds which run between, and at right angles to, the main screeds in defining the plane of a carefully ruled plaster surface.

Cure (to cure): the setting and hardening process of a plastic mix contain-ing a cementitious binder.

Dead-burnt dolomite: a chemically inactive form of dolomitic quicklime used for refractory linings.

Dead-burnt lime: Calcium oxide formed at extremely high furnace tem-peratures. It has a dense physical structure which does not allow it to hydrate under normal conditions.

Depeter: decoration of an external render by pressing in hard decorative stones or fragments of other materials to form a decorative pattern.

Diaper: a geometrical pattern carved on a wall, a screen or round openings repeated over the areas in regular formation as ornament.

Dolomitic limestone: a calcareous rock with a high content of the double carbonate of calcium and magnesium $CaCO_3.MgCO_3$. Dolomitic limes contain a high proportion of magnesium compounds whilst magnesian limes contain a significant but lower proportion. High calcium limes con-tain very little magnesium. ASTM C51–71 defines dolomitic limestone as a limestone containing from 35% to 46% magnesium carbonate ($MgCO_3$).

Dots (plaster dots): dabs of plaster which are carefully set up to define the eventual plane of a plaster surface. They are first joined up by carefully levelled strips called screeds and the plasterer's rule is worked across the surface of the screeds.

Drowned lime: lime which has been spoiled in slaking because it has failed to reach the necessary temperature for a satisfactory reaction between the water and a naturally slow-slaking (unreactive) quicklime. A skin of lime putty seals the quicklime preventing further fresh water from reaching the remaining quicklime. Further agitation or some careful external heating is needed to avoid the problem.

E.M.L.: expanded metal lathing.

Eminently hydraulic lime: Class C3 lime prepared from a limestone containing a high proportion of active clay. Most suitable for hydraulic engineering works. The distinction between this and a natural cement is that the eminently hydraulic lime still contains enough free lime to enable it to break up and slake when water is added. The cement must be finely ground to be able to hydrate.

Enrichment: carvings or other embellishments as added ornaments.

Entablature: the horizontal members carried by columns, normally in classical architecture.

Expanded metal lathing: a sheet steel material which is cut and stretched to form a perforated surface. It is used as an alternative to wooden laths but is a poor substitute when working with lime plasters.

Façade: exterior surface of a building, usually used in connection with the front or principal elevation.

Fallen lime: lime which has air slaked.

Fat lime: Class A lime putty having a good workability.

Fattening up: the slow absorption of water into a lime putty. This literally plumps it up and makes it more plastic.

Fatter: The fatter a lime is, the more sand it can carry cohesively and the smoother its putty.

Feebly hydraulic lime: slightly hydraulic lime; Class C1 lime. This contains a small proportion of active clay, typically less than 12%, and should set in water in fifteen to twenty days or even longer.

Fine stuff: a mixture of lime putty and very fine aggregate which is stored to mature for use as plaster finishing coats.

Fixing fillet: a band or wedge of wood or other material embedded in the structure to which woodwork or other materials are fixed.

Float (to float): a float is a laying on and smoothing tool for plastering.

Floating fair: to use the float to achieve a sound, smooth and flat finish on plaster.

Flocculation: the gathering together or clotting of fine particles in a dispersed state to form large agglomerations.

Fly ash: a very fine coal ash which may have pozzolanic properties. See also PFA.

Foraminifera: an order of the lowest class of Protozoa, a minute sea creature of one living cell with a shell usually perforated by pores (*foramina*). It can contribute to the formation of magnesian limestone as the shell is composed of up to about 11% magnesium carbonate.

Formaldehyde, formalin: formalin is a 40% solution of formaldehyde gas (H-CHO). Among other uses it is a disinfectant and preservative.

Free lime: lime in a mortar which remains as calcium hydroxide and has not yet carbonated or combined with a pozzolan. It may be transported by moisture in various forms such as calcium bicarbonate or calcium hydroxide and may heal fine cracks.

Fresco: painting with pigments into a freshly formed lime plaster surface.

Grappiers: lumps of clinker which are formed when certain hydraulic limestones are calcined. These are screened out from the remainder of the lime and ground to a fine powder which is either mixed back into the lime or sold separately as Grappier Cement.

Green state: the transitory state of a mortar or plaster which, in the process of drying out, has developed a little mechanical strength just from its loss of plasticity, but which has not yet developed significant strength from carbonation or hydraulic reaction. It may have a characteristic dull dark green colour.

Grey lime, greystone lime: a Class C1 lime from chalk containing a small proportion of clay. Limes of this sort were used for most of the brickwork in London up to about 1940. Confusion arises because the word greystone was sometimes abbreviated to 'stone', so that in old documents 'stone lime' may either be hydraulic (from greystone chalk) or non-hydraulic (from a pure limestone).

Ground lime: quicklime which has been ground down to a specified particle size range.

Grout: a mortar in a fluid state prepared and poured into place to fill fine joints or voids in masonry. Used for joints and crevices too small to access with mortar of normal consistency. Hydraulic lime, either natural or artificial, is generally preferred for grout due to the advantages of a hydraulic set in the depth of joint filled. Very fine sand, brick dust or a combination of these may be used as aggregate. Where joints are exceptionally fine (1–2mm), moderately or eminently hydraulic limes, and particularly the leaner limes, may be used on their own without aggregate.

Gypsum: $CaSO_4.2H_2O$. The dihydrate of calcium sulphate from which the various forms of gypsum plaster are prepared by dehydration, and to which they revert on setting.

Hack: to cut back and roughen the surface.

Hair hook: a tool like a broad-pronged rake for mixing hair into a lime plaster or mortar.

Hand picking: the process of handling large lumps of quicklime to assess their densities. The denser lumps are rejected as they are either over-burnt or contain an excessive core of unburnt material.

Hard (plastering on the hard): when plaster is placed straight on to the masonry rather than on to laths it is said to be on the hard. In damp conditions an air lime plaster on the hard will not set.

Hard-burnt quicklime: a quicklime which has been deliberately finished in the kiln at a high temperature so that it is protected by a less reactive shell. This is helpful for storage and handling.

Harling: a thrown finish of lime and aggregate, applied by throwing the material on to a well-prepared background. The heavily textured surface improves durability making it suitable for more severe climates. Traditional for external walls in Scotland.

Hawk (plasterer's hawk): a hand tool made of a rectangular board with a handle below, to carry plaster for laying.

High calcium lime: Class A lime. A pure form of calcium oxide or hydroxide containing no clay and with less than 5% of magnesium oxide.

High-speed pan mill: a powered mortar mixer in which a series of scrapers and blades connected to a rotating vertical shaft are moved through the mix to ensure a thorough combination of aggregate and binder.

Horse: the principal timber board used to support the stock and mould profile of a running mould.

Hot lime: lime mortar prepared by slaking quicklime in sand and mixing the ingredients in the hot state as the lime slakes. In the very few cases where expansion would be helpful the mortar can be used in that state (like an 'expanding cement'), but more often it is stored in moist conditions for a few days to complete the slaking. In this method there is no control to eliminate the defects which can be caused by late hydration of over burnt quicklime or contamination with under-burnt material other than by punching the mortar through a sieve.

Hydrated lime, dry hydrate: Calcium hydroxide as a dry white (or lightly coloured) powder, $Ca(OH)_2$. Bagged lime. In production, the heat of hydration drives off any slight excess of water to leave a dry powder which may be improved by sieving or by air separation to remove heavy particles. It may be stored in a silo for some days or weeks to allow for late hydration before the material is packed in containers, usually paper sacks, or distributed in tankers.

Hydrated hydraulic lime: a Class C lime which has been hydrated into a dry powder at the works to be sold to the users in bagged form.

Hydration: strictly hydration is the chemical combination of a salt and its water of hydration, but in this context it is used to describe the chemical combination of calcium (or magnesium) oxide with water to form the hydroxide. If carried out in a wet state this is called 'slaking to putty' and with minimum water 'dry hydrate' or powder is formed.

Hydraulic binder: a binder which sets and develops strength by chemical interaction with water. It can set under water.

Hydraulic cement: the formal term for a cement which takes a hydraulic set.

Hydraulic limes: Class C limes are natural hydraulic limes prepared from limestones or chalks with clayey impurities. Artificial hydraulic limes are manufactured by mixing pozzolan with calcium hydroxide which enable the limes to harden even in damp conditions. Hydraulic limes were originally used in areas subject to frequent saturation or continuously damp conditions, and for hydraulic engineering works such as harbours and bridge piers.

Hydraulic set (of limes): the chemical combination of lime, burnt clay or other pozzolanic material and water to form a stable compound, even under water. This can either be arranged by mixing an air lime (or any other) with a pozzolan and water, or by mixing a hydraulic lime and water. In the latter case the lime and clay will already have formed intermediate compounds in the firing.

Impervious: forming a barrier to water in its liquid state.

Impfing: seeding a liquid with a small crystal to begin a general process of crystallization. Inclusions of calcite crystals, for example in the form of crushed oyster shells, can promote crystal growth through a lime mortar as it carbonates and thus help to develop strength.

Intonaco: a relatively simple Italian stucco technique with sands, a little crushed brick and lime.

Jaghery, jaggery: a coarse dark brown Indian sugar made from the sap of the jaggery palm tree. This is used in small quantities in water used for mixing a mortar or render, particularly to strengthen the finishing coat in a plaster. Sugar greatly increases the solubility of lime in water.

Jamb: the side of a window or doorway.

Kankar: a pozzolanic ingredient of limes and aggregates used for hydraulic mixes in India.

Keratin: a protein found in horn, hoof, wool and hair. Traditionally used for the production of glues and sealants, but sensitive to moisture.

Key: a mechanical bond produced by the physical interpenetration of the first plaster coat with the background and of one plaster coat with another. The plaster key on lath background is made by the nibs that are formed between and behind the laths by pressure with the float when laying on the first coat. The nib is ideally a dovetail shape, but in practice just an irregular nib or scratching.

Large lump lime: quicklime in sizes over 200 mm which are thus suitable for hand picking.

Larry: a long-handled mixing tool for mixing lime putty and coarse stuff. It is like a hoe with a half-moon shaped hole in its blade.

Late hydration: normally, reactive quicklime combines with water to a large extent within a matter of minutes and entirely within a few hours. But quicklime burnt at a higher temperature, perhaps at a hot spot within the kiln, and some of the more hydraulic limes may be less reactive. It may not combine with water until some days or even months later. This can be a serious problem since the lime in its hydrated state may be almost double the volume of the quicklime. This situation can give rise to defects in the finished work.

Latent hydraulic binder: a pozzolan. It can combine with lime and water to give a hydraulic set.

Laterite, murram, red soil: soil formed as the result of tropical weathering of rocks rich in iron, alumina or both; often with varying proportions of free silica, quartz and clay. Typically the iron fraction, which can vary between 5% and 40%, is one of the principal causes of hardening when exposed to air and/or dried. This hardening quality is used, in tropical countries, to produce sun-dried bricks and earth structures without the need for firing or other stabilization methods. The addition of lime and/or compaction often has the effect of improving the durability of this soil as a construction material.

Lath, lathing: the riven or sawn wood which is nailed up to form the background to some plaster systems. Typical dimensions for a lath are 25 mm wide, 5 mm to 6 mm thick, and 900 mm to 1500 mm long. The word lathing is also used to describe alternative materials which do a similar task, for example, expanded metal, perforated and ribbed sheet materials, mesh and reeds.

Lean lime: Class B lime. A lime prepared from a limestone or chalk which contains impurities which do not contribute to a hydraulic set, but act instead as part of the aggregate in a mortar. For this reason comparatively more lean lime needs to be used in a mortar mix. Often the lean limes will also contain active clay ingredients (Class B from nil up to 8%) to give a slightly hydraulic set.

Lime: the root meaning of the word is a sticky substance and from that it has developed several later meanings. In this context, the word lime includes all of the oxides and hydroxides of calcium and magnesium, but excludes the carbonates. Thus quicklime and slaked lime we would call lime, but chalk and limestone we would not call lime. Farmers are not so pedantic and may 'lime' their fields with crushed chalk.

Lime concrete: a building material cast from aggregate (usually sand and stone) in a matrix of hydraulic lime or of lime and pozzolan, but not using Portland cement.

Lime cycle: a concept to warm the heart of environmentalists. When lime is used in buildings it eventually reverts to calcium carbonate which is the chemical from which it was originally prepared, so all the carbon dioxide gas driven off in the lime-burning is eventually replaced by carbon dioxide taken back from the atmosphere. The full sweep of the cycle is the conversion to calcium oxide (giving off carbon dioxide), the combination with water to form calcium hydroxide, and finally the carbonation in which water is lost and carbon dioxide regained to form calcium carbonate again.

Lime pit: a covered tank formed in the ground to store lime putty in moist conditions.

Lime putty: slaked lime stored in an excess of water to fatten up. This process also enables less reactive particles to be hydrated before use. In Roman times the lime putty for plastering of the highest standard had to be stored for three years before use. A distinction should be drawn between putty prepared from dry hydrate and putty run directly from quicklime. The overwhelming evidence on site shows the latter to be greatly superior, where excellent plasticity and good carbonation are needed. Dry hydrated lime should also be made up into a putty (paste) to fatten up before use, but this is rarely done due to the additional time and effort involved.

Lime water (limewater): a saturated solution of calcium hydroxide in water. When lime putty settles out from milk of lime the clear liquid above is limewater. As this evaporates it becomes covered with a clear layer of calcite. Lime water may be used for consolidation of porous materials. Dr Higgins, in the eighteenth century, recommended it for use in place of water for all lime work, for example for slaking lime and diluting limewashes.

Lime-ash floors: a method of forming floors, particularly upper floors, with a lightweight concrete formed on reeds or laths laid out over the timber floor joists. The composition varies greatly from one place to another and, for upper floors, most include a considerable amount of gypsum as part of the binder. Other ingredients are small lime and ashes from the limekilns. Crushed brick is often incorporated.

Limed wood: 1. limed oak, a finish given to oak furniture by rubbing a paste of chloride of lime and water into the grain. It may be finished with a wax polish. 2. A finish given to new or well-prepared and clean woodwork by painting or rubbing on thin limewash. When dry this may either be left as the finish or vigorously brushed off to leave the wood grain showing white.

Limestone: any rock or stone whose main constituents are calcium carbonate or calcium and magnesium carbonates.

Limewash: a simple form of paint prepared from lime, with or without various additives. It is most suitable for use on walls and on ceilings, both internally and externally.

Lump lime: Calcium oxide (quicklime) in lump form, rather than crushed form.

Magnesia: Magnesium oxide. It occurs in double compounds with calcium when dolomitic limestones are fired.

Magnesian limestone: a calcareous rock containing magnesium carbonate ($MgCO_3$) in lower proportions than dolomitic limestone. ASTM C51–71 defines magnesian limestone as a limestone containing from 5% to 35% $MgCO_3$.

Marl: 1. a soft calcareous rock, mostly made up of shells and usually containing appreciable quantities of clay and sand. 2. in some districts weathered chalk is known as marl.

Marmorino: a decorative Italian stucco technique using several coats of lime and various gradings of marble dust, usually mixed in the ratio of 2 parts marble dust to 1 part lime.

Masonry: either the craft of walling and vaulting, or the products of the mason's work – the units set in mortar. The exact scope varies from country to country; for example, in some areas stone would be included but not brickwork, and in others stone, brickwork and mud walling would all be included.

Masonry units: the blocks of stone or concrete, earth or bricks from which a masonry wall or other structure is built.

Milk of lime: a free flowing suspension of hydrated lime in water in such proportions as to resemble milk in appearance.

Moderately hydraulic lime: Class C2 lime which might be expected to set under water in about six to eight days, but possibly longer.

Mortar: Any material in a plastic state which can be trowelled, becomes hard in place, and which can be used for bedding and jointing masonry units.

Mortar mill: 1. See roller pan mill. 2. Similar to a roller pan mill in operation but with many variations including stone rollers and troughs of varying sizes in lieu of a pan. It may be animal, machine or man-powered.

Mountain lime: an archaic term for Class A lime prepared from carboniferous limestones. For example the high purity Buxton lime in England.

Natural cement: a fortuitous balance of chalk and clay, as in certain mudstones, can have the ideal proportions to produce a quick-setting cement when fired at its optimum temperature. The original patent for Parker's 'Roman' cement was taken out in 1796. Like other cements, natural cements need to be finely ground before they can hydrate.

Non-hydraulic lime: Class A lime. A lime with high purity.

O.P.C.: Ordinary Portland cement.

One-and-a-half coat (plaster) work: a thin second coat of very fat fine stuff applied over a coat of coarse stuff when it is still 'green'.

Over-burnt quicklime: if lime is burned at too high a temperature the lumps begin to contract, become less reactive and, particularly if there is a sufficient amount of clay in the stone, will eventually sinter. This gives them a wizened appearance. Over-burnt lumps will not slake readily and may lead to problems from late hydration.

P.F.A.: Pulverized Fuel Ash is a waste product from power stations burning pulverized coal. The product varies with different coals and different burning conditions, but some PFAs are pozzolanic. They are all contaminated with sulphates, some much more so than others. PFA is used in grouts with lime, and with cement where it serves two purposes: much of the material is in the form of tiny spheres of glass which help the grout to flow readily. The reactive parts will combine to set with lime (or with free lime in a cement) in a hydraulic reaction in a position where carbonation would not easily take place.

Pargeting, parging, to parge: 1: rich decoration on external plasterwork by modelling the surface. 2: lining a flue or other surface with a mix of lime putty and cow dung.

Particle size distribution: an assessment of the proportions of material of different sizes within a sand or aggregate. For good work with lime an even distribution is helpful.

Pebble lime: quicklime graded within a certain size range of between about 6mm and 65mm.

Performance standards: a way of specifying which describes the results required (the performance) rather than the materials or practices to be used.

Permeability: the ease with which a liquid or vapour can pass through a solid material.

pH value: a scale from acidity to alkalinity expressed on a measure of 0–14; 0 for extreme acidity and 14 for extreme alkalinity.

Phenolphthalein indicator: a widely available chemical indicator which can clearly show the difference between neutral and alkali conditions. Thus, on calcium carbonate it remains colourless whilst on calcium hydroxide it changes to deep purple-red. This can show the extent of carbonation in a lime mortar.

Pigments: colouring material from which paints may be made, and in the form of a very fine dry insoluble powder.

Pisé de terre: a technique of building earth walls by compacting a relatively dry and lean soil between stout shutters.

Pitting and popping: a defect in plasterwork caused by late hydration of over-burnt quicklime when it has been incorporated into a plaster. As the quicklime hydrates it tries to expand and pressure builds up behind the surface. This may be released with a small explosion as a cone-shaped section of plaster in front of the speck blows forward (pops) leaving a small crater (pit) in the surface.

Plain plastering: plastering to simple smooth surfaces without three dimensional relief or decoration.

271

Planted: a term applied to mouldings and other ornamental features that are moulded or cast separately and then attached and not formed in the solid.

Plaster of Paris: Calcium sulphate hemi-hydrate, $CaSO_4.\frac{1}{2}H_2O$ derived from gypsum. Casting plaster. A very quick setting plaster which expands as it sets.

Plaster: plaster may be any material used in a plastic state to form a durable finishing coat to the surfaces of walls and ceilings and other elements of a building. Typical materials are based on lime or gypsum or cement or soil, or any combination of those.

Plastic materials: in this context, plastic means readily moulded with very little pressure.

Plasticity: a measure of the ease with which a material may be moulded or distorted.

Plasticizer: an additive used to make a mortar or concrete more workable. Often this will be an air entraining agent to form tiny bubbles in the mix.

Plinth: the base of a wall above the ground with a projecting surface.

Pointing: the finished surface layer in the joints between masonry units.

Porosity: the extent to which a solid material has pores or voids.

Porous aggregate: aggregate composed of particles containing air-filled pores. These assist speed of set of lime-based mixes and reduce the weight of the finished material.

Portland cement, ordinary Portland cement, O.P.C.: the common form of cement conforming to certain standards and made by grinding a clinker formed by firing a slurried mixture of clay and limestone at high temperature in a kiln. Calcium sulphate is also ground in to modify the setting rate. Originally so called because when set it was said to be as hard as Portland stone.

Portlandite: a crystalline form of calcium hydroxide as hexagonal plates.

Pozzolan, pozzolanic material: a pozzolan is any material which contains constituents, generally alumina and reactive silica, which will combine with hydrated lime at normal temperatures in the presence of moisture to form stable insoluble compounds with binding properties. It may be used to give a hydraulic set to a mortar made with a Class A lime or to combine with the free lime in a naturally hydraulic lime or Portland cement mix to increase its durability. There are many naturally occurring pozzolanic materials, such as certain volcanic ashes, and several artificial materials such as crushed soft bricks. These contain clay particles mostly composed of alumina, silica and sometimes iron, which have been rendered active by heat. Fine grinding increases their reactivity.

Pozzolanicity: the extent to which a material can combine with calcium hydroxide and water at normal temperatures to produce compounds which can set and develop strength under water.

Profile: outline of a moulding or other ornament.

PVA: An emulsion of polyvinyl acetate designed for use as a primer and bonding agent to improve background adhesion for internal plaster. Similar qualities and uses as SBR but not suitable for use externally or areas subject to damp.

Quicklime: Lime which has not been slaked. Lump lime, burnt lime, calcium oxide, CaO. The quicklime from magnesian limes may be in two states: $MgO.CaCO_3$ or $MgO.CaO$ or a mixture of this and CaO. Called 'quick' because of its lively affinity for water. Commonly recognized sizes from ASTM C51–71 are:
1. *large lump* – 200mm (8") and smaller.
2. *pebble* – 65mm (2½") and smaller.
3. *ground, screened or granular* – 6.5mm (¼") and smaller.
4. *pulverized*, mostly all passing a No. 20 (850μm sieve).

Quoin: the external angle of a wall. The word is often used in connection with corner stones.

Reactivity (of lime): The ability of lime to combine quickly in chemical reactions. This can be seen immediately in the slaking reaction. It is partly dependent on the parent limestone and largely dependent on the temperature and duration of calcination. Reactive limes have porous structures with high surface areas. Hard-burnt limes are less reactive. Over-burnt and dead-burnt limes are very unreactive.

Rebate, rabbet: a rectangular sinking along the edge of a piece of material, usually of wood or stone.

Relief: prominent sculptured or modelled ornament partly projecting from the background on which it stands.

Render: 1: an external plaster system. 2: the first coat of two-coat work (render and set) or of three-coat work (render, float and set).

Rendering: applying a first coat of coarse stuff to a solid background.

Resin, rosin: a hard brittle substance formed by the secretion of the sap of certain plants and many trees. Exudes naturally or can be obtained by incision. Extensively used in making varnishes. Examples are amber, gum animé and copal.

Retarder: an additive which delays the setting of a binder, perhaps to allow more time to work a plaster in its plastic state.

Return: a continuation of a member or moulding in another direction, usually at right angles.

Reveals: the sides of an opening such as a window or a doorway between the frames and the face of the wall.

Rich mortar: one with a higher than normal proportion of binder to aggregate or with a particularly smooth binder. It would be particularly free flowing and comfortable to use, but more prone to shrinkage.

Riven battens, riven laths: formed by splitting rather than sawing the timber. This leaves the fibres intact and gives considerable extra strength compared to sawn timber of a similar size.

Roller pan mill: an edge grinder adapted for mixing mortars. There are several variations, but the mortar rests in a sturdy ring-shaped pan and is squeezed by heavy iron rollers. Either the pan rotates or the two rollers are guided around the pan. The mixing is very thorough, but the grinding action changes the particle size distribution of the aggregates.

Roman cement: the very first quick-setting natural cement was patented by James Parker in 1796. The patent was vigorously exploited and the material was very widely used for fifty years. It has a characteristic warm brown colour. There was production in England, Germany, Russia and USA.

Run of kiln quicklime: quicklime with all impurities and defects, just as it is drawn from the kiln. This may include over-burnt and under-burnt material, ash, and even unburned fuel. The quality of run of kiln quicklime produced depends on the skill of the lime burner.

Running lime (to run lime): slaking quicklime to form milk of lime and running that through a sieve into a lime pit to mature. The sieving and the storage as lime putty contribute to good quality control.

Running a moulding: forming a cornice or similar moulding in plasterwork by drawing a template (the running mould) along guides across the plaster.

Sacrificial pointing or rendering: a pointing mortar or a render deliberately designed to be less durable than the masonry it protects. Any harmful salts are drawn into its pores and away from the masonry units.

Salamander: a portable fire-pot or heating furnace used to accelerate the drying of plaster in cold or wet weather.

Sand: weathered particles of rocks, usually high in silica, smaller than gravels and larger than silts, typically between about 0.06 mm to 5 mm. The particles are hard and will not crumble. Sand is used as an aggregate in mortars, plasters and renders as well as a component in concretes. The properties of sand used in a mix have a major effect on its workability, final strength and durability. The types of sand normally used in building are:

1. *Sharp sand*: consists of predominantly sharp angular grains. Clean well-graded sharp sand for mortar, render and plaster is selected as the best for the strength and durability it imparts to the finished work. Workability is improved by mixing with fat lime as the binder and allowing this to stand as coarse stuff (not possible with OPC as a binder on its own).

2. *Coarse sand*: A sand which is composed of predominantly large and medium sized grains. The higher the proportion of large grains, then the coarser the sand. Coarse sand is used for external renders and mortars to improve durability. Very coarse sands usually require a lime

binder, blending with other sands or the addition of a plasticizer to assist workability. Sharp coarse sand is the most durable but the least workable, although suitable for roughcast and harling.

3. *Soft sand*: A sand which is composed of predominantly small and rounded grains. It often has a silt content, the proportion of which is variable. It feels soft in the hand when squeezed. The smallest rounded particles assist workability but can give rise to cracking and failure in the finished work.

4. *Well-graded sand*: A sand with an approximately even particle size distribution. As the smaller particles may fit in between the larger particles, this even distribution reduces the proportion of voids to solids and thus is less demanding on the binder than poorly-graded sand.

5. *Blended sand*: A blend of sands of different grain sizes and sharpness to achieve a good particle size distribution. This provides a balance between durability and workability. Used mostly in connection with plaster for backing coats and pointing mortar when the quality of available sand needs to be improved. Sand may be blended, either from one source by sieving it to adjust the particle size proportions, or by using sands from different sources.

SBR: An emulsion of styrene-butadiene rubber designed for use as a primer and bonding agent to improve background adhesion for plasters and renders. It can assist in consolidating friable surfaces as an alternative to more traditional primers such as size. It reduces the natural suction of backgrounds and permeability unless heavily diluted (up to 10 : 1, water : SBR). Satisfactory for use externally but not compatible with organic based pigments or with masonry cements.

Scouring: giving plaster a smooth hard surface by working it in a circular motion with a cross grained float. This draws the binder and finest particles (laitance) to the surface. The same process can actually reduce durability in external work by leaving a lean layer behind the surface, that is a layer with a reduced proportion of binder.

Screed: 1. (in plastering or flooring) a carefully levelled band of stuff to act as a guide for the rule, the tool which sets the level of the whole surface. 2. (in floor laying) the whole mortar layer levelled to receive the finished floor surface.

Scutch hammer: a hammer designed to be fitted with plain or toothed blades which can be replaced when worn out. Used for hacking backgrounds to form a key for plaster and render.

Semi hydraulic lime: Class C2 lime.

Septaria: cement stones occurring in the mud of certain river estuaries. They sometimes contain light lined markings with seven sides and can be in the form of squat seven-sided prisms. They were the basis of Parker's patent for Roman cement.

Setting stuff: a mix of lime and fine aggregates and possibly gauged with gypsum, for the finishing coat in two- and three-coat lime plasterwork.

Sgraffito: a decorative treatment of plaster achieved by cutting and scratching through a coat of one colour to reveal a different colour in the coat behind. This is done before the plaster has set.

Shale: an argillaceous type of rock, characterized by cleavage-planes, intermediate between clay and slate.

Shell lime: 1: Class A lime prepared from sea shells and highly valued. 2: A Scottish term for quicklime.

Silicates: the salts of silicic acid (H_2SiO_3); the most common type of minerals. Conveniently treated as if they were compounds of silica (SiO_2) and of a metal oxide. Normally available and readily recognized in sand. A most important pozzolanic component in active clay.

Silver sand: a very fine-grained sand with negligible iron impurities and hence no yellow colour. It has a whitish-grey colour. Sometimes suitable for use in lime plaster finishing coats and lime : sand grouts.

Sintered: coalesced at high temperature to form a single mass although not strictly melted.

Size (glue size): a glue derived from animal products and used in solution with water to reduce the suction on a porous surface before applying a paint.

Skimming stuff: a mix of lime and very fine aggregates for a thin finishing coat.

Slaked lime: calcium hydroxide, $Ca(OH)_2$. Prepared by hydrating quicklime in an excess of water to form a milk or putty.

Slaking: 1. Slaking to putty; the action of combining quicklime with excess water to form milk of lime or lime putty. 2. Slaking to dry hydrate; the action of combining quicklime with the minimum amount of water to form dry hydrate powder. 3. Air slaking; the exposure of quicklime to the air in sufficient quantity to promote hydration.

Slightly hydraulic lime: Class C1 lime. Feebly hydraulic lime.

Small lime: when it was usual for builders to select 'hand-picked lump lime' the remainder of the quicklime from a batch, including dust and ashes, was sold as small lime at a lower price. It was used for floors and foundations. The ash might have acted as a pozzolan.

Soapstone: a soft stone that feels greasy to the touch and in which silicate of magnesium predominates. Produced in powder form as talc.

Soffit: 1. The horizontal lining at the head of an opening. 2. The underside of features such a eaves, arch and stairs, etc.

Soft-burnt quicklime: highly reactive quicklime which has been deliberately prepared at a relatively low kiln temperature.

Soil: (earth) formed by the weathering of rocks and containing a mixture of clays, silts, sands, stones and other materials.

Steady up (allow to steady up): allow plaster to take its initial set by drying out to reduce plasticity.

Stone lime: a description used before the explicit understanding of hydraulic limes. Sometimes describing hydraulic limes (from greystone chalks) and sometimes fat limes from pure limestone deposits. It was wrongly believed from very early times that the setting strength of a lime depended on the strength of the material from which it was calcined. On that basis limes prepared from marble were believed to be particularly potent.

Stucco: the Italian for plaster now adopted into the English language and used as a rather smart word to suggest above average quality in an external render, often in imitation of masonry.

Stucco duro: a high-quality plastering material based on lime putty, marble dust and fine sands often containing finely ground pozzolanic aggregates.

Surkhi: a softly burnt clay which is ground together with lime in a mortar mill. This acts both as a porous aggregate and a pozzolan and makes particularly good mortar.

Tallow: a clarified animal fat. It is prepared from the hard fat from around the kidneys of ruminants (animals that chew grass and vegetation as their staple diet) by melting it, which separates the tallow from the residue.

Temper: 1. In respect of putties, mortars and similar mixes; to bring a material to a proper state and consistence by mixing and working up before use. 2. To allow the same material to stand undisturbed (in a wet state) to assist infusion and development of the binder in the mix before use. 3. The combination of 1. and 2. above.

Thermal conductivity: the ease with which a material conducts heat.

Throwing (throwing a render): quite literally throwing the coarse stuff at the wall, usually by flicking it from the edge of a trowel, but in some cultures by throwing balls of stuff straight from the hand. The impact helps adhesion, but tends to alter the balance of the mix, leaving it leaner in parts and richer in others.

Titration: to determine the amount of an element in a mixture by volumetric analysis. This can be done by adding to a solution of known proportion a reagent of known strength until a reaction occurs or ceases.

Torching: in this context, plastering or pointing on the underside of roofing slates or tiles to reduce penetration from wind-blown fine rain and snow.

Trass: a siliceous rock from near Andernach, Germany. A local description of tuff, a consolidated fine-grained volcanic ash from the Brohl and Nette valleys of the Eifel, Germany. Trass from Andernach was ground to a powder and extensively exported for use as a pozzolanic additive to mortars in the 18th and 19th centuries.

Travertine: porous but well consolidated limey precipitate from springs or calcium bicarbonate dissolved from calcium carbonate and chemically precipitated. In some types the pores of calcareous tufa are filled with calcareous cement. It can be sawn into slabs which can be used for floors and cladding. Easy to polish.

Trowelling up: hardening up a plaster surface by alternately sprinkling it with water and working it with the trowel.

Tuff, tufa: volcanic ash, the finest grained is called dust tuff, grains up to 2mm diameter sand tuff, and 2mm to 64mm grains are known as lapilli.

Under-burnt quicklime: quicklime which has not received enough heat to convert the whole lump from carbonate to oxide, leaving a core of unconverted material at the centre.

Unsoundness: in some mechanical processing the residue of overburnt and underburnt material is ground finely and reintroduced into the dry hydrate. If this is used for plastering without sufficient maturing as a putty (or if a putty run straight from quicklime is used too soon) then the overburnt particles will hydrate within the body of the plaster causing a general expansion. This breaks the bond between the plaster and the backing and can lead to hollowness behind the plaster. The Le Chatilier test shows if this will be a problem.

Washable: some water-based paints are not sufficiently cohesive to allow the surface to be washed down for routine cleaning. Improved paints were sold as 'washable emulsions'.

Water limes, water building limes: John Smeaton's term to describe hydraulic limes. Limes which were suitable for building work in water, such as canal locks or harbours or lighthouses.

Water retention: as lime putty matures it draws water into its body, far beyond what is needed for its hydration. This lubricates the mortars made from it, making them plastic (easily mouldable) and hence comfortable to use. When a mortar is applied to a porous masonry unit, the masonry tries to suck the water away from the mortar. To some extent this is helpful as it forms the bond between unit and mortar. With poor quality mortars, the suction reduces the plasticity of the mortar, making it harder to work. Water retentivity is the measure of the ability of a putty (or mortar) to retain the water it holds against the suction of the backing.

Water-burnt lime: if the slaking is badly handled, temperatures may rise too high and this hard, gritty, form of calcium hydroxide may be produced.

Weathering qualities: the durability of a material against the destructive actions of the weather and atmosphere. These actions include cycles of heating and cooling, frosts, wind abrasion and airborne chemicals.

White chalk lime: Class A lime produced from white (not grey) chalk and used mainly for plastering.

White lime: Class A limes. Non-hydraulic limes. In many cases these limes are white, but this is not a sure guide.

White Portland cement: a white coloured Portland cement which is made from clays containing no iron. Where cement must be used in the conservation of old buildings it is sometimes selected because it contains fewer soluble salts than OPC.

Whitewash: a simple form of paint. The word has more than one meaning. Sometimes it is used to describe low quality limewash prepared from lime and water. In other circumstances it is used to describe a paint made with whiting (very finely ground chalk) with glue size as a binder.

Workability: the ease with which a mortar may be used. This important property is not easily defined, but it includes high plasticity and good water retention. A highly plastic binder, say a good lime putty, can allow the use of much sharper sands than are possible with, say, a cement binder. These sharp sands contribute to the long-term durability.

Appendix 1

Proposed classification of building limes by hydraulicity

Research by Stafford Holmes and Michael Wingate current as at November 1996. The burning and evaluation tests on limestones are on-going. Due to the extensive variation of limestone types there will be those whose characteristics fall across two classes. Acknowledgements to L.J. Vicat (1818, trans. 1837) who carried out the initial research and A.D. Cowper (1927) for information on which this table is based. The figures for slaking rates and setting times are given on the basis of Vicat's test to immerse the quicklime specimen in water for six seconds (p. 205).

	CLASS					
	Non-hydraulic lime		Hydraulic lime			Natural cement
Classification	A	B	C1	C2	C3	D
Common description of the lime type	Pure	Lean	Slightly hydraulic	Moderately hydraulic	Eminently hydraulic	Roman cement (UK)
Other names Commonly used terms not always specific to this classification	Fat, rich, white chalk, high calcium air lime	Grey chalk, stone lime, poor lime, common lime	Feebly hydraulic, grey chalk, stone lime, semi-hydraulic, common lime	Pure natural XHN 30 (France), semi-hydraulic	Pure natural XHN 60 (France)	Parkers cement, Medina Cement, natural XHN 100 (France), eminently hydraulic lime (Italy), hydraulic lime (EU)
Slaking rate	Rapid: much heat	Moderately slow – 5 minutes	Slow – 5 to 60 minutes	Very slow – over 60 minutes	Extremely slow – residue requires fine grinding	Clinker must be ground to powder
Expansion on slaking	2–3 times	Large – up to 2 times	Small	Very small	Very small to nil	Nil

Appendix 1 (cont.)

Set in water This is initial putty setting time. Hardening continues for 12 months or more	None	None but residue is much firmer than pure lime	15 to 20 days or more (Rivington, 1899)	6 to 8 days (Rivington, 1899)	2–4 days	Initial set in the order of 15 minutes to 2 hours or more, mostly less than one day
Consistence after one year in water	Fat rich lime putty	Lean coarse dense putty	Soap-like	Hard soap	Stone-like	Hard stone within 28 days
Residue on solution in much water	Very small to nil	Small; devoid of consistence	Appreciable	Insoluble	Insoluble	Insoluble
Residue ditto in HCl	Very small to nil	Small; devoid of consistence	Appreciable	Moderate	Large	Very large
Composition (approximate) $CaO + MgO$	Over 94%	Over 70%	Over 65%	Over 60%	Over 55%	Over 45% – generally over 55%
$SiO_2 + Al_2O_3 + Fe_2O_3$ (may contain up to 5% impurities)	Negligible – up to 2%	2% to 8% (up to 20% inert impurities)	Under 12% active clay	12% – 18% active clay	18% – 25% active clay (up to 36%, Cowper, 1927)	Up to 55% – generally up to 45% active clay according to Sir Humphrey Davey
Compressive strength* – approximate at 28 days 1:3 lime:sand 1:1 lime:sand for class D.	No crushing strength requirement, anticipated only (44 to 74 psi)	No crushing strength requirement, anticipated only (44 to 191 psi)	1.30 N/mm² 191 psi 13 kg cm²	2.60 (2.0 DIN) N/mm² 383 psi 26 kg cm²	6.00 (5.0 DIN) N/mm² 883 psi 60 kg cm²	10+ N/mm² 1472 psi 100 kg cm²
Proposed range – N/mm² at 28 days for classes C to D	**0.3 to 0.5**	**0.3 to 1.3**	**1.3 to 2.0**	**2.0 to 5.0**	**5.0 to 10**	**10 and above**

*Conversion of compressive strength is based on 1N/mm³ = 147.2 psi. Pounds per square inch is abbreviated to psi.

Appendix 2
Pozzolans, natural and artificial

Natural pozzolans

	Comments and principal source
Italian pozzolans	Volcanic tuff normally found in a fragmentary state; principal sources near Rome, Naples and Vesuvius include the original pozzolana.
Rhenish trass	A consolidated rock-like form; principal source Andernach, Germany, traditionally used in Germany and Holland since 1682 (Cowper, 1927).
Pumice	A low density, glassy honeycomb rock formed from lava.
Santorin earth	Volcanic ash from Santorin, Greece.
Tettin	From the Azores.
Tosca	Principal source, Teneriffe, Canary Islands.
Volcanic ash	Unchanged surface deposits of ash ejected by volcanic activity.
Volvic pozzolan	Volcanic pozzolan, south-eastern France.
Volcanic tuff	Consolidated volcanic ash or volcanic rock of an earthy texture.

Volcanic material deposits are widely distributed over the globe and can be found in many other countries including the USA, Canada, Japan, New Zealand, Kenya, Tanzania, Rwanda, Indonesia and Vanuatu. Other naturally occurring materials that may have pozzolanic qualities include:

Diatomaceous earths	Widely distributed and have been discovered and used in California, Canada, Algeria, Denmark, Germany, and parts of the UK. They are formed from the skeletal remains of certain algae.
Moler	A Tertiary-aged diatomaceous earth from Denmark.
Siliceous rocks	Only siliceous rocks with a high soluble silica content.

Cowper (1927) gives an analysis by Eckel of natural pozzolans from 31 samples. The table is reproduced below.

Average analysis, natural pozzolans

Element	Percentage of element
Silica	42–66
Alumina	15–17
Iron oxide	4–19
Lime	3–7
Magnesia	5–7
Water	4–9

(Source: Eckel, 1922).

Artificial pozzolans

Burnt clays

Including kaolinite, illite, and montmorillonite, sediments with particle sizes less than 0.039mm (39 microns). Soft burnt clay, at about 900°C, appears to provide a much better pozzolanic reaction than hard burnt material.

Ground bricks and tiles

Other ways of obtaining burnt clays in powder form. These have been used worldwide and from before Roman times, when Vetruvius recorded that ground potsherds were used as a pozzolan. Ground clay pozzolan is common in many countries where it is known by other names such as *surkhi* and *kankar* in India, *homra* in Egypt, and *semen merah* in Indonesia. It was reported in Egypt that the lime/burnt-clay mortar used initially in construction of the Aswan Dam was found to be more water-tight than a 1 : 4 Portland cement : sand mix. Its only disadvantage is that it is slow to set.

Lime-surkhi mortar is prepared by grinding lime and burnt clay together in a mortar mill, a common practice in India. Oversized particles also act as beneficial porous aggregates which help free lime to carbonate.

Burnt gaize

Prepared from a soft porous, clay-rich sandstone from the Ardennes and Meuse valley areas of France. It contains silica in a gelatinous condition and has been used in the raw state as a pozzolan but it is usually burnt at about 900°C.

Burnt moler

A pozzolan deposit of Tertiary age of diatomaceous earth containing a considerable portion of clay, formerly used in its raw condition but at present burned at about 750°C for brick production (Hepworth Refractories).

283

Bauxite	Burnt at low temperatures 250–300°C. Le Chatelier reported finding mortars made from pulverized bauxite and lime in the ruins at Baux in the Rhone valley, France (7th int. congress appl. Chem. London, 1909).
Calcined basalt stone	Calcined basalt stone ground to a fine powder (Smith, BRE OBN 198, 1993).
Si-stoff	A silicious waste product from the manufacture of alum in Germany, not very often used as there is a danger that it may contain high concentrations of sulphur trioxide.
Iron slag	Ground granulated blast furnace slag.
Flyash or PFA	Crushed coal cinders have been used as a pozzolan. Pulverized fuel ash, a residue from the combustion of pulverized coal in power stations has similar properties. PFA from some sources has a high sulphate content which would be unsuitable for renders.
HTI powder	Finely ground fired china clays prepared for high temperature insulation.
Agricultural wastes	Silica is taken up by many plants during their growth. Wood ash was used in the eighteenth century by slaking fresh lime surrounded by wood ash, and then mixing, allowing it to go cold, then beating thoroughly again – ratio 3 wood ash to 2 lime. Current research and development of the use of ash from burning agricultural residues looks most promising. Pozzolans have been produced with ash from rice husks, bagasse (sugar cane after extraction of the sugar), and rice straw (Smith, 1993).
Minion	Burnt and crushed ironstone, i.e. stone containing a high proportion of ferric oxide.
Forge scales and ashes	Waste material from a forge or ironworks containing a high proportion of finely divided iron oxide particles.

Appendix 3

Sieve gauge and mesh size conversion table

Aperture size mm British (BS 410)	Tyler mesh gauge number British	American mesh gauge number USA (ASTM E11–70)	DIN aperture size mm German (DIN 4188)
5.600	¼"	3½	5.600
* 5.000	³⁄₁₆"	4	–
4.000	⁵⁄₃₂"	5	4.000
3,350	⁵⁄₁₆"	6	–
2.800	6	7	2.800
* 2.360	7	8	–
2.000	8	10	2.000
1.400	12	14	1.400
* 1.180	14	16	1.180
1.000	16	18	1.000
0.850	18	20	0.800
0.710	22	25	0.710
* 0.600	25	30	0.630
0.500	30	35	0.500
0.425	36	40	0.425
0.355	44	45	0.355
* 0.300	52	50	0.315
0.250	60	60	0.250
0.180	85	80	0.180
* 0.150	100	100	–
0.125	120	120	0.125
0.090	170	170	0.090
* 0.075	200	200	–
0.063	240	230	0.063
0.045	350	325	0.045

Note: The Tyler and ASTM mesh gauge number remains in use for the description of sieves currently produced for practical site operations and to supply the building industry. The Tyler gauge number is based on the number of spaces between wires per inch. Variations in the number of spaces per inch occur from one country to another due to difference in the standard wire thickness selected.

The aperture sizes given in millimetres and microns are normally used in connection with sieves for more accurate laboratory testing and for specialist conservation work.

Standard sieve aperture sizes for gravel are 6.7mm (¼"), 10mm (⅜"), 14mm (½"), 20mm (¾"), 37.5mm (1½"), 63mm (2½") and 75mm (3").

* Indicates sieve sizes normally used for aggregate grading purposes.

Appendix 4
Select list of national standards

Indian Standards
IS:1624 – Methods of Field Testing Building Limes
IS:1635 – Code of Practice for Field Slaking of Building Lime and Preparation of Putty
IS:712 – Specification for Building Limes
IS:2394 – Code of Practice for Application for Lime Plaster Finishes
IS:1727 – Methods of Test for Pozzolanic Materials
IS:1344 – Specification for Burnt Clay Pozzolana
IS:3812 (Part 1) – Specification for Fly Ash
      Part 1: For Use as Pozzolana
IS:4098 – Specification for Lime-Pozzolana Mixture
IS:7873 – Code of Practice for Lime Concrete Lining for Canals.

Published by: Indian Standards Institution, Manak Bhavan, 9 Bahadur, Shah, Zafar, Marg, New Delhi 110002, India.

NBO Publication – Lime and Lime Pozzolana, Mortars and Plasters, edited by Sunil Bery for the Government of India National Buildings Organisation, New Delhi 1988.

Netherlands (Dutch) Standards
N.488 – IID:691.5: Definition and Specification for Trass (for use as a pozzolan in mortar) (1932)
N.931 – UDC:691.51: Definition and Specification for Building Limes (1952)

Published by: The Secretariat, Centraal Normalisatie Bureau, 'sGravenhage, Lange Houtstraat 13A, Holland.

Zimbabwe Standards
RNS No. A15:1963 – Building Limes
RNS No. A19:1964 – Materials for Soil Stabilization
      Part 1: Hydrated Lime (high calcium content)

Published by: Standards Association, Pax House, 87 Union Avenue, Harare, Zimbabwe.

European Standards
The British, French and German standards (see below) are gradually being phased out or amended to fall in line with, or be superseded by, European ENV standards under the guidance of the European Committee for Standardization (CEN).

BS EN 459–1:2001 – Building Lime – Part 1: Definitions, specifications and conformity criteria
BS EN 459–2:2001 – Building Lime – Part 2: Test methods
BS EN 459–3:2001 – Building Lime – Part 3: Conformity Evaluation
BS EN 196 – *Part 3*: Methods of Testing Cement, determination of standard setting time and soundness.

Contact address: CEN-European Committee for Standardization, Central Secretariat, Rue de Stassart 36, B-1050, Brussels, Belgium. European Standards are also available from the institutes of member countries.

British Standards
BS 890:1995 – Specification for Building Limes
BS 6463:1984 – Quicklime, Hydrated Lime and Natural Calcium Carbonate
   Part 1: Methods of sampling
   Part 2: Methods of chemical analysis
BS 6463:1987 – *Part 3*: Methods of test for physical properties of quicklime
   Part 4: Methods of test for physical properties of hydrated lime and lime putty
BS 4550: *Part 3*: 1978, Section 3.5, Methods of Testing Cement.
BS 1377 – Methods of test for Soils for Civil Engineering Purposes, London, 1975.
BS 6677: *Part 1*: Calcium Silicate Pavers
BS 187: Calcium Silicate (Sandlime and Flintlime) Bricks
BS 4551:1980 – Methods of Testing Mortars, Screeds and Plasters
BS 1199:1995 – Sand for Rendering and Plastering
BS 1200:1976 – Sand for Mortar
BS 3892: 1996 – *Part 2* – Pulverized Fuel Ash for Use in Concrete
BS 3148:1980 – Water – Tests for Suitability
BS 4721:1981(86) – Ready Mixed Lime : Sand for Mortar
BS 4887: 1987 – *Part 2* – Quality of Admixtures to Mortars
BS 5262:1991 – Code of Practice for External Renderings
BS 5492:1990 – Code of Practice for Internal Plastering
BS 6100:1984 – *Part 6*: British Standard Glossary of Building and Civil Engineering Terms, *Section 6.1*: Binders
BS 812 (31 parts) – Methods for the Sampling and Testing of Mineral Aggregates, Sands and Fillers
BS 4123:1967 – Schedule of Preferred Chemical Indicators
BS 882:1992 – Specification for Aggregates From Natural Sources for Concrete
BS 1369:1987 – Steel Lathing for Internal Plastering and External Rendering
   Part 1: Specification for expanded metal and ribbed lathing
BS 8000:1995 – Workmanship on Building Sites
   Part 10: Code of Practice for plastering and rendering (amendment 9271:Nov 96)

BS 3797:1990 – Specification for Lightweight Aggregates for Concrete (amendment 6796)
CP 211 – Internal Plastering
CP 221 – External Rendered Finishes

Complete editions of the Standards can be obtained by post from BSI Customer Services, 389 Chiswick High Road, London W4 4AL, UK.

BRE Digest No. 139 – Control of Lichens, Moulds and Similar Growths
BRE Digest No. 163 – Drying-out Buildings
BRE Digest No. 157 – Calcium Silicate Brickwork

Contact address: BRE Bookshop, Building Research Establishment, Garston, Watford, WD2 7JR, UK. Tel: 01923 664444, Fax: 01923 664400.

French Standards
NF P 15 – 310: 1969 – Natural Hydraulic Limes, XHN
NF P 15 – 461 – Chemical Characteristics
NF P 15 – 451 – Compression Strength Tests
NF P 15 – 432 – Expansion Test (Chatelier)
NF P 15 – 101 – Hydraulic Binders Definitions
NF P 15 – 300 – Hydraulic Binders Clauses and General Conditions – Marking, Packing, Receipts, Ordering and Delivery
NF P 15 – 311 – Designation of Limes
        High Calcium Lime
        Hydrated Lime
        Natural Hydraulic Lime
        Dolomitic Lime

Test Methods
NF P 15 – 401 – General Descriptions
NF P 15 – 403 – Standard Sand and Standard Mortar
NF P 15 – 411 – Mixer
NF P 15 – 412 – Choice of Apparatus
NF P 15 – 413 – Moulds for Prismatic Tests and Accessories
NF P 15 – 414 – Vicat Apparatus and Truncated Cone Mould
NF P 15 – 431 – Taking Tests (sampling)
NF P 15 – 432 – Test for Expansion to Hot and Cold
NF P 15 – 451 – Mechanical Tests: Deflection and Compression
NF P 15 – 461 – Chemical Tests

Code of Practice – Dossier Technique no. 17 Hydraulic Lime Mortars

Contact address: Centre Scientifique et Technique du Batiment, 4 Avenue du Recteur-Poincaré, 75782 Paris Cedex 16, France.

American Standards (USA)

ASTM C219 – 76a – Standard Definition of Terms Relating to Hydraulic Cement
ASTM C114 – 81 – Standard Methods of Chemical Analysis of Hydraulic Cement
ASTM C270 – Mortar for Masonry
ASTM C1489 – Lime Putty for Structural Purposes
ASTM C1324 – Analysis of Hardened Mortar

Standard Specifications

ASTM C5 – 79 – Quicklime for Structural Purposes
ASTM C25 – 81 – Methods of Chemical Analysis of Limestone, Quicklime and Hydrated Lime
ASTM C110 – 76a – Methods of Physical Testing of Quicklime, Hydrated Lime, and Limestone
ASTM C141 – 67 (78) – Hydraulic Hydrated Lime for Structural Purposes
ASTM C206 – 79 – Finishing Hydrated Lime
ASTM C207 – 79 – Hydrated Lime for Masonry Purposes
ASTM C593 – 76a (81) – Fly Ash and Other Pozzolans for Use with Lime
ASTM C821 – 78 – Lime for use with Pozzolans
ASTM C6 – 49 (74) – Normal Finishing Hydrated Lime
ANSI/ASTM C10 – 76 – Natural Cement
ASTM C50 – 27 (52) – Methods of Sampling, Inspection, Packing and Marking of Quicklime and Lime Products
ANSI/ASTM C51 – 71 (76) – Definitions of Terms Relating to Lime and Limestone
ANSI/ASTM C144 – 76 – Aggregate for Masonry Mortar
ASTM C191 – 52 – Method of Test for Time of Setting of Hydraulic Cement by Vicat Needle

Contact address: ASTM Headquarters, 1916, Race Street, Philadelphia, Pa. 19103, USA.

German Standards

DIN 1060 – Building Limes
　　　　Part 1: Terminology, requirements, supply, inspection
　　　　Part 2: Methods of chemical analysis
　　　　Part 3: Methods of physical test
DIN 1053: *Part 1*: Masonry of Simplified Design – Design and Construction
DIN 4226: *Part 1*: Aggregates for Concrete – Aggregates of dense structure (heavy aggregates), terminology, designation and requirements.
DIN 18 550: *Part 1*: Plaster and Rendering; Terminology and Requirements
　　　　Part 2: Plaster and Rendering Made From Mortars with Mineral Binders; Application
DIN 18 506 – Hydraulic Binders for Road Bases, Soil Stabilization and Soil Improvement; Hydraulic Road Base Binders
DIN 4211 – Plaster and Masonry Binders

Appendix 5

Minerals associated with common limestone chemicals

Minerals composed of chemicals associated with limestone

Name	Composition	Colour	Common Form	Other Properties
Iron	Fe	Iron-grey	Usually massive, if crystalline, found as octahedra.	Strongly magnetic.
Fluorite (Fluor Spar)	CaF_2	Variable; Blue John is the purple variety.	Cubes with octahedral cleavage. Also massive.	Vitreous lustre.
Quartz	SiO_2	When pure colourless, but many coloured varieties.	Crystals with hexagonal prisms and rhombohedra, also massive.	Vitreous lustre.
Calcite	$CaCO_3$	Usually white.	Hexagonal crystals, good rhombohedral cleavage.	Effervesces with cold dilute hydrochloric acid.
Aragonite	$CaCO_3$	White or greyish.	Orthorhombic crystals, often with re-entrant angles owing to twinning, also massive or fibrous.	
Dolomite	$CaCO_3.MgCO_3$	White, often tinged with yellow.	Hexagonal crystals usually rhombohedra with curved faces. Also massive and granular. Perfect rhombohedral cleavage.	Pearly lustre on crystal faces, does *not* effervesce with cold dilute hydrochloric acid (compare calcite).
Magnesite	$MgCO_3$	White.	Usually massive or fibrous.	Earthy lustre if fibrous, otherwise vitreous.
Gypsum	$CaSO_4.2H_2O$	White.	Monoclinic crystals (selenite), compact form (alabaster), fibrous form (satin spar).	Earthy lustre on crystal faces, fibrous varieties have silky lustre.
Anhydrite	$CaSO_4$	White, often tinged with grey or blue.	Orthorhombic crystals, also compact, fibrous and granular.	Pearly lustre on cleavage planes.
Olivine	Mg.Fe silicate	Shades of green, yellow or brown.	Orthorhombic crystals, also massive or granular triclinic.	
Serpentine	Hydrated Mg, silicate	Shades of green, brown, black, red or yellow.	Massive granular or fibrous.	Colours shown veining or brecciation.
Talc	$3MgO.4SiO_2.H_2O$	White or green.	Usually massive (soap-stone) also granular or in scales.	Pearly lustre, greasy feel.

Common limestone chemicals

Alumina	Al_2O_3	Phosphorus pentoxide	P_2O_5
Carbon dioxide	CO_2	Potassium oxide	K_2O
Chlorine	Cl	Silica	SiO_2
Iron sulphide	FeS_2	Sodium oxide	Na_2O
Lime (calcium oxide)	CaO	Sulphur	S
Magnesia	MgO	Sulphur trioxide	SO_3
Manganese oxide	MnO	Titanium dioxide	TiO_2
Oxides of iron	$FeO,$	Water	H_2O
	Fe_2O_3		

Appendix 6

Chemical analysis of limestones, hydraulic limes and natural cements – percentage by weight

	No. 1	No. 2	No. 3	No. 4	No. 5	No. 6	No. 7	No. 8	No. 9	No. 10	No. 11	No. 12	No. 13
Insoluble siliceous matter	3.43	7.311	7.70	2.27	3.603	1.031							
Silica	1.73	2.315	1.23	1.46	17.496	12.230	15.42	14.27	16.00	15.28	17.14	38	47
Alumina	1.02	0.530	1.65	0.79	5.120	4.640	5.63	5.81	6.50	4.50	6.87	7	3
Ferric oxide					8.972	2.907	6.81	5.97	8.60	1.61	4.83		
Calcium carbonate	92.98	83.095	87.36	93.47						71.21		55	49
Magnesium carbonate	0.49	3.605	1.92	1.42						5.67			
Lime					57.393	72.980	45.12	46.20	46.80		47.35		
Magnesia					0.618	2.479	0.83	0.67	1.50		3.39		
Manganese							0.54	0.83			0.17		
Loss on ignition		0.834											
Loss on calcination, moisture and carbonic acid					2.480	1.062	25.65	26.25	20.60		20.25		

(Sources: Redgrave and Spackman, 1905; Millar, 1897)

No. 1: Lower or Grey chalk, Kent, England
No. 2: Blue Lias limestone, Newport, Monmouthshire
No. 3: Carboniferous limestone, Charlestone, Scotland
No. 4: Carboniferous limestone, Lancashire, England
No. 5: Blue Lias, Leicestershire ground lime (a natural cement)
No. 6: Blue Lias, Leicestershire lump lime
No. 7: English Roman cement
No. 8: Boulogne cement, France
No. 9: Cement of Vassy, France
No. 10: Cement rock, Lehigh valley, Pennsylvania, USA
No. 11: Cement of Pouilly, France
No. 12: Cement stones for Sheppey Roman cement (Millar, 1897)
No. 13: Cement stones for Harwich Roman cement (Millar, 1897)

Appendix 7

Effects of the addition of pure limes to natural hydraulic limes

Classification	French standard	Natural hydraulic lime Active clay proportion		Lime addition	Final lime:active clay ratio	Final active clay percentage proportion	Revised classification following addition of pure lime at 1:1
		Approx. active clay	Approx. pure lime				
Hydraulic limes							
D Natural cement	XHN 100	35%	60%	+ 100%	160:35	22%	C3
C3 Eminently hydraulic	XHN 60	25%	70%	+ 100%	170:25	14.7%	C2
C2 Moderately hydraulic	XHN 30	15%	80%	+ 100%	180:15	8%	B
C1 Slightly hydraulic		10%	85%	+ 100%	185:10	5.4%	B
Non-hydraulic limes							
B Lean		2 to 8%	over 70%				
A Pure		0.1 to 2%	over 94%				

Lime: $CaO + MgO$
Active Clay: $SiO_2 + Al_2O_3$ ($+FeO_2$)

Fat lime putty is sometimes added to hydraulic lime mortars and renders to improve workability. This table is included to illustrate that care must be taken with the proportion of putty added to the mix and class of hydraulic lime selected if a hydraulic set is required.

293

Appendix 8

Suitability of soils for the addition of lime

Soil	Shrinkage and swelling	Sensitivity to frost action	Bulk density (kg/m^3)	Voids ratio	General suitability for the addition of lime
Clean gravel Well graded	Almost none	Almost none	2000	0.35	Suitable for lime concrete. The addition of sand will improve performance.
Clean gravel Poorly graded	Almost none	Almost none	1840	0.45	Suitable for lime concrete but grading and addition of sand will improve performance.
Silty gravel	Almost none	Slight to medium	1760	0.50	Not suitable.
Clayey gravel	Very slight	Slight to medium	1920	0.40	Suitable for stabilization.
Clean sand Well graded	Almost none	Almost none	1920	0.40	Suitable for mortars, plasters and render.
Clean sand Poorly graded	Almost none	Almost none	1600	0.70	Suitable for mortar but grading will improve performance.
Silty sand	Almost none	Slight to high	1600	0.70	Not suitable.
Clayey sand	Slight to medium	Slight to high	1700	0.60	Suitable for daub and soil structures. Suitable for weak render coats particularly in connection with weak backgrounds.
Low-plasticity clay	Medium to high	Slight to high	1520	0.80	Suitable for stabilized road formation and stabilized earth render, improves with the addition of sand.
Organic silt	Medium to high	Medium to high	1440	0.90	Not suitable.
Clays with low plasticity	Medium to high	Medium to high	1440	0.90	Suitable for stabilization
Highly plastic clay	High	Very slight	1440	0.90	Suitable for road stabilization and, if sand is added, for soil structures.
Highly plastic silt	High	Medium to high	1600	0.70	Not suitable.
Highly plastic organic earth	High	Very high	1600	0.70	Not suitable.
Peat	Very high	Slight	1600	0.70	Not suitable

(Source: UNCHS, 1987).

294

Appendix 9

Recommended quantities of gypsum for gauging internal lime plaster Based on British Standard Code of Practice CP 211 'Internal Plastering'

Background	Nominal Mix by Volume					
	Undercoats			Finishing Coat		
	Gypsum-plaster	Lime	Sand	Gypsum-plaster	Lime	Sand
Brickwork, building blocks and wood-wool slabs	⅓ or more	1	2–4	¼–½	1	0–1
	2	1–1½	5–6	¼–1	0–⅓	—
				1		—
In-situ and pre-cast concrete (hair may be included in undercoat mixes)	2	1	5	¼–½	1	0–1
				¼–1	1	—
				1	0–⅓	—
Wood or metal lath (hair should be included in all undercoat mixes)	⅓ or more	1	2–4	¼–½	1	0–1
	2	1	5	¼–½	1	0–1
				½–1	1	—
				1	0–⅓	—

(Source: Limestone Federation, 1963).

Notes: In this table, references to lime are to those that are not eminently hydraulic, i.e. Classes A, B, C1 and C2. Lime plaster does not have to be gauged with gypsum. Gauging the mix, particularly finishing coats, became common practice, however, when gypsum was readily available as its addition to the mix accelerated setting time. A hard surface can be achieved within hours of gauging, which enables all work to be progressed at a faster rate. The quick set and hard finish that results assists the preparation of intricate shapes, for decorative work. The disadvantages of gauging the mix for large areas are the additional cost and hard and brittle surface that results. Gypsum is water-soluble and should therefore not be used externally and may swell in damp conditions internally.

Appendix 10
Comparative crushing strengths of mortars and associated building materials

Test cubes mixed in the proportion of 1:3 binder:sand, with a standard sand and crushed at 28 days

Lime class	Binder	Crushing strength			Approximate Ratio (Class A=1)	French Standards for hydraulic limes
		N/mm²	kg/cm²	lbs/in² (psi)		
A	Fat lime (non hydraulic)	0.4	4	60	1	
C1	Slightly hydraulic	1.3	13	190	3	
C2	Moderately hydraulic	2.6	26	380	6	XHN 30
C3	Eminently hydraulic	6.0	60	880	15	XHN 60
D	Natural cement and French hydraulic (other limes to be researched)	10.0	100	1472	25	XHN 100
–	Ordinary Portland Cement	28.0	280	4120	70	

Standard OPC:Lime:Sand mixes	lbs/in² (psi)
1:3:12	99–212
1:2:9	284–426
1:1:6	426–711

Comparative crushing strengths

	N/mm²
Internal non-loadbearing walls (GLC Byelaws 1972)	**1.5**
Loadbearing walls for 1 and 2 storey bldgs. (UK Building Regulations, 1976)	**2.75**
London Stock Bricks	6.25
Bath Box Ground Limestone	11.7
Hand-made bricks	12–35
Guiting Limestone	16.3
Machine-made facing bricks	20–120
Hollington sandstone	32.4
Portland Whitbed Limestone	42.8

Crushing strength variables with differing sands

All sands mixed in the proportion of 1:2 with moderately hydraulic Blue Lias from Nelson's Yard, Stockton and tested *after 2 years.*

	lbs/in²	N/mm²
Charlton fine sand	257	1.75
Standard sand (Leighton Buzzard)	538	3.65
Pit sand	605	4.11
Thames sand	785	5.33
Ground brick	910	6.18

Conversions based on 1/Nmm² = 147.2 lbs/in²   (Source: Dibdin, 1911).

Appendix 11

Properties of bricks and blocks

Properties of Ghanaian compressed soil blocks stabilized with 6% lime

	Kumasi blocks				Fumesua blocks			
Compaction pressure (MN/m²)	2 (Cinva-Ram)*	4	8	16	2 (Cinva-Ram)*	4	8	16
Water content of mix (Wt%)	20.0	19.0	16.0	13.0	17.0	16.0	14.0	13.0
28 day compressive strength (MN/m²)	1.05	1.85	2.90	3.55	0.70	1.70	2.75	3.05
24 hr compressive strength – cured at 95°C (MN/m²)			4.85	5.45			4.45	4.60
Water absorption (Wt%)	19.6	19.1	18.4	14.2	15.8	14.7	12.2	12.4
Dry density (kg/dm³)	1.51	1.74	1.82	1.84	1.75	1.79	1.86	1.93
Moisture movement (drying shrinkage percent of length)	0.16	0.11	0.06	0.04	0.13	0.07	0.05	0.03

Range of properties of building bricks and blocks

Property	Calcium Silicate Bricks *	Fired Clay bricks *	Concrete Bricks (Dense) *	Aerated Concrete Blocks (Autoclave)	Light-weight Concrete Blocks *	Stabilized Soil Blocks =
Wet compressive strength (MN/m²)	10–55	10–60	7–50	2–6	2–20	1–40
Drying shrinkage (percentage of length)	0.01–0.035	0.00–0.02	0.02–0.05	0.05–0.10	0.04–0.08	0.02–0.2
Thermal conductivity W/m°C	1.1–1.6	0.7–1.3	1.0–1.7	0.1–0.2	0.15–0.7	0.5–0.7
Durability under severe natural exposure	Good to moderate	Excellent to very poor	Good to poor	Good to moderate	Good to poor	Good to very poor
Properties affecting laying and plastering	Good	Good to poor	Good	Good	Good	Good to very poor
Density (kg/dm³)	1.6–2.1	1.4–2.4	1.7–2.2	0.4–0.9	0.6–1.6	1.5–1.9
Aesthetic value of surface =	Good but sensitive to dirt	Good	Poor	Good but sensitive to dirt	Normally rendered	Good to poor

= Properties are based on limited worldwide date of cement- and lime-stablized soil blocks.
* Properties reproduced from Overseas Building Notes No. 154. Calcium Silicate Bricks.

Reproduced from Overseas Building Notes no. 184, M.G. Lunt, Building Research Establishment, HMSO, 1980.

Appendix 12

Comparative compressive strengths of traditional British lime mortars with those given in some European standards

Cement: Lime:Sand Mixes to Achieve Equivalent Compressive Strengths (ii)	Traditional Building Limes — In common use up to the beginning of 20th century — Class (iii)	Description	Anticipated Compressive Strength N/mm² (iv)	French Standards NF P 15–310, 1969+ NF P 15–510, 1981 — Description	(v) Min. N/mm²	German Standard DIN 1060 part 1 1986 — Description	(v) N/mm²	European Standard for Building Limes pr. EN 459–1 1998 — Description	(v) 0–20 N/mm² Total Range	European Standard for Masonry Mortars pr. EN 998–2 1997 — Description	(v) N/mm²
–	A	Fat lime (pure, non hydraulic)	0.1 – 1.3	Slaked lime	–	Non hydraulic	–	Air limes	–	–	–
1:3:12–1:2:9	C1	Feebly (slightly) hydraulic	1.3 – 2	Light lime	<3	Feebly hydraulic	<2	NHL2 2 – 7 N/mm²		M1	1
1:2:9–1:1:6	C2	Moderately hydraulic	2 – 6	XHN 30	3	Moderately hydraulic	/ 2	NHL3.5 3.5 – 10 N/mm²	NHL5 5 – 15 N/mm² (upper limit 20 N/mm²)	M2.5	2.5
1:1:6–1:½:4	C3	Eminently hydraulic	6 – 10	XHN 60	6					M5	5
1:1:6–1:½:4	D	Natural cement (Roman cement)	10 – 15	XHN 100	10	Eminently hydraulic	5 – 15			M10	10
1:½:4–1:¼:3				XHN 100	10			NHL2 10 N/mm² upper limit; NHL3.5 14 N/mm² upper limit		M15	15
1:¼:3 with selected aggregate				Standard NF P 15–310 stipulates a minimum free lime content of 10% for all hydraulic limes.						M20	20

i) The compressive strength achieved with the cement:lime:sand mixes shown are minimum. Variations in the type of aggregate and Portland Cement will produce different results. In general in the UK compressive strengths are likely to be higher to between 30 and 40 N/mm² for a 1:3 cement:sand mix.

ii) These values are derived from the relationship between minimum compressive strength and mix proportions given in table 2 of pr. EN 998–2:1997 Specification for Masonry Mortar.

iii) Class and description of building limes given by L.J. Vicat, 1818, and by A.D. Cowper, 1927, in Lime and Lime Mortars report for the B.R.S. published by HMSO London.

iv) These values are derived from an assessment of the French and German standards for traditional building limes of the same class and description.

v) These values are derived from the test methods utilized in the cited standards.

Key to hatched areas of graph illustrating compressive strength range

Range of strength requirement given in EN 459.

Upper Strength limit given in EN 459.

The upper limit for single compressive test results is:-
NHL 2 – 10N/mm², NHL 3.5 – 14N/mm²,
NHL 5 – 20N/mm²

The lower limit for single available (free) lime is:-
NHL 2 – 8%, NHL 3.5 – 6%, NHL 5 – 3%

NB: A lime given the designation of NHL 3.5 by the manufacturer may produce any compressive strength (at 28 days) between 3.5 N/mm² and 10 N/mm² under this standard. An NHL 3.5 lime may therefore vary in strength from an equivalent of the weaker traditional moderately hydraulic (C2) building lime to the stronger end of the traditional eminently hydraulic (C3). The precise strength (traditional classification C1, C2, C3, D) of the lime should be verified by the manufacturer before purchase to ensure it is fit for purpose.

All strengths are given for a lime:aggregate ratio by mass (weight) of 1:3 tested at 28 days unless stated otherwise. These figures are given for comparison and ease of testing only. There will be considerable gains in strength for up to at least 2 years curing time particularly for lime rich mixes. An equivalent lime:aggregate ratio by volume is between 1:1 and 1:2.

Appendix 13
Conversion tables

MEASUREMENT OF VOLUME (Dry Measure Volumes for Lime or Sand)

1 Load =	36 Bushels =	1 Chaldron (coal) =	1.3107 cu. metres
1 Measure (1 cart load) =	21 Bushels =	1 cu. yard (27 cu. ft.) =	0.7646 cu. metres
1 Quarter =	8 Bushels =	64 gallons =	290.94 litres
1 Bushel (12" × 12" × 15⅜") =	**2218.19 cu. ins. =**	**8 gallons (1.284 cu. ft.) =**	**36.368 litres**
1 Peck (8"× 8" × 8⅞") =	¼ Bushel =	2 gallons (544.246 cu. ins.) =	9.092 litres
1 Gallon =	8 pints =	272.123 cu. ins.	4.546 litres
A Hod	contains 1 peck =	4 pints =	2.273 litres
1 Pint =	4 gills =	34.015 cu. ins. =	0.568 litres

Bushels given are Winchester stricken measures, i.e. the "struck" bushel measure of 1.28 cubic feet, lightly filled, and struck smooth at the top with a straight edge (Rivington).

AVOIRDUPOIS OR WEIGHT

16 Drams =	1 Ounce (oz) =	28.35 g
16 Ounces =	1 Pound (lb) =	0.4536 Kg
14 Pounds =	1 Stone (st) =	6.3504 Kg
2 Stones =	1 Quarter (q) =	12.7008 Kg
4 Quarters =	1 Hundredweight (cwt) =	50.80 Kg
20 Hundredweight =	1 Ton (tn) or 2240 lbs =	1016.06 Kg

CAPACITY OR VOLUME (liquid)

4 Gills =	1 Pint (pt) =	0.568 litres
2 Pints =	1 Quart (qt) =	1.137 litres
4 Quarts =	1 Gallon (gal) =	4.546 litres
2 Gallons =	1 Peck (pk) or 1 Hod =	9.09 litres
4 Pecks =	1 Bushel =	36.369 litres
8 Bushels =	1 Quarter (qr) =	290.94 litres
4 Quarters =	1 Load (1 cu. yd). =	0.765 cu. metres

Sources: Gwilt (1894), Nicholson's Dictionary of Architecture (c.1850), Millar (1897), Rivington (1899).

Index

This index should be read in conjunction with the Glossary, pages 259–279

accelerators 87–8, 259
adhesion (bond) 2, 58, 260
adobe (mud brick) construction 152, 259
aggregates 259
  core as 10, 263
  grading 285
  for limewash 56
  for mortar 46, 48, 63–5, 72, 73
agricultural lime 259
air entrainment 259
  for mortar 66–7, 69
  for plaster 87
air limes 4, 11, 259
air slaking 10, 209, 259
Alizarian Red 203
alum 55, 178, 284
alumina 13, 153
aluminates 108, 259
aluminium nitrate 202
aluminium silicates 153
ambient conditions 223
American standards (ASTM) 289
ammonites 198
amphorae (hollow clay pots) 183
aqueducts 184
Arayash 118
arches 187
argillaceous material 198, 259
arks 12
armatures 141, 259
ashes 174, 177, 284, 286, 271
Atterberg limits 158
autoclaves, high pressure steam 168, 230
autogenous healing 3, 260

backgrounds for plaster 260

earth 78–9
  for decorative plaster 132
  lathing 80–3
  solid walling 79–80
backgrounds for renders 106, 120–1, 260
  preparation 122
  separation from 123, 125
bag-rubbed finish 112
bagged lime 11, 71, 260
bankers 20, 260
barium chloride 223
beds, limestone 203
'beef' (fibrous calcite) 202
binders 163, 260
  active hydraulic 259, 267
  for limewash 53–5
  for mortars and renders 120, 123, 126
binding power 209
block making 157, 161
Blue Lias lime 188, 198–9, 260
bolsters 44
bonding agents 79, 87
Bordeaux mixture 56, 260
boriti (mangrove) poles 175–6
Boynton, R. S. 13
brandering 82, 260
breathability xi, 2, 49, 54–5, 260
brick dust 164
bricks and blocks, properties of 297
bridges 184, 187–8
British Standards (BS) 287–8
brushes
  bench (dusting) 40
  splash 40
  stock 39, 98
  tool 40
building lime 260
  physical requirements 6
building specifications, local 6–7
buildings, medieval 68

buildings, protection of 3
bulking, sand 219–20
Bullard, Tony viii
bullocks' blood 176
burning and slaking 9, 205–6

calcareous material 197, 261
calcium carbonate (aragonite and
    calcite) 9, 123, 194, 202–3, 259, 261
calcium oxide 9, 203–4, 261
calcium silicates 153
  bricks and components 168–70
Californian Bearing Ratio (CBR)
    181–2
canals 184, 189–90
carbon dioxide 4, 9, 211, 215–16,
    228–9
carbonation 4, 9, 50, 54, 62–3, 64, 67,
    73–6, 123–4, 125, 152–3, 245, 261
  rate of 222
care of materials 240
care of tools 16
Carson Blotter Test 214
carved plaster 144–5
casein (skimmed milk) in limewash 55,
    261
ceilings 90–1, 99–101
  cracks 246
  inspection 246–9
cement 261
  in mortar 65–6
  mixers 70
  natural 13, 280–1, 292
  Portland, ordinary (OPC) 108, 192,
    121–2, 272
  setting time 206–9
  stones 202
cementation 152
  index (C. I.) 13, 261–2
chalk 9, 83–4, 154, 165, 197, 262
chalk lines and reels 25, 27, 99
charcoal 174
chemicals, limestone 290–1
chicken wire 164
chimney flues 120
chisels 40
chunam 118, 262
civil engineering 185

classification of limes 6, 65, 109, 205–8,
    280–1
clay 262
  active 191, 198–9, 203–4, 221, 259
  burnt 283, 286
  field tests 224
  puddled 188
  residue from limestone 13
  structures 153
coarse stuff 262
  plaster 84, 86–7, 90, 133
  renders 116
coats, plaster 88–98
cob walls 243, 262
cobble paving 171–2
coccoliths 197
colours
  fastness 59, 262
  limewash 53, 58
  renders 111
comfort conditions, buildings 63
compaction
  mortar joints 46
  renders 125
  soil 158–9
  sub-base 171
compasses 27
concrete 2, 5, 171–92, 262
conservation, building 238, 262–3
consistency 214–15, 232, 236, 281
containers, storage 17
coral rocks 9, 145, 175–6, 195
core (in quicklime) 10, 263
cornices 129–34, 263
cow dung 120, 154, 163
Cowper, A. D. 13
cracking 122, 123, 240
crazing 123, 125
crystallization of salts 61, 65
curing 119, 125, 138, 237, 263
  compressed blocks 161

damp walls 80–1
damp-resistant floors 174–5
damping down 72, 75, 97, 125
dampness 123
  rising 61
darbies 24, 89

dashings
  dry 112–14
  harling 116–17
  wet (rough cast) 114–17
daub construction 120, 154–6
decorative finishes, repairing 244
density vessels 232–3
depeter 143–4, 263
diaper 128, 263
distempers 146
  maintenance of 245
diversity of limes 4
dolomite 14–15, 198, 202–3, 209, 228, 263
Dorking stone lime 186
drags 20, 37
drainage 103, 172, 175
  maintenance 242
drying, rapid 126
durability of structures 63, 73

earth bricks and blocks 157–62, 297
earth structures 5
  internal plasters 166
earth walling 156–7, 166
egg white 176, 178
eminently hydraulic limes *see* hydraulic limes
emulsion paints, maintenance of 245
enrichment (decoration) 5, 264
environmental benefits of limes 1
European standards (CEN) 286–7
evaporation from renders 103
expansion on slaking 207–8, 280

Faija apparatus 216
falls, paving 172
fat limes 4, 264
feather-edge rules 23–4
ferric oxide 13
ferrous sulphate 222
fibres in plaster 86
field investigations and tests 193, 203–27, 286
files (tools) 40
fineness 213, 215, 228, 229, 232
finishes
  plaster 89, 101

renders 110–12
fire resistance 5, 77, 82, 163
firing temperatures 13
firing trials 205
floating rules 23–4
floats, hand 93, 98, 111, 264
  cross-grained 32
  devil 33–4, 89, 95–6
  felt 33, 111, 112
  skimming 33
  special 34
  sponge 99
flocculation, clay particles 153, 181, 264
floors
  concrete 171–5
  insulation 174
  loading 246
  maintenance 249, 250
  surfaces 172–3, 177–8
  suspended 175–6
flow table 233–4
fly ashes, power station 65, 265
formaldehyde 55, 265
fossils 195, 198
foundations, lime concrete 186–9
French standards 288
frost damage 61, 72, 91, 126, 223; *see also* weather, severe

gauging 120–2
  gypsum 102, 295
  trowel 29–30
German standards 289
geological observations 193–5
glue size in limewash 54, 276
gouges 40
grading, sand 217, 220
gravel 285
Greek classical orders 129
grey limes 14, 110–11, 265
grip floor 174
gums and resins in limewash 55
gypsum 101–2, 134, 135, 177, 265, 295

hair hooks 20, 265
hair in plaster 86
hammers
  brick 44

club (lump) 44
  lath 35
hand picked lump lime 10, 266
harbours 184, 189
hardcore sub-base 171
hardeners 87–8
  surface 178
harling 104, 116–17, 266
hawk, plasterers' 28–9, 266
health 83
hoggin (wall ballast) 181
hop ups 22
horsing up 130, 266
hot lime 112, 117, 187, 266
hydrate, dry 9, 11, 109, 266
  field tests 215–16
hydration 10–11, 124, 266–7
  pressure 208
hydraulic engineering works 12, 264
hydraulic limes 4, 6, 12–14, 107, 108–10,
    148, 189, 204, 205–7, 264, 267
  buff colour 13
  burning temperature 208
  chemical analysis 292
  classification 236, 280–1
  grinding 208
hydraulic mortars 71–2, 75, 185–9
hydraulicity 13
hydrochloric acid 202–3, 228

igneous rocks 195
impervious finishes 47, 267
impurities, active clay 4
Indian renders 117–19
Indian standards (IS) 286
induration 62–3
iron dust and slag 178, 187, 188
Italian stuccos 148–51, 267, 270

jaggery 117–18, 267

kankar 190, 267
kerbs, cobble paving 171
keys 267
  plaster 79, 81, 91
  renders 104, 164
kiln temperatures 9
kilns, test 203, 205

knocking up 109

laitance 74
lard in limewash 54
larries 20, 268
laterite 268
lateritic earth 165
lathing 80–3, 113, 123, 263, 268
  repairs 247–9
  wetting 90
laying on, plaster 90
Le Chatelier moulds 230–2
lean limes 14, 204, 212, 228, 268, 280–1
lean mortar mix 63
levelling, plaster
lime 268
  available 169
  characteristics 2–4
  classes A, B, C and D 195, 197, 206,
    207–8, 262, 280–1
  cycle 8–9, 268–9
  definitions 259–71, 274, 276–9
  fat and lean 228
  proportion, optimum 158
  well matured 12
lime pit 11, 84, 269
lime putty 4, 9, 12, 50–2, 70, 83–4, 109,
    111, 124, 209, 269
  field tests 212–15, 220
  standards and tests 231–4
lime water 12, 81, 98, 269
lime-ash floors 175–6, 269
lime-soil reactions 152–3
limestones 269
  burning, under- and over- 209–10,
    211, 228, 271
  carboniferous (mountain) 199, 270
  chemicals in 290–2
  clay content 204
  density 200
  evaluation 203
  formation 193
  fossiliferous 195–6
  hydraulic lime 198–9
  igneous 195
  magnesium 197–8, 208–9
  metamorphic 199–201
  oolitic 196–7

precipitated 202
recognition 193–204
sedimentary 6
limewashes 5, 107, 118, 120, 167–8, 269
    additives 53–6
    application 56–8
    maintenance 245
    mould growth 54, 55–6
    preparation 50–3
    trial mixes 58–9
    uses and qualities 49–50
line bobbins 43–4
lines and pins 43
local materials, untried 6
lump-lime *see* quicklime

Madras chunam 118, 167
Madras plaster 119
magnesia *see* magnesium oxide
magnesium carbonate 14, 197–8, 208
magnesium limes 14–15, 208–9, 270
magnesium oxide (magnesia) 15, 169,
    203–4, 208, 269
maintenance 240–51
marble 195, 201
    powdered 119
marine works 188, 184–6, 188
marmorino *see* Italian stuccos
masonry, inspection of 244
masons' tools 42–8
materials specification 6
metalwork, inspection of 249
metamorphic rock 195
metrication 237
military engineers 61, 65
milk of lime 11, 220, 270
minerals 290
mist spraying 72, 75
mixes, soil-lime 181
Moh hardness scale 202
moisture, construction 79, 101
moisture movements 156
moisture/air equilibrium 243
mortarmen, master 67
mortars 5, 60, 270
    additives 65–7
    applications 72–5
    crushing strengths 296

clay and lime 162
field tests 221–3
hot lime 47
hybrid 293
hydraulic 185–9
joints 46
lime-soil 162
Lyme Regis (Blue Lias) 188, 198–9,
    260
materials 63–5
mills (roller pan mixers) 46–8, 67–70,
    71, 270
mixes 72, 244
mould growth 66
performance 60–3
preparation 67–70
quicklime 70–2
repairs 244
for soil blocks 161
strength 221
trial mixes 75–6
water for 190–2
mosaic 172, 177
mould box 136
mould inhibitors 54, 55–6
moulds, cast 134–8
moulds, running 129–30, 133, 274
mucus 163
muffles 133

national standards 6, 227–8, 237–9,
    286–90
Netherlands standards 286
nibs, plaster 81

oils 54, 66, 107, 121, 176, 178
organic additives 145

paint, emulsion 54
Pantheon temple in Rome 2, 3, 183–4
pargeting 120, 138–40, 163–4, 271
Paris, carved plaster in 145
particle size, sand 217, 220, 271
pat tests 230–1
paving, cobble 171–2
pebble-work 177
performance specification 6
permeability 271

mortar 72, 73
slurries 165
tar and bitumen 168
phenolphthalein 76, 211, 215, 222, 229, 271
pigments 53, 58, 147, 271
pinnings 91, 116
pisé de terre (rammed earth) 152, 156–7, 271
pisolite 196
pitting and popping 71, 88, 124, 230, 271
plaster casts 135
plaster dots 93, 264
plaster of Paris 101, 135, 272
plasterers' tools 28–42, 77
    small 36–7, 134
plasters 5, 272
    cleaning 245
    field tests 221–3
    gauging 295
    internal for earth structures 166
plastering 272
    application (coats) 88–98, 271
    backgrounds for 78–83
    cast plasterwork 40
    ceilings 99–101
    finishing coat 29, 32, 34
    gauging 101–2
    materials 83–8
    texture and finishes 98–99
    wood float finish 32
plasterwork, decorative 102
    carved and diapered 144–5
    cast moulds 134–8
    depeter 143–4, 263
    discolouration 246
    hand-modelled stucco 140–3
    Italian stuccos 148–51, 267
    maintenance 246–9
    pargeting 138–40
    run mouldings 127–34
    sgraffito 146–8
plasticity 2, 163, 181, 272
plumb bobs and reels 26, 94
pointing 73, 244, 251, 272
    irons 46

jointers 45–6
trowels 45
Portland cement, ordinary (OPC) *see* cement
pouncing a pattern 147
pozzolanic mortars 47, 64
pozzolanic reaction 153
pozzolanic set 10
pozzolans, artificial and natural 14, 65, 107, 108, 121, 165–6, 185, 198, 260, 272, 282–4
    field tests 221
    specifications 286
    surkhi 65, 69, 277, 283
    trass 282, 286
pugs 154, 187–8
pulverizing machine 182
pumice stone 178, 183, 282
pure lime 6, 209–10, 280–1

quality, lime 6, 228
    hand picking 10
quicklime 8, 9, 50, 52, 78, 164, 270, 273
    field tests 209–12
    grinding 169, 212
    hard-burnt 10
    mortar 67, 70–2
    over-burnt 10, 209–10, 270
    reactivity 211
    soft-burnt 10
    solubility 209–10
    under-burnt 10, 209–10, 211, 278

rainwater goods and fixings 241
Ramad 167
rasps 40
Rajasthan aryash 167
reactivity of limes 9, 212, 273
red lime 171
renders, external 5, 89, 273
    backgrounds 106
    daub 163, 166
    durability 103
    faults 122–6
    gauging 120–22
    gypsum-lime 166
    Indian 117–19
    keys 104, 164

lime and cow dung 163–4
lime-soil 164–5
materials 106–10
mixes and application 110–12
shrinkage 164–5
soil structures 162, 164–6
thrown finishes 112–17, 277
tools 105
repairs, building 240
retarders 87–8, 273
ribbon test, soil 224
roads 178–82
maintenance of 250
Roman cement 188, 202, 270, 274,
280–1
roof finishes 166–7
roof maintenance 241
rules (straight edges) 23–4, 89, 93, 95,
97, 101, 111
joint 35–6, 134
notched 248–9
running 130, 132, 134
run mouldings 127–34
run of kiln quicklime 9, 274
running lime 18, 274
running moulds 129–30, 133,
274

sacrificial materials 60, 274
safety procedures 8, 12
lime slaking 50, 52
salt crystallization 223
salts
in limewash 55
in mortar 65
in plaster 83, 84
in sand 123
sand 260, 274–5, 296
aggregates 63–4
alternatives 85
arénes 259
field tests 216–20
in plaster 84–5
in renders 106, 109–12, 116
silver 87, 97, 276
'standard' 237
washing 19
sandcrete blocks 157

sanitary fittings 242
scaffolding 21, 105
scouring, plaster 77, 88, 89, 93, 98, 101,
275
scratchers 39, 91, 96, 132
screeds, levelling 93–5, 100, 101, 263,
275
sediment 6, 85
field test 217–18
sedimentary rocks 194–5
sedimentation analysis 153
selenitic lime 148
septaria 201–2, 275
setting out 99–101
setting-out tools 23–8, 99–101
setting stuff, plaster 84, 87, 89, 276
setting time, mortars and plasters 72,
101, 223
standards 235–6
sgraffito 146–7, 276
shell lime 117, 119, 276
shells 9, 145, 152, 198
shovels 17
shrinkage 12, 69, 74–5
earth walling 156
mortar 162
renders 164–5
sieves 18, 84–5
gauges 285
sieving limewash 50
silica 13, 153
silica gel 153
silt 85, 123, 217
traps 242
skill and experience 1
skimming 99, 276
slaking 8, 10–12, 70–1, 88, 264, 276, 280,
286
tanks 17
slurries 164–6
small lime 10, 276
Smeaton, John 69, 185
soapstone 118, 119, 178, 276
soil blocks 297
soils 277
building 5
compaction 158–9
composition 152–3, 294

stabilization 5, 158, 286
  field tests 223–6
  suitability 294
soundness 10, 228, 230–2, 278
  dry hydrate 216
  lime putty 212, 232
spatterdash 106
  machine 41–2
specifications, concrete 186–9
specifications, performance 6
spirit levels 27
spot boards 21
squares, setting-out 25, 26, 27
stabilization with lime 152–70
  roads 178–82
stabilized clay sub-base 171
stabilized earth 121, 152–3
stabilizing friable surfaces 78
stalagmites and stalactites 202
standard tests 227–37
standards
  lime 6
  limewash 58–9
  national 6, 227–8, 237–9, 286–90
statumen 173
steam cabinets 216, 230, 231
steam in lime burning 9
stickiness of limes 2
stilts 22
stone limes 14, 110–11, 277
stone paving, repair of 249–50
stone preservation 49
storage, lime 209
storage containers 17
straining limewash 50
straw, chopped 154
streaking on limewash 56
strength, mortar 72
strength tests, 281
  mortars and plasters 236–7, 296
  soil blocks 224–7
structural movement 240
stuccos 277
  bastard 112
  common 109, 110–11
  Italian 148–51, 267, 270
  Indian 118
  modelling in situ 140–3

one and two coat 117–18
polished 149
rough 111
trowelled 111–12
substructures 171–92
sugar 56, 66
sulphate contamination 10, 106, 223
superstructures, lime concrete 183
surfactants in mortar 67

tallow 54, 66, 136, 277
tar and lime coating 167–8
tempering 214, 277
templates 129–30
terrazzo 172, 177
  maintenance of 250
textured surfaces 95, 98, 105, 112
thermal conductivity 2, 277
thrown finishes see renders,
    external
tools and equipment 16–48
  damping 72
  limewashing 57–8
  mortar preparation 67–70
  plastering 77, 89–90
  rendering 105
tracery 145
travertine rubble 183, 202
trestles 21–2
trial mixes
  limewash 58–9
  mortar 75–6
  plastering 87
  renders 107
trowels 111
  angle (twitcher) 31–2
  brick (laying) 42–3
  dashing 116
  finger (margin) 45
  gauging 29–30
  harling 31, 105
  laying-on 29, 91, 97–8
  pointing 45
  polisher 98
  throwing 30, 105
tuck joints 46
tufa 183, 202, 278
tyrolean machine 41–2, 105

unsoundness *see* soundness

vegetation, control of 250–1
ventilation, dry lining 81
viaduct, Bawtry 188
Vicat apparatus 215, 223, 234–5
Vicat L. J. 118, 185, 189, 222, 259
Vicat's classification 13, 280

walls, lime concrete in 183
walls, maintenance 243–4
washable paints 49, 278
waste, quarrying 14
waste products, using 169
water, jaggery 117–18, 267
water absorption 78, 232
water mortars 190–2
water quality 65

water retention 2, 63, 214, 278
water-resistant finishes 167
waterlogged ground 179–81
waterproofing 120
wattle and daub 154–6
weather, severe 122, 125, 179; *see also* frost damage
weathering, renders 107
whitewash 49, 50, 54, 279
wood ash 167, 284
wooden stamps 139
workability 2, 63, 66, 67, 88, 95–7, 109, 214, 222, 232–4, 279
workmanship specification 6

Xisto 127, 146

Zidaka 145
Zimbabwe standards 286
zinc sulphate 178